Bedford Women's Club

Bedford, New Hampshire

by
Bedford Women's Club

Additional copies of *Tasteful Treasures* may be purchased by contacting:

Bedford Women's Club
P.O. Box 10015
Bedford, New Hampshire 03110

ISBN 0-9647574-0-0

First Printing	September 1995
Second Printing	August 1997
Third Printing	January 2000

Printed in the USA by

1-800-548-2537

Table Of Contents

Cookbook Committee

Chair
Madonna Lovett Repeta

Marketing
Maureen McIntyre

Distribution
Merrie Edgar

Nite Beale
Nancy Bechard
Bonnie Becker-Jones
Nancy Chase
Anna Curtis
Rita Fitzgerald
Emily Griffith
Anne Hoffman
Stephanie Johnson
Luana Jones
Karen King
Barbara Kuenzig
Barbara Lanteigne
Grace Newell
Hannah Perutz
Roberta Peimer
Sheila Roberge
Bobbie White
Ex Officio: Lynn Tuttle

Original Committee

Project Coordinator/Chair
Patricia Nichol

Recipe Chair/Cookbook Co-Chair
Janet Jespersen

Marketing Co-Chairs
Christina Barley
Madonna Lovett Repeta

Typesetting/Copy Chair
Bess Morrison

Art Consultants
Hannah Perutz
Margaret Rooney

Publication Chair/ Cookbook Co-Chair
Merrie Edgar

Jacqueline Aiken
Sally Balog
Eunice Brine
Patricia Cobb
Barbara Friedman
Martha Glasheen
Doris Guimont
Phyllis Hickey
Anne Hoffman
Suzanne Hyman
Donna Joas
Pat Korcuba
Patricia Lauer
Wesley Maloney
Carol Molitoris
Elisabeth Place
Carol Skelly
Tish Smith
Jeanne Thibault
Lynn Tuttle

Cookbook Dedicated in Memory of Margaret Rooney

Acknowledgments

The Cookbook Committee is most grateful to our many friends who generously shared their recipes with us. Their contributions ultimately aid the organizations and charities supported by the Bedford Women's Club. We thank the Bedford Historical Society for their assistance with historical information. It is our hope that the sale of this cookbook will help support our outreach ventures for many years.

Bedford Women's Club

In 1905, ten women met and started our organization, calling it the Child Study Circle. The first President was Mrs. George H. Wiggin. (She is pictured below.) These women soon expanded their interests and in 1906 changed the name to Home Study Club. Families planned their work so one of the farm horses would be free for the woman's use on club day each month. Dues were 25 cents. The subject and meetings pertained to child rearing, character building and responsibilities of citizenship.

The fund raising projects began in World War I with raising money for the war fund, Red Cross, and gifts for soldiers in 1917-1920. Baby clinics and dental clinics were established and supported by this group. They enjoyed sewing, bridge, and reading circles. (It is interesting to note that within the larger group today, many small groups meet and enjoy these same interests.)

With World War II, the group had fewer meetings due to gas rationing. They sent packages of food to American prisoners of war. In 1949, the group changed their name to the Bedford Woman's Club. Every spring, the women displayed their flair for cooking by giving a smorgasbord which was open to the public.

Today's Bedford Women's Club has 105 members who are involved in many activities. We have organized Day Trips once a month, in addition to our monthly business meeting with a planned program and petite luncheon. Some of our fund-raisers have been dances, harvest dinners, fashion shows, photography portraits, and Whale of a Sale. Our most recent venture is the cookbook project. All of the proceeds of these activities are donated to community charities and scholarships.

Introduction

The Bedford Women's Club is a non-profit organization of women. We strive to foster social and cultural relationships among our members by promoting the best interests of the community. The Bedford Women's Club has provided 90 years of community service. Our new cookbook venture commemorates this achievement.

Tasteful Treasures highlights both sumptuous recipes for all occasions and lifestyles, as well as accentuates the beauty, treasures and history of the Bedford, New Hampshire area.

The beauty of Bedford is also exhibited through its volunteers and caring spirit. The Bedford Women's Club provides funds, scholarships and service to help those in need and to make our community a better place for all. Our members eagerly volunteer their time and talents. The success of our fund raisers provides us the opportunity to continue our work. All proceeds from the sale of this cookbook will be donated to the community through charities and scholarships.

We thank you for your support and hope you enjoy our culinary offering.

The Bedford Women's Club
Bedford, New Hampshire

About The Cover

The cover was designed to highlight even more of New Hampshire treasures — lilacs, apples and granite. The purple lilac, syringa vulgaris, is our state flower. Hillsborough county in which Bedford is located, produces 45% of the annual one million bushel apple crop. New Hampshire is called the Granite State for its extensive granite formations and quarries. Some of the most beautiful buildings and monuments in the United States have used our granite.

New Hampshire's treasures are "like jewels in a showcase," said Robert Frost who lived in New Hampshire during his most productive years. We are happy to share our treasures with you.

Bedford, New Hampshire

Bedford was incorporated in 1750 and named after the Duke of Bedford, who was one of two secretaries of state under King George II. Its fertile land lining the Merrimack River was ideal for farming, and by 1836, Bedford had become the largest hop-growing town in New England.

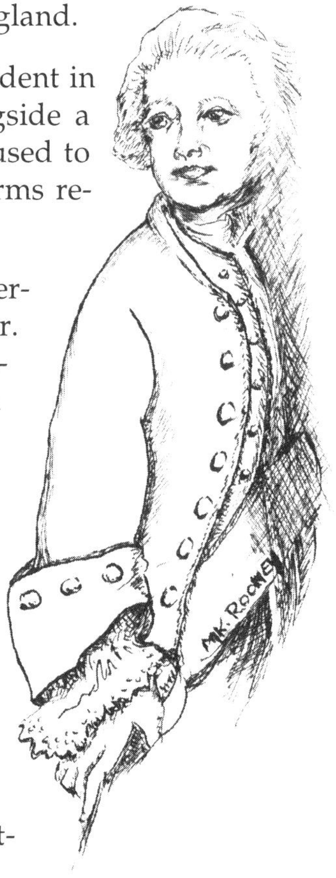

Bedford's agricultural heritage is still evident in the occasional hops seen growing alongside a road and the rambling stone walls that used to divide farm from farm. Few working farms remain in the town.

Despite substantial residential and commercial growth, Bedford retains a rural flavor. A Presbyterian Church, Town Hall, Library and antique colonial homes mark the town center. Surrounding rolling hills hide the single-family homes tucked away throughout the area.

The beauty and rural character of Bedford is only half of its appeal. The other half is the town's commercial development, which is contained along the town's two major thoroughfares, Routes 3 and 101. This area is teeming with shopping centers, restaurants and office buildings, including a major department store and malls.

In the wake of major highway construction during the 1950's, Bedford has repositioned itself as an exclusive commercial, office, and research and development address.

The convenience of nearby shopping and office parks that are clearly set apart from the town's residential sections enables Bedford to offer a seemingly paradoxical combination of urban convenience and rural character.

About The Artists

HANNAH PERUTZ created many of the sketches illustrating our theme of Bedford History and Treasures. They are featured as chapter division pages for this cookbook. She was also the creator/photographer for the cover of *Tasteful Treasures*. Hannah has degrees in science, education and commercial art. She has enjoyed successful careers involving research with Sloan-Kettering Institute for Cancer, enriching and expanding the experiences of her two children, creating visual displays for department stores and museums, and graphic design for corporate and philanthropic organizations. Hannah lives in Bedford with her husband and is a past president of the Bedford Women's Club.

MARGARET K. ROONEY was our second artist who ably created many of the chapter division theme pages and illustrations in the *Tasteful Treasures* cookbook. She also was a past president of the Bedford Women's Club. Margaret's *joie-de-vivre* was exemplified by her uncanny ability to do so many things well. In her different projects she exuded the confidence and willingness to help many — including the mentally handicapped, the sick and those in need. The background for this energy was a college degree, art school and many advanced courses of study in different areas. These studies led to teaching, interior decorating, gourmet cooking, floral designs and decorative painting to list a few — sharing all with those interested. Margaret passed away in 1997.

Appetizers

Pennacook Indians

The original inhabitants of Bedford were tribes of Indians known as the Pennacook Indians. Their great Indian Chief Passaconnaway roamed this area in the late 1600s. This particular group lived very peacefully in the same area with the settlers.

Some seemed not to belong to any tribe and lived a solitary life, rightly called Praying Indians. One such Indian was Cristo, who lived on the river bank by "Hunter John" Goffe's ferry.

This was the home of the Indians but nothing remains to tell of their existence except the meaningful names they gave to the striking natural objects nearby. On the east rolls the current of the majestic Merrimack River expressed by its name Merruh (of strong current) and Auke (place). Further west towers the Monadnock, the word derived from Manit (the Great Spirit) and auke (place). There are many more names proving that they thrived in the beautiful surroundings of Bedford where Nature had endowed many natural resources.

Harvest Table

soup

Curried Butternut Squash with Apple Soup

salad

Salad with Nuts and Seeds

entrée

Yankee Pot Roast

Crisp Onion Roasted Potatoes

Heidi's Cranberry Chutney

desserts

New England Indian Pudding

Pumpkin Chiffon Pie

Apple Crisp

APPETIZERS

Hot Artichoke Crostini

1 French baguette
1 cup mayonnaise (reduced fat)
1 cup fresh grated Parmesan cheese
1 (4.5 ounce) can chopped green chilies, drained
1 (14 ounce) can artichoke hearts, drained and chopped
2 cloves garlic, minced

Preheat oven to 400 degrees. Slice baguette into ¼ inch slices and place on a cookie sheet sprayed with Pam. Bake for 5 minutes until lightly browned. Combine mayonnaise, Parmesan cheese, chilies, garlic and chopped artichokes. Spread on bread slices. Bake for 5 minutes or until cheese melts.

Garnishes:
chopped green onions
chopped tomatoes
4 slices crumbled bacon

Top with garnishes and serve immediately. Yield: 3 dozen.

Note: Crostini means "little crusts."

Margaret K. Rooney

Hot Artichoke Dip

2 (14 ounce) cans artichoke hearts, not marinated
1 cup Parmesan cheese
1 cup shredded mozzarella cheese
1 cup mayonnaise
1 teaspoon salt
1 clove garlic, minced

Preheat oven to 350 degrees. Drain and chop artichoke hearts. Mix all of the ingredients in a large bowl. Spoon mixture into a buttered casserole dish. Bake for 25 to 30 minutes. Serve hot with crackers.

Martha M. Glasheen

Artichoke Nibbles

2 (6 ounce) jars marinated artichokes
1 small onion, minced
1 clove garlic, minced
4 large eggs
¼ cup fine, dry bread crumbs
pinch of salt
⅛ teaspoon oregano
⅛ teaspoon pepper
⅛ teaspoon Tabasco sauce
2 cups shredded Cheddar cheese
2 tablespoons minced parsley

Preheat oven to 325 degrees. Drain artichokes, reserving the marinade. Put half of the marinade into a frying pan. Place the onion and garlic into the pan and simmer until tender. Set aside. Chop the artichokes and set aside. Beat the eggs and stir in the bread crumbs and seasonings. Add the chopped artichokes, cheese and parsley. Add the onion, garlic and marinade (in which they were cooked) and mix well. Place the assembled ingredients into a 7 inch by 11 inch greased baking dish. Bake uncovered for 30 minutes. Cut into 3 to 4 dozen little squares. Let cool slightly before cutting.

Note: The remaining marinade may be used for salad dressing. This appetizer is a little different. I always like to take it to a party when I am asked to bring something.

Louise Langley

Homus Dip

1 can chick peas, retain half of the juice
1 tablespoon Tahini (pureed sesame seeds)
1 tablespoon lime juice
⅓ cup olive oil
1 medium size clove garlic, pressed
Pinch of salt

Place all ingredients into a blender. Blend on high speed. Add more lime juice and olive oil for a richer taste. Serve with parsley and pomegranate (when in season) and pita bread.

Note: May double or triple this recipe.

Alice Asadourian

Puree of White Bean Dip

1 clove garlic, minced
⅓ cup chopped fresh cilantro
1 (16 ounce) can butter beans, rinsed and drained
¾ teaspoon ground cumin
1 tablespoon plus 1 teaspoon fresh lemon juice
3-4 tablespoons olive oil
salt and freshly ground pepper to taste
Vegetables for dipping
Cilantro sprigs for garnish

Place garlic and cilantro in a food processor with the metal blade and process until minced. Add beans, cumin, lemon juice, oil, salt and pepper. Pulse until mixture is almost pureed, but still slightly chunky. Refrigerate for at least 1 hour. Serve with assorted vegetables. Garnish with cilantro sprigs. Preparation time: 15 minutes. Chill time: 1 hour. Yield: 1⅓ cups.

Note: This dip is a creamy, yet low-fat dip for vegetables. It may be refrigerated up to 4 days or frozen up to 1 month.

Rita Fitzgerald

Ginger Beef Sticks

½ cup soy sauce
⅓ cup rice vinegar
1 tablespoon sesame oil
1 tablespoon grated fresh ginger
4 teaspoons packed brown sugar
3 cloves garlic, minced
1 to 1½ pounds flank steak, cut diagonally into thin strips
1 bunch cilantro or parsley
1 tablespoon sesame seeds, toasted
Bamboo skewers, soaked in water

In a ziplock bag, combine first 6 ingredients. Add beef and refrigerate for several hours or overnight. Thread 2 strips of beef onto each skewer. Grill or broil for 3 minutes per side. Arrange the skewers on a bed of cilantro or parsley and sprinkle with toasted sesame seeds. Yield: 6 servings.

Bonnie Venn

Red Pepper Dip

1 (7.25 ounce) jar roasted red sweet peppers, drained, or 1-2 red sweet peppers, roasted, peeled and cut up
½ cup blanched whole almonds, toasted
¼ cup plain low-fat yogurt or sour cream
2 teaspoons anchovy paste
2 cloves garlic, quartered
¼ teaspoon ground cumin
red pepper strips
assorted vegetables

For dip, in blender container or food processor bowl combine first six items. Cover and blend or process until smooth. Chill until serving time. For a creamier dip stir in extra ¼ cup yogurt or sour cream. Place dip in a small dish, top with red pepper strips. Serve on a platter with assorted vegetables. (Blanching broccoli, cauliflower and carrots will bring out the color.) Yield: 12-20 servings.

Anne C. Hoffman

Brie en Croute

1 sheet Pepperidge Farm frozen Puff Pastry Dough
1 pound brie cheese
¼ cup sliced, toasted almonds
¼ cup parsley, chopped
1 egg, beaten with 1 teaspoon water to make an egg wash

Preheat oven to 400 degrees. Thaw pastry for 20 minutes and on a floured surface, roll pastry into a 14-15 inch circle. Slice chilled brie in half horizontally. Layer with almonds and parsley. Top with remaining half of brie. Place layered cheese in the center of the pastry.

Brush edges of pastry with egg wash and pull up sides to enclose the brie. Pinch closed. Place seam side down on ungreased baking sheet. If desired, decorate top with pastry scraps. Brush top with egg wash. Cover with foil. Bake for 20 minutes. Let cool at least 10 minutes prior to serving. Serves 12.

Note: May replace almonds and parsley with apricot preserves.

Anne C. Hoffman

Caviar Pie

5 hard-boiled eggs
1 (3 ounce) jar black lumpfish caviar, drained
½ small onion, finely chopped
1 teaspoon lemon juice
1 cup sour cream
Paprika
Parsley

Rice the eggs into a Pyrex or decorative 8 inch pie pan. Mash down the eggs with the bottom of a spoon, covering the bottom and sides of the pie pan to form a 'crust'. Spread caviar evenly over the egg crust. Add a very thin layer of chopped onion and sprinkle with lemon juice. Top with a smooth layer of sour cream. Garnish with paprika and parsley. Chill at least 2 hours. Cut into wedges to serve.

Note: This is a recipe from a Women's Club that I belonged to over 10 years ago!

Bonnie Venn

Cranberry Topped Brie

⅓ cup cranberry orange sauce
3 tablespoons brown sugar
¼ cup chopped pecans
1 tablespoon brandy
1 round (2 pounds) brie cheese

Preheat oven to 500 degrees. Combine first 4 ingredients in a small bowl. Carefully remove the rind from the top of the cheese. Place the cheese on an oven-proof plate or platter. Cover the top of the cheese round with the cranberry mixture. Bake for 5-8 minutes until heated but not melted. Serve with crackers. Serves 10-12.

Wesley Maloney

Crab Dip

1 (8 ounce) container whipped cream cheese
Several dashes Worcestershire sauce
1 can crab meat, pick through to remove cartilage

Preheat oven to 325 degrees. Mix all ingredients together and place in an oven-proof dish. Bake for 30 minutes. Serve with crackers.

Bonnie Venn

Ceviche

1 pound firm white fish, cut into small chunks (have fish market check fish carefully on a light table as the fish will not be cooked)
juice of 6-8 limes
1 teaspoon minced garlic
1 small tomato, peeled, seeded and chopped
1 small onion, finely chopped
2 jalapeño chili peppers, seeded and chopped (optional)
3 tablespoons Pace or Shorty's Roadhouse Chunky Salsa
1 small handful of parsley, finely chopped
salt
12 flat corn tostada shells

Arrange fish in a deep dish and cover with lime juice. Refrigerate for 8 hours, turning once. Drain liquid and pat dry. Combine garlic, tomato, onion, chilies, salsa, parsley, and salt to taste. Pour sauce over fish and toss. Place a heaping spoonful of fish on a flat tostada and enjoy!

Note: This is a chilled appetizer of fish "cooked" by marinating in lime juice. It is a tangy summer favorite served with an iced-cold beverage.

Karen White
Town of Bedford Planning Director

Cheese Crisp Bites

¼ pound margarine, room temperature
½ pound grated cheddar cheese, sharp or extra sharp at room temperature
1 cup flour
1 teaspoon Lawry's seasoned salt
⅛ teaspoon cayenne pepper
dash paprika
2 cups Rice Krispies

Preheat oven to 350 degrees. Mix margarine and cheese well. Add remaining ingredients, Rice Krispies last. Roll into marble size balls and place on an ungreased cookie sheet. Flatten with the tines of a fork. Bake for 15-20 minutes.

Barbara Weigold

Olive and/or Sausage Covered Cheese Balls

2 cups sharp cheddar cheese, finely grated
1 stick softened butter
½ cup flour
1 teaspoon paprika
1 jar (48) pimento-stuffed olives and/or 48 small sausages

Blend cheese and butter with mixer. Add flour and paprika and combine thoroughly. Shape 1 tablespoon of this mixture around each olive or sausage. Freeze. Preheat oven to 400 degrees. Bake frozen balls for 20 minutes, or until golden brown.

Caroline Williams
Catherine T. Liotta

Nutty Cheese Ball

1 package Wispride sharp cheddar cheese, room temperature
1 (8 ounce) package cream cheese (can use no-fat) room temperature
½ teaspoon garlic salt
½ teaspoon garlic powder
chopped nuts are optional

Mix all ingredients with electric mixer. Refrigerate until chilled. Shape chilled mixture into one large ball and roll in chopped nuts.

Note: Instead of forming a large ball, the mixture may be spread directly on crackers.

Madonna Lovett Repeta

Peter's Cheese Spread

2 large packages of cream cheese
1 cup walnuts, coarsely chopped
1 cup golden raisins
¼ cup amaretto liqueur

Combine and serve with crackers and/or fruit.

Note: This recipe was given to me by a bachelor friend in New York.

Wesley Maloney

Cheese Pennies

8 teaspoons soft butter
½ pound grated Cheddar cheese
¾ cup sifted flour
½ teaspoon salt
⅛ teaspoon cayenne
½ teaspoon ground mustard

Preheat oven to 350 degrees. Use ungreased cookie sheets. Cream butter until light and fluffy. Beat in cheese, then flour, ¼ cup at a time. Add salt, cayenne and mustard. If too soft to be formed into a ball, add 1 teaspoon flour at a time until right consistency. On lightly floured surface, shape into a roll about 1¼ inch wide and 12x14 inch long. Wrap in wax paper and refrigerate until firm (approximately 1 hour). Slice chilled dough into ¼ inch rounds. Arrange ½ inch apart on ungreased cookie sheet. Bake in middle of oven for 8-10 minutes. Cool on rack. Yield: 3 dozen.

Note: Freezes well.

Mrs. Lester J. Grant

Barbecued Chicken Wings

1 cup soy sauce
1¼ cups brown sugar
2 teaspoons garlic powder
2 cups water
1 teaspoon ginger
⅔ cup cider vinegar
10 pounds chicken wings

Heat all ingredients (except chicken wings) until brown sugar melts. Pour mixture over chicken wings and refrigerate for two days. Place chicken on foil lined cookie sheet. Bake at 350 degrees for one hour. Broil last 5 minutes to make it crispy. Serve warm. Yield: 14-16 servings.

Note: The longer you marinate the meat the tastier it gets. The effort is well worth it.

Doris Guimont

Marinated Chicken Drumsticks

4-5 pounds chicken thighs (mini drumsticks)
1 cup soy sauce
1 cup light brown sugar, packed
½ cup butter
1 teaspoon dry mustard
¾ cup water

Preheat oven to 350 degrees. Arrange chicken pieces in a shallow baking dish. Combine the remaining ingredients. Heat until butter and sugar dissolve.

Cool and pour over chicken. Refrigerate for at least two hours, turning occasionally. Pour off half of the marinade. Bake chicken for 45 minutes, turning once and baste every 15 minutes. Do not allow liquid to be completely absorbed. Drain on wire rack and serve.

Christina Barley

Crab Cocktail over Cream Cheese

2 (8 ounce) packages cream cheese, room temperature
1 small onion, minced
½ cup mayonnaise
1 tablespoon lemon juice
1 tablespoon Worcestershire sauce
1 teaspoon garlic salt
¾ cup chili sauce
2 (5 ounce) boxes frozen crab meat, thawed, drained and shredded

Mix first 6 ingredients and blend well. This mixture may be refrigerated overnight.

To Serve: Shape the cream cheese mixture onto a serving plate. Top with chili sauce. Cover entire top with crab meat. Serve with crackers.

Beth Squeglia

Seafood Mold

1 can tomato soup
1 large package cream cheese
1½ packages Knox Gelatin (small envelopes)
1 cup celery, finely chopped
¼ cup green pepper, finely chopped
2 small onions, finely chopped
3 tablespoons Worcestershire sauce
1 pound of lobster, crab or shrimp (or any mixture)
1 cup Hellmann's Mayonnaise

Mix soup and cream cheese in top of double boiler. Let it get just hot enough to mix. Dissolve gelatin in ¼ cup cold water and stir into the mixture. Add everything else and pour into an oiled mold (wipe with vegetable oil on a paper towel). Chill overnight. Unmold. Garnish with parsley.

Note: For the seafood, you can use 3 small cans of baby shrimp and 3 small cans of crab meat. Serve with crackers.

Wesley Maloney

Cocktail Meat Balls

½ pound ground sirloin
1 egg, beaten
¼ cup Italian flavored bread crumbs
1 clove garlic, finely chopped
2 tablespoons finely chopped scallions
½ teaspoon salt
¼ teaspoon basil leaves, crushed
dash pepper
½ cup grape jelly
½ cup chili sauce
1 tablespoon prepared mustard

In medium bowl, combine the first 8 ingredients. Mix lightly and shape into 24 bite sized meatballs. In a 2-quart casserole, combine jelly, chili sauce and mustard. Mix until well blended. Add meatballs and cover with glass lid or microwave safe plastic wrap. Heat on high 6 minutes, then on medium-low 9 minutes, stirring twice. Stir and let stand uncovered for 3 minutes before serving. Preparation time: 15 minutes. Microwave time: 15 minutes. Yield: 24 meatballs.

Catherine Quackenbush

Cocktail Meatballs in Italian Tomato Sauce

Sauce:
6 large cans tomato paste
10 cans of water
2 teaspoons sugar
2 teaspoons salt
½ teaspoon pepper
2 cloves garlic
1 heaping teaspoon basil
½ teaspoon fennel seeds

Sauce: Mix all sauce ingredients together. Cook all afternoon on lowest setting. Sir occasionally.

Meatballs:
3 pounds hamburger
2 packages sweet sausage
2 eggs, beaten
6 slices bread, soaked in water and squeezed
1 teaspoon garlic powder
Add about 1 cup of the tomato sauce from above
salt and pepper to taste

Meatballs: Mix all ingredients together. Form small round balls and fry until brown. Add to tomato sauce and serve.

Note: Leftovers may be frozen.

Donna Joas

Kielbasa Appetizer

½ cup brown sugar
1½ cups ketchup (one 14 ounce bottle)
¾ cup whiskey
2 pounds Kielbasa sausage

Preheat oven to 350 degrees. Slice the Kielbasa into coin shaped pieces. Mix all of the ingredients and put into a casserole dish. Bake for 1 hour. Transfer to a chafing dish or a crock pot to keep warm.

Note: This is a good dish to take to someone's house. It travels well.

Carol Molitoris

Mexican Pie

1 (4.5 ounce) can chopped green chilies
½ bar extra sharp Cheddar cheese, grated
3 eggs
2 tablespoons milk
Tortilla chips

Preheat oven to 350 degrees. Spray Pam on bottom of square Pyrex or pie pan. Beat eggs with milk. Add cheese and chilies. Pour into dish. Bake about 35 minutes. Cut into small pieces and serve on tortilla chips. Serves 6.

Note: Easy appetizer when company drops in.

Barbara Weigold

Quesadilla with Gary's Guacamole

Guacamole:
¼ cup fresh cilantro
1 clove garlic
1 lime
1 jalapeño chili
½ small onion
2 ripe avocados
salt & pepper

In food processor, add cilantro, garlic, juice of ½ of lime, jalapeño, onion and salt & pepper. Process till chunky paste. Add avocados and rest of lime juice. Process only until mixed. Do not overprocess.

Quesadillas:
2 bunches of scallions
1-2 limes
salt
12 flour tortillas
8 ounces Monterey Jack jalapeño cheese, thinly sliced

Clean scallions and sprinkle with lime juice and salt. Grill scallions on hot grill until slightly limp. Remove from grill and cut into 1 inch pieces. Set out 6 tortillas, top with thinly sliced cheese, scallions and then a second tortilla. Grill until cheese starts to melt and tortillas have grill marks. Cut into quarters and serve immediately with guacamole and salsa. Yields: 24 pieces and serves 6-8.

Anne C. Hoffman

Ham-Stuffed Mushrooms

1 cup cooked ham, finely chopped
1 tablespoon Dijon mustard
1 tablespoon chutney, minced
1 teaspoon vinegar
sour cream and mayonnaise, just enough to bind the other ingredients
14-16 small to medium mushrooms, stems removed

Combine first 6 ingredients and mound into mushroom caps. Chill until ready to serve. Serves 4-6.

Note: May be prepared several hours in advance.

Doris Peck Spurway,
Supervisor of the Checklist

Stuffed Mushrooms

1 pound fresh mushrooms, medium size
1 clove garlic
3 tablespoons butter
¾ teaspoon oregano
¾ teaspoon parsley flakes
1 teaspoon Worcestershire sauce
⅛ cup white wine
2 tablespoons Parmesan cheese
½ cup bread crumbs

Preheat oven to 350 degrees. Clean mushrooms, remove stems and chop. Chop garlic. Sauté chopped stems and garlic in a medium size fry pan. Add seasoning and cook until mixture is tender. Remove from heat and add remaining ingredients. Mix until stuffing resembles a pate or chopped liver mixture. Place a small amount of stuffing into each mushroom cap. Place on a pie pan or cookie sheet. Sprinkle with paprika. Bake for 20-30 minutes until caps are tender.

Donna Joas

Savory Stuffed Mushrooms

3 to 4 dozen mushrooms, wiped clean with damp paper toweling
1 pound hot or sweet Italian sausage, casings removed
1 medium onion, finely chopped (about ¾ cup)
4 cloves garlic, minced
2 tablespoons unsalted butter
2 teaspoons dried basil, crumbled
1 teaspoon chili powder
1 teaspoon dried oregano, crumbled
½ teaspoon fennel seeds, crushed
½ teaspoon sugar
½ teaspoon salt
¼ teaspoon ground white pepper
Pinch of ground cinnamon
Few drops of hot red pepper sauce
¾ cup fine dry bread crumbs
¼ cup freshly grated Romano or Parmesan cheese
4 tablespoons dry sherry
2 tablespoons unsalted butter, melted

Heat oven to 400 degrees. Separate stem from mushroom caps and finely chop stems. Measure out ½ cup chopped stems. Reserve caps and chopped stems separately. Cook sausage meat in large heavy skillet over medium heat, breaking it up into small pieces until browned, 7 to 8 minutes. Add onion and garlic. Sauté, stirring frequently, until onion is softened, 2-3 minutes. Stir in chopped mushroom stems, 2 tablespoons butter, the basil, chili powder, oregano, fennel seeds, sugar, salt, pepper, cinnamon, and hot red pepper sauce. Sauté until mushroom pieces are tender, 4-5 minutes. Stir in bread crumbs and cheese until well combined. Add 2 tablespoons of sherry, stir to moisten mixture. Remove mixture from heat. Allow to stand at room temperature until cool enough to handle. Using fingers, gently press sausage mixture into mushroom caps, dividing evenly. Brush filled caps with melted butter. Sprinkle tops with remaining 2 tablespoons sherry. Arrange on foil lined baking sheet, baking until stuffing is bubbly and mushrooms are browned, about 7 minutes. Remove to warmed platter, garnish with parsley. Serve immediately. Yields: 36-48 mushroom caps.

Anne C. Hoffman

Marinated Mushrooms

1 pound small fresh mushrooms
¼ cup olive oil
3 tablespoons lemon juice
1 clove garlic, halved
½ teaspoon salt
⅛ teaspoon pepper
⅛ teaspoon oregano

Remove the mushroom stems (save them for use in another dish). Wipe caps with a paper towel, and place the mushroom caps into a jar. Combine the other ingredients in a saucepan and heat just to the boiling point. Pour over the mushrooms and let cool. Cover and refrigerate for at least 2 days, shaking twice per day. When serving, drain and present with toothpicks. Serves 12.

Janet Jespersen

Hot Pecan Beef Dip

1 cup chopped pecans
2 teaspoons butter
2 (8 ounce) packages cream cheese
¼ cup finely chopped onion
4 tablespoons milk
3 ounces dried beef, minced
1 teaspoon garlic powder
1 cup sour cream
Dash of garlic salt

Preheat oven to 350 degrees. Combine and mix all ingredients and place in a buttered 9 inch pie plate. Bake for 20 minutes. Serve with unsalted crackers. Serves 8.

Peggy Rooney Bozzard

Pepperoni Puffs

1 egg
1 cup flour
½ stick pepperoni, cut into small pieces
½ cup grated Romano or Parmesan cheese
1 teaspoon baking powder
1 cup milk

Preheat oven to 350 degrees. Mix ingredients together and half fill well-greased miniature muffin pans. Fills 3 pans. Bake for 20-30 minutes. Yield: 32-36.

Note: Best eaten warm! May be made in advance and frozen. Reheat in oven or microwave.

Rose Marie Borelli

Vera's Roasted Pepper Appetizer

2 packages refrigerated crescent rolls
¼ pound American cheese, sliced
¼ pound Swiss cheese, sliced
¼ pound ham, sliced
¼ pound pepperoni, sliced
1 jar large roasted peppers
3 eggs
3 tablespoons Parmesan cheese

Preheat oven to 350 degrees. Grease bottom of a 9 x 13 inch pan and line with 1 package of the rolls, sealing seams together. Layer American and Swiss cheeses, ham and pepperoni, then add peppers. Beat eggs with Parmesan cheese. Spread ⅔ of egg mixture over the peppers. Cover with the remaining package of rolls, sealing the seams together. Brush with remaining egg mixture. Cover with foil. Bake for approximately 30 minutes. Remove foil and brown. Cut into squares to serve.

Note: This is delicious! This recipe comes from my sister-in-law in Orange, Connecticut.

Rose Marie Borelli

Pizza Dip

1 (8 ounce) package cream cheese, softened
½ cup sour cream
1 teaspoon oregano
⅛ teaspoon red pepper
½ cup pizza sauce
½ cup chopped pepperoni
¼ cup chopped green pepper
¼ cup chopped onion
½ cup shredded mozzarella cheese
dash garlic powder

Preheat oven to 350 degrees. In a small bowl, beat cream cheese, sour cream, oregano, garlic powder and red pepper. Spread evenly in a 9-10 inch pie plate. Spread pizza sauce over top. Sprinkle with pepperoni, onion and green pepper over top. Bake for 10 minutes, top with cheese and bake an additional 5 minutes. Serve with crackers or chips.

Martha Harris Gaudes
Executive Assistant to the Bedford Town Manager

Bacon-wrapped Scallops

2½ pounds bacon, strips cut in half
2½ pounds sea scallops
¾ cup butter, melted
2½ tablespoons lemon juice
salt & pepper

Preheat oven to 400 degrees. Cut bacon strips in half and cook until partially done. Drain. Rinse scallops. Drain and dry on paper towels. Combine butter and lemon juice, brush mixture over scallops. Sprinkle with salt and pepper. Wrap each scallop in half a slice of bacon. Secure with a toothpick. Broil 5 inches from heat for 3 minutes. Turn scallops, broil 2 to 3 minutes longer. Serve hot. Yield: 60 pieces.

Anne C. Hoffman

Spinach Soufflé Triangles

1 (11 ounce) package frozen spinach soufflé
9 sheets fillo or strudel dough leaves
¼ pound melted butter

Preheat oven to 400 degrees if cooking immediately. Thaw spinach soufflé. Lay 1 leaf of fillo or strudel dough on a flat surface. Cover remaining sheets with a damp towel. Brush the sheet with melted butter. Fold in half crosswise. Brush again with butter. Cut lengthwise into 4 equal strips about 2 inches wide. Place a scant teaspoon of spinach soufflé in a corner of each strip. Do not overfill as filling will rise as it bakes. Fold the dough over the spinach soufflé, enclosing it and forming a triangle at the top of the strip. Continue to fold the strip, maintaining a triangular shape. Brush the top with melted butter. Repeat with the remaining dough and spinach soufflé. Triangles may be refrigerated completely covered overnight or frozen.

Lightly butter baking sheets. Place thawed or frozen triangles on baking sheets. Bake in a preheated 400 degree oven for 15-20 minutes or until golden. Top with powdered sugar and cinnamon. Yield: 36.

Bonnie Venn

Hot Shrimp Dip

1 (8 ounce) package cream cheese (may use reduced or no fat)
½ stick butter
1 can cocktail shrimp, drained

Preheat oven to 350 degrees. Beat cream cheese, add melted butter and mix well. Add drained shrimp and stir. Place in oven proof dish. Bake for 20 minutes. Accompany with crackers or crusty bread. Serves 6 to 10.

Madonna Lovett Repeta

Surprise Spread

1 (8 ounce) package cream cheese
½ cup sour cream
¼ cup mayonnaise
2 (3-4 ounce) cans small shrimp, drained and rinsed
1 cup cocktail sauce
2 cups shredded mozzarella cheese
1 cup chopped green pepper
2 small chopped scallions
1 diced tomato

Mix first three ingredients and spread over a 12 inch pizza pan. Scatter shrimp over the cheese mixture. Add remaining ingredients in order in layers. Cover and chill until ready to serve. Accompany with assorted crackers or toast cups. Serves 10-12.

Sheila Roberge

Crab Dip Supreme

2 pounds Velveeta cheese
1½ cups mayonnaise
½ cup sour cream
¾ cup chopped chives
3 cans crab meat or 1½ pounds fresh crab meat

Add first four ingredients into top of double boiler and melt. Add crab last. Serve hot with chips and crackers.

Note: This recipe is from the early Sixties from La Canada, California. It is still as delicious as it was then, when it was served at nearly every party.

Virginia Larson

Soused Shrimp

2 pounds large raw shrimp
1 lemon, thinly sliced
1 red onion, thinly sliced
½ cup pitted black olives, drained
2 tablespoons chopped pimento
½ cup fresh lemon juice
¼ cup olive oil
1 tablespoon wine vinegar
1 clove garlic, crushed
½ bay leaf, broken up
1 tablespoon dry mustard
¼ teaspoon cayenne pepper
1 teaspoon salt

Shell and devein raw shrimp. Add shrimp to boiling water for 3 minutes. Drain shrimp and put into a pretty glass serving bowl. Add all of the remaining ingredients and toss. Cover and refrigerate for at least 2 hours.

Wesley Maloney

Taco Dip

1 (8 ounce) package light or regular cream cheese, softened
2 cups (16 ounces) Dannon plain non-fat or low fat yogurt
1 (1.25 ounce) package dry taco seasoning mix
1 (8 ounce) jar taco sauce
½ head lettuce, shredded
2 tomatoes, chopped
½ cup sliced black olives
½ cup sliced scallions
1 (4 ounce) cup shredded Cheddar cheese

Beat cream cheese until smooth, stir in yogurt and taco seasoning mix. Chill one hour. Spread yogurt mixture on bottom of large serving bowl or platter. Spread taco sauce over yogurt mixture. Layer with lettuce, tomatoes, olives, scallions, and cheese. Serve with your favorite chips. Yield: 3 cups of dip.

Sharlene Genest

Veggie Melts

½ cup shredded carrots
¾ cup shredded zucchini
1 cup sliced fresh mushrooms
2 scallions, finely chopped
2 tablespoons chopped green pepper
1 cup shredded Monterey Jack cheese
2 tablespoons mayonnaise
¼ teaspoon seasoned salt
24 slices party rye, toasted

Combine first 8 ingredients. Place a rounded teaspoonful of the vegetable mixture on each toast round. Microwave on high for 2½ to 3 minutes or until cheese melts.

Margaret K. Rooney

Veggie Pizza

2 cans of crescent rolls
2 (8 ounce) packages of cream cheese
1 cup mayonnaise
1 small package Hidden Valley Ranch Dressing mix
1 cup broccoli florets
1 cup pitted black olives
1 cup chopped scallions
1 cup grated carrots
1 cup grated Cheddar cheese

Preheat over to 375 degrees. Press the crescent rolls flat (like a crust) onto a cookie sheet and bake according to package directions until lightly browned. Mix together the cream cheese, mayonnaise, and ranch dressing and spread over cooked crust. Top with the vegetables and sprinkle the grated cheese over all. Cut into finger size pieces.

Martha M. Glasheen

Jane's Dip

1 pint sour cream
1 teaspoon salt
1⅓ tablespoons white horseradish
1 teaspoon tarragon
1 clove garlic, crushed
1 tablespoon minced chives
⅛ teaspoon white pepper
1 tablespoon paprika

Mix together the above ingredients. Put in sealed container and chill thoroughly. Can be made a day ahead. Serve as vegetable dip with assorted raw or blanched vegetables. Serves: 8-12.

Anne C. Hoffman

Beverages

Merrimack River

The Merrimack River runs north to south through the center of New Hampshire and passes through the state's largest cities before draining into the Atlantic Ocean.

The easterly border of Bedford is the Merrimack River. In olden times it was renown for fishing and boating. The plains along its banks were very fertile. In the southern part of town, there was an abundant supply of clay suitable for brick making. At one time there were twenty brickyards in operation in that area. Record has it that 150,000 bricks were shipped down the river every day.

Before the river was obstructed by mill dams and canal locks, as many as fifty or sixty salmon were taken at a haul. The river also teemed with shad, lamper eels and alevines.

New England Summer Clam Bake

soup

New England Clam Chowder

entrée

New England Clam Bake

Good Old Baked Beans

desserts

Cranberry Crisp

Hermit Cookies

BEVERAGES

Bourbon Sour Slush

2 cups hot tea
1 cup sugar
6 ounces frozen orange juice
6 ounces frozen lemonade
6 cups water
2 cups bourbon

Mix well and freeze. Serve partially thawed, as slush.

Note: Popular at parties. Delicious but potent!

Wesley Maloney

Spanish Coffee

½ shot Amaretto
½ shot Kahlua
coffee
whipped cream

Put Amaretto and Kahlua in bottom of fancy mug. Fill cup with hot brewed coffee. Top with whipped cream. Enjoy.

Note: This was served at the Red Jacket Mountainview Motor Inn in North Conway, NH.

Alberta Dieter

Hannah's Healthful Hot Toddy

½ lemon
1 ounce honey
1 ounce bourbon or Irish whiskey
1 cup boiling hot water
dash of cinnamon

Squeeze lemon into a glass and add the rest of the ingredients. Drink as hot as possible.

Note: Great for flu and colds.

Hannah Perutz

Egg Nog

6 eggs
¾ cup sugar
1 pint whiskey
1 ounce brandy
1 ounce rum
1 pint whipping cream
1 pint half and half or whole milk
nutmeg

In large bowl, beat egg yolks together with ¼ cup sugar. Add liquor slowly while constantly beating. Let stand at least 12 hours in a cool place. 24 hours is better.

Beat egg whites until they form stiff peaks. While still beating, slowly add ½ cup sugar. Slowly fold in egg whites to liquor mixture. Whip the cream until it has stiff peaks. Slowly fold in whipped cream to above mixture. Add half and half and stir until blended. Cover and store in cool place for at least 6 hours. If there is a strong whiskey flavor, add a little more rum. Serve in punch cups and sprinkle nutmeg on top when served. Serves: 8-10.

Anne C. Hoffman

Raspberry Champagne Punch

2 (10 ounce) packages frozen red raspberries in syrup, thawed
⅓ cup Real Lemon lemon juice concentrate
½ cup sugar
1 (750 ml) bottle red rose wine, chilled
1 quart raspberry sherbet
1 (750ml) bottle Asti Spumante or Champagne, chilled

Puree raspberries in a blender. In a large punch bowl combine raspberries, lemon juice, sugar and wine. Stir until sugar dissolves. Just before serving, scoop sherbet into punch bowl. Add champagne. Stir gently. Makes 3 quarts.

Doris Guimont

It would be easier by far to lose weight permanently if replacement parts weren't so handy in the refrigerator.

Christmas Fruit Punch

1 (6 ounce) can frozen orange juice
2 (6 ounce) cans frozen limeade
1 (6 ounce) can frozen lemonade
1 large can pineapple juice
1 pint cranberry juice cocktail
2-4 cups cold water
1 quart frozen strawberries
2 quarts chilled ginger ale
1 quart plain chilled soda water

Mix juices and water. Let stand until frozen juices are thawed. Stir well. Add frozen strawberries. Pour in ginger ale and soda water.

Doris Guimont

Concord Coach Punch

2 quarts tea, using 8 tea bags
1 (12 ounce) can frozen lemonade, diluted
1 (12 ounce) can frozen orange juice, diluted
1 (12 ounce) can frozen lemonade, undiluted
1 quart cranberry juice
2 quarts ginger ale

Prepare tea with boiling water to desired strength. Cool. In a large container prepare diluted juices according to directions on can. Add undiluted lemonade, cranberry juice and tea. Divide into 2 one gallon plastic containers and chill. When ready to serve, pour one container into punch bowl with ice. Add 1 quart ginger ale. Use second quart of ginger ale when serving the rest of the punch. Makes 9 quarts.

Note: This recipe was given many years ago by a member of the Concord Coach Square Dancers. My family prefers the tea base be omitted.

Margaret G. Comiskey

How come some lemonade is flavored with artificial lemon, while furniture polish and dish soap are made with real lemon?

Non-Alcoholic Punch

5 pineapple slices
5 cherries
2 (6 ounce) cans orange juice
1 (6 ounce) can frozen lemonade
8 cans water
2 cups grenadine
juice of 3 lemons
3 quarts chilled ginger ale

Using a round mold, arrange pineapple slices in a ring. Center a cherry on each slice. Add enough water to cover and freeze.

Mix remaining ingredients in a punch bowl. Float the fruit ring.

Doris Guimont

Sparkling Cranberry Punch

1½ quarts of cranberry juice cocktail
2 cups orange juice
¼ cup lemon juice
1 quart bottle of ginger ale or 2 bottles of champagne
2 cups of vodka, if not using champagne

Combine cranberry juice with orange juice and lemon juice. Chill well. Just before serving, pour into punch bowl and add the ginger ale and vodka or the champagne. Serve in punch cups or champagne glasses. Serves: 20 six ounce servings.

Anne C. Hoffman

Raspberry Lime Rickey

Ice
1 package of frozen raspberries in light syrup, thawed
2 limes, quartered
2 liter bottle of seltzer water or soda water

Place several cubes of ice in 10 to 14 ounce glass. Add 1 heaping tablespoon of raspberries with a little juice. Squeeze a quarter of a lime into glass and then add the piece of lime. Fill with seltzer water and stir. This makes a refreshing low calorie drink for a summer lunch. Serves: 8.

Anne C. Hoffman

Breads and Muffins

Our Apple Tree

Bedford is listed in the National Register of Big Trees in Washington, D.C. with the largest recorded apple tree in the United States.

Our Apple Tree, Common Malus Sylvestris, measures:

circumference 183 inches
height 44 feet
spread 49 feet (average of widest & narrowest)
age 150 - 200 years old

Our Apple Tree is located at the beginning of Bedford's first mile of the Heritage Trail along the Merrimack River at the end of Moore's Crossing Road. Further along the Trail you can picnic, overlook the river, and visit Eagle Park, which is a winter roosting area for American Bald Eagles.

Leaf Peepers Dinner

soup

Pumpkin Soup

bread

Dinner Rolls

salad

Green Salad

with Shaker Village Salad Dressing

entrée

Pork Tenderloin

Rice Pilaf

dessert

Cranberry-Raisin Pie

BREADS AND MUFFINS

Spicy Applesauce Muffins

1 cup flour
1/3 cup sugar
1/2 teaspoon salt
4 1/2 teaspoons baking powder
1/4 teaspoon baking soda
1/4 teaspoon allspice
1/4 teaspoon ground cloves
1/4 teaspoon cinnamon
4 dashes pepper
1/8 pound butter
1 beaten egg
2/3 cup milk
1/3 cup applesauce
1 1/3 cups quick oats

Preheat oven to 400 degrees. Mix together flour, sugar, salt, baking powder, baking soda, allspice, cloves, cinnamon and pepper. Cut in the butter. Mix together with egg, milk, applesauce and oats. Bake 22 minutes. Makes 9 muffins.

Lee Tebbetts

Banana Nut Bread

1 cup mashed bananas
2 cups all-purpose flour
1 1/2 teaspoons baking powder
1 teaspoon salt
1/2 teaspoon baking soda
1/2 cup softened butter
1 cup granulated sugar
2 eggs
3 tablespoons sour cream
1 tablespoon fresh lemon juice
1 cup chopped pecans

Heat oven to 350 degrees. Grease 9x5x3 inch loaf pan and set aside. Peel bananas and mash. Sift flour, baking powder, salt and baking soda into a medium size mixing bowl. Set aside. Put butter and sugar in a large mixing bowl and beat until mixture is creamy. Add eggs, sour cream, lemon juice and mashed bananas to butter mixture and beat well. Stir in pecans. Add flour mixture and stir just enough to combine all ingredients. Pour mixture into pan and bake in oven 50 to 60 minutes, until bread is golden brown on top and a knife inserted comes out clean. Remove from oven and cool 10 minutes. Set bread on a rack to cool completely.

Alice Asadourian

A Different Kind of Banana Bread

½ cup shortening or butter
1 cup sugar
2 eggs, beaten
1½ cups mashed bananas (3 to 5)
¾ cup grated carrots
2 cups sifted flour
1 teaspoon salt
½ teaspoon baking soda
1 teaspoon vanilla
⅔ cup nuts (pecan or walnuts)
⅔ cup chopped prunes
1 teaspoon lemon juice

Preheat oven to 325 degrees. Cream shortening. Add sugar slowly. Add beaten eggs, bananas and carrots. Sift together flour, salt, and baking soda and add to the mixture. Add nuts, prunes and lemon juice. Using a greased 2 quart loaf pan bake for 1 hour and 15 minutes. Test with a toothpick to make sure it is done. Cool. May store in refrigerator or freezer. Best served the next day.

Note: This is an old Texas recipe from a family friend. It is delicious.

Virginia Larson

Lemon Bread

¾ stick butter
1 cup sugar
2 eggs
½ cup milk
1½ cups flour
½ teaspoon salt
1 teaspoon baking powder
½ cup chopped nuts
grated rind of 1 lemon

Preheat oven 350 degrees. Grease 9x5 inch loaf pan. Cream butter and sugar. Add eggs one at a time, beating after each addition. Add milk, alternating with sifted flour, salt and baking powder. Add nuts and grated lemon rind. Bake for 1 hour. Allow to cool for 5-10 minutes.

Topping:
⅓ cup sugar
juice of 1 lemon

Mix sugar and lemon juice. Pour over bread. Let stand ½ hour before removing from pan. Preparation time: 15 minutes.

Janet Jespersen

Banana Nut Bread

2 eggs
1 cup sugar
⅔ cup oil
3 mashed bananas
¾ teaspoon baking soda
1½ cups flour
½ teaspoon salt
¼ teaspoon cloves
¼ teaspoon nutmeg
½ cup chopped walnuts

Preheat oven to 350 degrees. Grease one 5x9 inch loaf pan. Beat eggs, add sugar and oil until well creamed. Add bananas. Add dry ingredients, mixing well. Add nuts. Bake for 1 hour.

Barbara Fox Friedman

Cream Cheese Braids

1 cup sour cream
½ cup sugar
½ cup melted margarine
¾ teaspoon salt
2 packages dry yeast
½ cup warm water
2 eggs, beaten
4 cups flour

Heat sour cream over low heat. Stir in sugar, margarine and salt. Cool to lukewarm. Sprinkle yeast over warm water in a large mixing bowl stirring until yeast dissolves. Add sour cream mixture, eggs, flour. Mix well. Cover tightly and refrigerate overnight or about 8 hours.

Filling:
2 (8 ounce) packages cream cheese, softened
¾ cup sugar
1 egg, beaten
⅛ teaspoon salt
2 teaspoons vanilla

Next day, mix together the ingredients for the filling. Divide dough into 4 parts. Roll out each part on a floured board to 12x8 inches. Spread ¼ of the cream cheese filling mixture on each rectangle. Roll up jelly roll style and place seam side down on a greased cookie sheet. Slit at 2 inch intervals about ⅔ way through the dough. Cover and let rise for one hour. Bake at 375 degrees for 12 minutes (until nice and brown). Let cool before slicing. May top with a powdered sugar glaze while still warm. Makes 4 braids.

Rita Fitzgerald

Cinnamon Twists

1 cup sour cream
3 tablespoons sugar
⅛ teaspoon baking soda
1 teaspoon salt
1 cake compressed yeast (or one package instant dry yeast)
1 large egg
2 tablespoons soft shortening
3 cups sifted flour
2 tablespoons soft butter
⅓ cup light brown sugar
1 teaspoon cinnamon

Preheat oven to 375 degrees. Use a greased baking sheet. Heat the sour cream in large saucepan to lukewarm. Remove from heat and stir in sugar, baking soda and salt. Crumble yeast into this mixture and stir until dissolved. Add the egg, shortening, and flour. Mix well, using hand if necessary. Turn dough onto a floured board and fold over several times until smooth. Roll into an oblong shape, 24 x 6 inches. Spread with butter. Sprinkle half of the dough with a mixture of the brown sugar and cinnamon. Fold the other half of the dough over this. Cut into about 24 1-inch wide strips. Hold strip at both ends and twist in opposite directions. Place on baking sheet 2 inches apart. Press both ends of twists to baking sheet. Cover and let rise until light, about one hour. Bake 12-15 minutes. While still warm frost with the icing.

Powdered Sugar Icing:
1 cup sifted powdered sugar
1-2 tablespoons warm milk or cream
½ teaspoon vanilla (or lemon juice with a bit of grated lemon rind)

Icing: Mix above ingredients. Spread or drizzle over twists.

Mary Dambach

Biscuits and sermons are improved by shortening.

Jalapeño Cheese Biscuits

1 cup unbleached all-purpose flour
pinch of sugar
¼ teaspoon salt
2 teaspoons baking powder
4 tablespoons (½ stick) unsalted butter, cold
6 tablespoons half and half
2 ounces Monterey Jack cheese with jalapeño peppers, grated (½ cup)

Preheat oven to 425 degrees. In a large bowl, sift together the flour, sugar, salt and baking powder. Cut the butter into small pieces. Using a pastry blender or your fingertips, work the butter into the flour until the mixture resembles coarse crumbs. Add the half and half. Stir well. Work in the grated cheese. Transfer the dough to a lightly floured surface. Knead it for about 30 seconds. Pat out until it is 1 inch thick. Cut out rounds with a 2 inch cookie cutter. Arrange the biscuits about 1 inch apart on a baking sheet. Bake 15 minutes until puffed and golden. Transfer biscuits to a wire rack and allow to cool. Makes 6 biscuits.

Evelyn Letendre

Cranberry-Corn Muffins

¾ cup all-purpose flour
½ cup whole-wheat flour
1 cup yellow cornmeal
⅓ cup sugar
2 teaspoons baking powder
½ teaspoon baking soda
¼ teaspoon salt
⅔ cup buttermilk
⅓ cup orange juice
⅓ cup canola vegetable oil
2 egg whites or 1 egg
4 teaspoons grated orange rind
1 cup fresh cranberries, coarsely chopped

Preheat oven to 400 degrees. Grease and flour a 12 cup muffin pan. In a large bowl, combine white flour, whole wheat flour, cornmeal, sugar, baking powder, baking soda and salt. In a small bowl combine the buttermilk, orange juice, oil, egg and orange rind. Add the buttermilk mixture to the flour mixture, stirring the ingredients until they are just moist. Stir in the cranberries. Pour into the muffin pan. Bake for 20 to 25 minutes. Makes 12.

Rita Fitzgerald

Jalapeño Skillet Cornbread

1 cup cornmeal
½ cup presifted flour
½ teaspoon baking soda
1 teaspoon salt
½ teaspoon sugar
1 cup creamed-style corn
1 medium onion, chopped
2 jalapeño chili peppers, chopped
¼ pound grated Cheddar or Velveeta cheese
½ cup vegetable oil
2 eggs, lightly beaten
1 cup buttermilk

Preheat oven to 450 degrees. Grease an 8 inch cast iron skillet. In a mixing bowl, combine dry ingredients. Stir in corn, onions, chilies and cheese. Combine with oil, egg and buttermilk. Turn into skillet. Bake for 20-25 minutes or until lightly browned.

Note: I grew up in Texas and this recipe reflects the unique blend of Deep South and Mexican cooking that is my southwestern heritage.

Karen White
Bedford Planning Director

Date Nut Bread

1½ cups whole-wheat flour
⅓ cup white flour
3 teaspoons baking powder
½ teaspoon baking soda
¾ teaspoon salt
¾ cup brown sugar
beaten white of an egg
1½ cups water
5 tablespoons powdered milk
1 cup Special K cereal, coarsely chopped
1 cup All-Bran cereal, coarsely chopped
1 tablespoon chopped nuts
½ cup pitted dates, coarsely chopped

Preheat oven 375 degrees. Mix all ingredients together. Pour into a greased loaf pan. Bake for 1¼ hours.

Note: Nephew of William Riddle McAllaster. Mother grew up on Vose Farm and his father grew up on Gendrons Farm on McAllister Road.

Lee Tebbetts

Zucchini Nut Bread

1 medium zucchini
1¼ cups sugar
⅔ cup vegetable oil
2 large eggs
2 cups unbleached flour
1 tablespoon baking powder
2 teaspoons cinnamon
½ teaspoon baking soda
1 teaspoon salt
¼ teaspoon ground allspice
2 teaspoons vanilla
1 cup minced walnuts

Preheat oven to 350 degrees. Prepare 1 large loaf pan or 2 smaller pans plus 1 mini loaf. In a food processor, using the metal blade, pulse the machine while adding chunks of zucchini. Zucchini should be well shredded but not over processed. If doing this step by hand, grate the zucchini. Set aside.

In a large mixing bowl, mix sugar, oil and eggs until smooth. Fold in dry ingredients, including the spices. Add zucchini, vanilla extract and nuts. Stir. Pour batter in to the prepared pans. Bake large loaf for 60 minutes, smaller loaves for 45 minutes and mini loaf for 30 minutes. Allow to cool in pan for 10 minutes, then turn out onto a cake rack to cool completely. Wrapped airtight, the loaves can be held at room temperature for four days or stored in a refrigerator for several weeks. The bread also freezes well up to 4 months.

Jeanene Procopis

Chocolate Zucchini Bread

3 eggs
¾ cup oil
2 cups sugar
3 cups grated zucchini
2 teaspoons vanilla
3 cups flour
2 tablespoons cocoa
3 tablespoons baking soda
¼ teaspoon baking powder
½ cup chocolate chips

Preheat oven to 325 degrees. Grease two 9x5 inch loaf pans. Mix together eggs, oil, sugar, zucchini and vanilla. Sift together the flour, cocoa, baking soda and baking powder. Add to egg mixture and stir well. Pour into 2 loaf pans. Sprinkle chocolate chips on top. Bake for 45-55 minutes.

Doris Guimont

Steph's Irish Raisin Bread

3 cups flour
1 teaspoon baking soda
1 teaspoon baking powder
1 teaspoon salt
½ cup sugar
2 teaspoons butter
1 egg
1¾ cups buttermilk
1 cup raisins

Preheat oven to 350 degrees. Grease and flour a 9x5 inch loaf pan. Sift together flour, baking soda, baking powder, and salt. Cream together sugar, butter, egg and buttermilk. Combine both mixtures. Add raisins. Bake for 1 hour. Place on a wire rack to cool. Preparation time 15 minutes.

Stephanie Gallagher Rooney
Mary Dambach

Pumpkin Apple Bread

3 cups flour
¾ teaspoon salt
2 teaspoons baking soda
1½ teaspoons cinnamon
1 teaspoon nutmeg
1 teaspoon ground cloves
¼ teaspoon ground allspice
1 (16 ounce) can of solid pack pumpkin
¾ cup vegetable oil
2¼ cups sugar
4 large eggs, beaten lightly
2 Granny Smith apples, peeled and chopped (2 cups)

Preheat oven to 350 degrees. Grease and flour 2 loaf pans. In a large bowl mix flour, salt, baking soda and spices. In another bowl whisk together the pumpkin, oil, sugar and eggs. Combine with the flour mixture, stirring until well mixed. Fold in the apples. Divide the batter between 2 pans.

Topping:
1 tablespoon flour
5 tablespoons sugar
1 teaspoon cinnamon
1 tablespoon softened butter

Mix together the topping ingredients until it resembles coarse meal. Sprinkle topping on the loaves. Bake 50 minutes. Let loaves cool in pans on a rack for 45 minutes. Then remove and cool completely. Makes 2 loaves.

Wesley Maloney

Pumpkin Bread

3 cups flour
2 cups sugar
2 teaspoons soda
1½ teaspoons ground cinnamon
1 teaspoon ground nutmeg
½ teaspoon baking powder
½ teaspoon salt, optional
¼ teaspoon ground cloves
2 eggs
2 cups (16 ounce can) pumpkin
⅔ cup oil

Bake at 350 degrees in two greased 8½ x 4½ inch loaf pans. Stir together flour, sugar, soda, cinnamon, nutmeg, baking powder, salt and cloves in large mixing bowl. Lightly beat eggs. Beat in pumpkin and oil. Add to flour mixture, stirring just to combine. Spoon into pans. Batter will be stiff. Bake for 55-60 minutes, or until wooden pick inserted near center comes out clean. Cool 5 minutes; remove from pans. Cool completely and wrap.

Note: Freezes well.

Doris Guimont

English Rich Scones

8 heaped tablespoons flour
1 level teaspoon baking powder
1 level tablespoon sugar
1 egg, beaten
2 level tablespoons margarine
milk

Preheat oven to 450 degrees. Cook on hot baking sheet. Sift together flour, baking powder and salt. Rub in margarine and add sugar. Mix with egg and enough milk to make a soft dough. Turn on to lightly floured board and knead quickly. Roll to ½ to ¾ inch thick. Cut with knife or floured cutter. Place on baking sheet and brush with milk. Bake 12-15 minutes.

Note: Delicious with jelly or jam and cream.

Caroline Williams

Morning Glory Muffins

1¼ cups sugar
2¼ cups flour
1 tablespoon cinnamon
2 teaspoons baking soda
½ teaspoon salt
½ cup shredded coconut
½ cup raisins
2 cups grated carrots
1 apple, shredded
1 (8 ounce) can crushed pineapple, drained
3 eggs
1 cup oil
1 teaspoon vanilla

Preheat oven to 350 degrees. Grease muffin tins. Makes 16 large muffins. In large bowl mix together sugar, flour, cinnamon, baking soda and salt. Add coconut, raisins, carrots, apple, pineapple and nuts. In a separate bowl whisk eggs, oil and vanilla. Combine all ingredients and blend well. Spoon into large cupcake papers and fill to brim. Bake for 35 minutes for large muffins.

Note: It took me two years and a sister-in-law in New Jersey to find this recipe!

Wesley Maloney

Shirley's Stock Market Muffins (Guaranteed to Rise)

4 cups Post Raisin Bran
1½ cups sugar
2½ cups flour
2½ teaspoons baking soda
1 teaspoon salt
1 stick melted margarine
2 eggs
2 cups buttermilk

Mix Raisin Bran, sugar, flour, baking soda and salt by hand. Add margarine, eggs and buttermilk. Refrigerate a few days before baking. Bake in muffin tins at 400 degrees for 15 to 20 minutes.

Note: This recipe was taken from the Beardstown Ladies Book, a Ladies Investment Club in Illinois.

Hannah Perutz

Brunch

The Old Town Hall

The first Old Meeting House was built in 1755 and was mainly used as a church until the Presbyterians built their own structure. The building lasted until 1876 when it was taken down and another built on the same location. This town hall served Bedford well until 1909 when a fire completely destroyed the building.

In 1910, the town appropriated $8,000.00 to rebuild the structure. The finished building is an imposing structure in the Greek Revival style, approximately 50x70 feet in size. There is a full basement, a kitchen, and an ample stage on the second floor. Four Doric columns support the porch roof. The Bedford Town Hall is a handsome, well-maintained structure standing at the southern end of the common, a most fitting image of a traditional New England village. Today it is used for community functions and recreational programs.

All Around The Neighborhood

(Progressive Dinner)

beverages

Concord Coach Punch   Bourbon Sour Slush

hors d'oeuvres

Bacon-wrapped Scallops

Savory Stuffed Mushrooms   Brie en Croute

Red Pepper Dip with fresh vegetables

entrée

Boeuf Bourguignonne   Egg Noodles

Tomato Aspic   French Bread

dessert

Scandinavian Baked Pears   Flan

Spanish Coffee

Apple Pan Dowdy

4-5 apples, peeled and sliced
cinnamon
nutmeg
2 eggs, well beaten
1 cup sugar
1 cup flour
1 teaspoon baking powder
4 tablespoons margarine, melted

Preheat oven 375 degrees. Bake in 9 inch square ovenproof dish. Fill dish with sliced apples. Sprinkle cinnamon and nutmeg over apples. In bowl, mix eggs, sugar, flour, baking powder and margarine. Drop mixture over apples. Bake 30-40 minutes. Yield: 6 servings.

Bess Morrison

Jewish Sour Cream Apple Coffee Cake

1 cup sugar
½ cup shortening
2 eggs
1 cup sour cream
1 teaspoon vanilla extract
2 cups flour
pinch salt
1½ teaspoons baking powder
½ teaspoon baking soda
1 cup diced apples

Preheat oven to 350 degrees. Grease tube or bundt pan. Cream sugar with shortening. Add eggs, sour cream, vanilla and sifted dry ingredients. Beat until smooth.

Filling:
½ cup sugar
2 teaspoons cinnamon
1 cup chopped nuts

Mix sugar, cinnamon, and nuts. Pour half the batter into the pan, then half the filling, and all of the apples. Add the rest of the batter and then the rest of filling. Bake for one hour or until toothpick comes out clean. Top can be drizzled with icing for a fancy effect.

Elisabeth P. Place

Orange Coffee Cake

2 cups flour
1 teaspoon cinnamon
1 teaspoon baking powder
¼ teaspoon nutmeg
1 teaspoon baking soda
Dash of salt
1 cup sugar
1 beaten egg
1 cup milk
½ cup oil
1 whole orange, ground

Preheat oven to 325 degrees. Sift flour, cinnamon, baking powder, nutmeg, baking soda, salt and sugar. Mix together egg, milk, oil and orange. Add to dry ingredients. Stir together and pour into a greased and floured 9x13 inch pan.

Topping:
⅓ cup brown sugar
½ stick margarine
1 cup chopped nuts

Mix together brown sugar, margarine and chopped nuts. Spread on top of batter. Bake for 30 minutes.

Glaze:
¾ cup powdered sugar
1 teaspoon milk
orange flavoring chunks

Make the glaze of powdered sugar, milk and orange chunks. Drizzle over the warm cake. Yield: 12 servings.

Doris Guimont

Cheese Grits Supreme

1 cup grits
½ cup butter or margarine, softened
1 (6 ounce) roll bacon-cheese
3 eggs, beaten
⅔ cup milk
½ cup Cheddar cheese, grated

Preheat oven to 325 degrees. Cook grits as package directs. Add butter and bacon-cheese to hot grits. Blend well. Cool. Combine eggs with milk. Stir into grits. Pour into greased casserole. Sprinkle with grated Cheddar cheese. Bake for 50 minutes.

Note: Too good to be true.

Bonnie Venn

Sour Cream Raisin Coffeecake

¾ cup butter
1½ cups sugar
3 eggs
1½ teaspoons vanilla
1½ cups sour cream
3 cups sifted all purpose flour
2¼ teaspoons baking powder
1½ teaspoons baking soda
¼ teaspoon salt

Preheat oven to 350 degrees. Cream together butter and sugar until mixture is fluffy. Add eggs and vanilla. Beat well. Blend in sour cream. Sift together remaining cake ingredients and stir into cream mixture. Mix well. Spread ⅓ of batter in angel food cake pan.

Filling/Topping:
1½ cups chopped walnuts
¾ cup sugar
1½ teaspoons ground cinnamon
1½ cups raisins

Combine nuts, sugar and cinnamon for filling. Sprinkle ⅓ of this mixture over the batter in the pan. Then sprinkle nuts on top. Spoon another ⅓ of batter over filling and repeat the layers ending with a topping of raisins. Bake for 55 minutes or until cake tester comes out clean.

Great to serve at a brunch.

Christina Barley

How to Preserve Children

To Preserve Children take:
1 large grassy field
½ dozen children
2 or 3 small dogs
a pinch of brook and some small pebbles

Mix all the children and dogs well together and put them in the field, stirring constantly. Pour the brook over the pebbles, sprinkle the field with flowers, spread over all a deep blue sky, and bake in a hot sun. When thoroughly browned, remove and set to cool in a bath tub.

Crumb Cake

½ cup shortening
2 cups brown sugar
2 cups all purpose flour
¼ teaspoon salt
1 egg
1 cup sour milk
1 teaspoon baking soda
1 teaspoon vanilla

Preheat oven to 350 degrees. Grease 8x8 or 7½x11 inch cake pan. Blend shortening, sugar, flour, and salt thoroughly. Measure ¾ cup of this mixture and set aside for topping. To the remaining mixture add egg and sour milk to which the baking soda has been added. Add vanilla and stir. Pour batter into prepared pan and sprinkle crumbs over the top. (May add chocolate chips to the topping or sprinkle cinnamon over the top if desired.) Bake for 35-40 minutes or until a toothpick comes out clean.

Harriet Bortis

Pull-Apart Cake

6 packages buttermilk biscuits
1½ cups sugar
3 teaspoons cinnamon
½ cup margarine, melted
Karo syrup
pecans
cherries

Preheat oven to 350 degrees. Grease a tube pan. Mix sugar and cinnamon together. Roll each biscuit into a ball. Drop into margarine then into sugar mixture. Put a little Karo syrup in pan. Arrange 5 cherries and nuts on the bottom of the pan. Place biscuits in pan (not too close together). Repeat, making 2 more layers of syrup, cherries and nuts. Sprinkle remaining cinnamon mixture on top along with a little Karo syrup. Set pan on cookie sheet (liquid might leak out) and bake 1 hour or until brown and done.

Note: During the holiday season a red candle can be placed in center of the cake.

Louise Padfield

Use baby powder or corn starch on exposed areas of skin before child plays in sandbox. Sand will brush off easily after play has ended.

Danish Puff

1 cup butter or margarine
2 cups flour
1 cup plus 2 tablespoons water
1 teaspoon almond extract
3 eggs
½ cup chopped nuts

Preheat oven to 350 degrees. Use ungreased baking sheet. Cut ½ cup butter into 1 cup flour. Sprinkle 2 tablespoons water over mixture. Mix and round into a ball. Divide in half. On baking sheet, pat each half into a 12 x 3 inch strip. The strips should be 3 inches apart. Heat ½ cup butter and 1 cup water to rolling boil in medium saucepan. Remove from heat and quickly stir in almond extract and 1 cup flour. Stir vigorously over low heat for about 1 minute until mixture forms a ball. Remove from heat and beat in eggs until smooth and glossy. Divide the mixture in half and spread each half evenly over the strips. Bake for 60 minutes or until topping is crisp and brown. (Topping will shrink and fall, forming the custardy top of this puff). Cool.

Sugar glaze:
1½ cups powdered sugar
1½ teaspoons vanilla
2 tablespoons butter or margarine, softened
1-2 tablespoons warm water

Mix glaze ingredients until smooth and of spreading consistency. Frost Puff with glaze and sprinkle with nuts. Cut into squares.

Sharlene Genest

Rice Pudding Cereal

3 cups cooked white or brown rice
2 cups skim or low fat milk
1 egg white plus 1 whole egg, lightly beaten
1 tablespoon sugar
¼ cup raisins
¼ teaspoon cinnamon

Preparation time: 10 minutes. Combine all ingredients in a medium saucepan and mix well. Cook over moderate heat, stirring occasionally until it has thickened (about 5 minutes after the milk reaches a boil). Serves 3 to 4.

Louise Langley

Jalapeño Cheese Grits

3 cups boiling water
1 teaspoon salt
¾ cup quick cooking grits
2 beaten eggs
¾ stick margarine or butter
8 ounces sharp Cheddar cheese
1 (8 ounce) roll jalapeño cheese
1 (4 ounce) can green chilies, chopped
3 or 4 shakes of Tabasco sauce
paprika

Preheat oven to 250 degrees. Add grits gradually to water and salt, stirring until thick — about 5 minutes. Add eggs and let come to a good boil. Add margarine and cheese. Stir until melted. Add green chilies and Tabasco sauce. Stir until blended. Put in a greased 9 inch square dish and sprinkle with paprika. Bake for 1 hour. Serve hot. Yield: 4-6 servings.

This can be prepared ahead. Makes an excellent brunch dish.

Anne C. Hoffman

Night Before French Toast Casserole

1 long loaf French bread
8 large eggs
3 cups milk
4 teaspoons sugar
¾ teaspoon salt
1 tablespoon vanilla
2 tablespoons butter, cut into small pieces

Grease 13x9 inch baking dish with butter. Cut bread into 1 inch slices. Arrange in one layer on bottom of the pan. Beat eggs, milk, sugar, salt, and vanilla together. Pour over bread. Cover pan with foil and refrigerate overnight. Uncover and dot with butter pieces. Bake at 350 degrees for 45-50 minutes (until puffy and brown). Remove from oven and let stand 5 minutes before serving. Serve with syrup. Yield: 8 servings.

This is an easy do-ahead breakfast recipe.

Betty Ober
Jacquelin Lavoie

Sausage and Cheese Casserole

1 pound Jimmy Dean bulk hot sausage
12 slices white bread, crusts removed, butter on one side
3 cups sharp Cheddar cheese, grated
3 cups milk
4 large eggs
¾ teaspoon salt
¼ teaspoon pepper

In skillet crumble and cook sausage. Drain on paper towels. In 13x9 buttered casserole, place one layer of bread, buttered side down. Cover with half the sausage mixture and half the cheese. Layer remaining bread, sausage and cheese. In bowl whisk milk, eggs, salt and pepper. Carefully pour over. Cover and refrigerate overnight. Remove from refrigerator 30 minutes before putting into the oven. Bake at 350 degrees 45-50 minutes.

Janis Clover

LJ's Breakfast Casserole

16 slices white bread, cubed
1 pound bacon, crisp and crumbled
1½ cups Swiss cheese, grated
1 pound Cheddar cheese, grated
6 eggs
3 cups milk
½ teaspoon onion salt
½ teaspoon prepared mustard
2 garlic cloves, crushed (optional)
2½ cups cornflakes

Grease 9x13 inch pan. Spread half the cubed bread on bottom. Sprinkle crumbled bacon and ½ the cheeses over the bread. Cover with the remaining bread cubes. Beat together eggs, milk, salt, mustard and garlic. Pour mixture over the bread. Cover with the remaining cheese. Refrigerate overnight. In the morning crush 2½ cups cornflakes and spread over the top. Bake at 375 degrees for 40 minutes. Cut into squares and serve.

Eugene Van Loan
Bedford Town Moderator

Breakfast Casserole

1 pound pork sausage
6 eggs (or egg substitute)
2 cups milk
1 teaspoon salt
1 teaspoon dry mustard
3 slices white bread, cubed
1 cup grated Cheddar cheese

Sauté sausage until brown and drain well. In bowl beat eggs. Add milk, salt and dry mustard. Mix well until all lumps are gone. In a greased 13x9 inch baking dish, layer the bread cubes, sausage and cheese. Pour egg mixture over all. Cover and refrigerate overnight. This gives the bread time to absorb the egg mixture. In the morning, bake at 350 degrees for 45 minutes. Serves 8.

Madonna Lovett Repeta

French Toast Soufflé

4 tablespoons unsalted butter
½ cup packed brown sugar
2 loaves Challah or 1 Portuguese Sweet Bread or other white bread
6 eggs
2 cups whole milk
2 teaspoons vanilla
dash salt

In bottom of 9x13 pan, place cut-up butter. Sprinkle with brown sugar. Place slices of bread in one layer (can be squeezed in). If using regular white bread do not remove crust, but do not use the two ends. In bowl mix eggs, milk, vanilla and salt. Pour over bread making sure entire surface is soaked. Cover, refrigerate overnight (this step cannot be omitted or soufflé won't puff up). Bake uncovered in 375 degrees oven for 40-50 minutes until puffed and lightly browned. Sprinkle with confectioner's sugar and serve immediately. Serve with fruit.

Note: This is a good breakfast/brunch casserole that is made the night before and refrigerated overnight — wonderful at holidays and any time you have overnight guests.

Evelyn S. Letendre
Bedford Representative
NH State Legislature

Oatmeal Pancakes

1½ cups rolled oats
2 cups buttermilk
½ cup flour
1 teaspoon sugar
1 teaspoon baking soda
1 teaspoon salt
2 eggs, beaten

Mix together rolled oats and buttermilk. Let sit 5 minutes. Beat in flour, sugar, baking soda, salt and eggs. If desired, fruit may be added to the batter. Makes a thin batter. Cook on griddle.

Bonnie Venn

Mickey's French Pancakes

1 cup flour
2 teaspoons baking powder
½ teaspoon salt
2 beaten eggs
1¾ cups milk
2 tablespoons melted butter

Preheat pancake griddle. Mix flour, baking powder, and salt together in large bowl. Add eggs and milk. Beat until well blended. Add butter and blend until well mixed. Rub hot pancake griddle with salt bag before cooking first batch of pancakes. (To make salt bag, put about 2 tablespoons of salt in the center of a square piece of old cotton sheet. Gather the ends and secure with a rubber band). With a small ladle, pour 1 ladle of batter per pancake onto prepared griddle. When the batter starts to have air bubbles in the center, turn the pancake. Pancake is ready when it is a consistent light golden brown color. The first pancakes cooked may not have a consistent color. Serves: 4-6.

Note: This recipe makes thin, light pancakes. One serving would have 4-6 small pancakes. Leftover batter will keep for 24 hours in refrigerator.

Anne C. Hoffman

German Pancakes

1 cup milk
1 cup flour
6 eggs
¼ teaspoon salt
6 tablespoons butter, melted in pan

Preheat oven to 450 degrees. Mix all ingredients together. Pour into 9x13 inch pan and bake for 20-25 minutes. Serve immediately.

Bonnie Venn

Ricotta and Spinach Pie

1 package chopped spinach (cooked and drained)
2 pounds ricotta cheese
1 cup grated cheese (mozzarella, feta or Cheddar)
4 eggs, lightly beaten
2 teaspoons oil
1 teaspoon onion salt or garlic salt
1 teaspoon salt
½ teaspoon fresh ground pepper
½ zucchini, sliced and sautéed
¼ pound fresh mushrooms, sautéed
½ green pepper, diced and sautéed
½ cup chopped ham or cooked sausage
2 teaspoons oil or butter

Preheat oven to 350 degrees. Add spinach to rapidly boiling water (¾ cup). Cover and cook 5 minutes. Drain and squeeze out all water. Combine ricotta cheese, spinach, grated cheese, eggs, oil seasonings, vegetables and meat. Pour mixture into a spring form pan or deep pie plate which has been lightly oiled. Bake for 40 minutes. Yield: 4-8 servings.

Hints: If you double the recipe, double the cooking time. If knife comes out clean when inserted in center, it is done. This is a nice brunch or lunch entrée. The pie can also be sliced thin and served as an appetizer.

Donna Joas

Salads

John Goffe's Mill

Mills were almost by necessity the first industry to exist in town. In 1748, John Goffe built a gristmill, and later a sawmill on Crosby's Brook. People came from far away to use them. Soon there were many mills on this Goffe property. One mill was used to make old-fashioned slat curtains, called jalousies.

At the mouth of Crosby's Brook, Goffe built a forge with a trip hammer and wrought ore into iron in considerable quantities. It was here that iron cannon balls for the Continental Army were made during the Revolutionary War. He also made nails used by Bedford's famous Dunlap furniture makers.

Mother's Day Brunch Buffet

beverages

Raspberry Champagne Punch

dishes

French Toast Soufflé

Maple Syrup

Crustless Quiche

Sausage and Cheese Casserole

Jalapeño Cheese Grits

Ricotta Spinach Pie

Fruit Salad with Fruit Salad Dressing

desserts

Banana Cake

Dutch Apple Pie

SALADS

Broccoli Salad

2 bunches fresh broccoli florets
1 small red onion
½ cup raisins, chopped
¼ cup sliced almonds
½ pound bacon (optional)

Cut broccoli into small florets (no stems), rinse and dry. Slice onion into rings and add to broccoli. Add raisins and nuts, set aside. Cook bacon until crisp, break into small pieces and add to above.

Dressing:
1 cup mayonnaise, low calorie
⅓ cup sugar
2 teaspoons sugar
2 teaspoons cider vinegar

Mix dressing well. Pour over broccoli and lightly toss. Chill thoroughly and serve on chilled salad plates lined with red leaf lettuce, if desired. Serves 6.

Cathy Rooney Ashley

Broccoli Salad

1 large bunch chopped broccoli
1 sweet onion, diced
½ cup grated sharp Cheddar cheese
1 pound bacon, cooked and crumbled

Combine all salad ingredients.

Dressing:
½ cup Miracle Whip dressing
¼ cup sugar
1 tablespoon vinegar

Combine all dressing ingredients well. Toss salad with dressing just prior to serving.

Alberta Dieter

Sweet and Sour Broccoli Salad

1 large head broccoli
½ cup chopped onions (optional)
8 bacon strips, fried and crumbled, or ⅛ cup Bacos
¼ cup raisins
¾ cup mayonnaise
¼ cup sugar
2 tablespoons vinegar

Cut broccoli into florets (peel stems and cut those up too). Combine broccoli, onions and bacon. Set aside. Mix mayonnaise, sugar and vinegar. Pour over broccoli mix and stir. Add raisins. Stir again. Chill or serve immediately. Serves 4.

Mary Jo Smith
wife of US Senator Bob Smith - NH

Cabbage Salad

1 large head cabbage, finely chopped
1 large green pepper, diced
2 medium onions, finely chopped
1 cup cider vinegar
1 cup salad oil
1 teaspoon salt
1½ cups sugar
1 teaspoon celery salt

Put cabbage, pepper and onion in a large bowl. In a saucepan combine the vinegar, oil, salt, sugar and celery salt. Bring to a boil. Pour over cabbage mixture and stir well. The mixture may also be placed in an air tight container and refrigerated. Marinate 3 days before serving. Stir or shake mixture 2 or 3 times daily. Can be kept 1 month in refrigerator.

Martha H. Gaudes

Vinegar - Low percentage natural acid, generally acetic acid. Used as a preservative for all pickling of vegetables and fruit. To give zest or tangy flavor to salad dressing; for meat, fish and vegetable sauces. Different kinds are wine vinegar, malt or beer vinegar, white vinegar, cider vinegar, tarragon vinegar.

Purple Cabbage Salad

½ head purple cabbage, thinly sliced or shredded (not chopped)
2 tablespoons cider vinegar
2 teaspoons salt
½ cup sour cream
pepper to taste

Add vinegar and salt to cabbage. Leave in the refrigerator so the salt can brine the cabbage overnight (or at least for a few hours). Drain the juice and pat dry the cabbage. Put shredded cabbage in a serving bowl and mix with the sour cream. Serve cold.

Note: This is easy and can be done in advance and left in refrigerator until needed.

Artie Robersen
Bedford Town Manager

Spicy Marinated Pepper Slaw

3 large bell peppers, cut into matchstick size strips (use one each of yellow, orange and red to add color)
2 jalapeño chilies, minced
⅔ cup olive oil
½ cup red wine vinegar
3 tablespoons sugar
12 cups thinly sliced red or green cabbage (about 2 heads)

Toss peppers and chilies in large bowl. Bring oil, vinegar and sugar just to the boiling point in a small heavy saucepan over medium heat, stirring often. Pour over peppers in the bowl and toss to coat. Cool. Add cabbage and toss. Season with salt. Can be prepared 1 hour ahead. Cover and chill. Serves 12.

Anne C. Hoffman

Storing vegetables improperly can cause a change in flavor or hasten spoilage.

7 Layer Salad

1 head lettuce
2 cups chopped celery
1 package cooked frozen peas, cooled
1 chopped red onion
1 chopped green pepper
1 pint mayonnaise
1 tablespoon sugar
1 cup grated mild cheddar cheese
bacon bits

Tear lettuce into a glass bowl. Add vegetables in layers. Spread mayonnaise all over top, sealing edges. Sprinkle with 1 tablespoon sugar, then with cheese. Top with bacon bits. Cover with plastic wrap and refrigerate at least 8 hours or overnight. Toss before serving. Serves 10 to 12.

Harriet Bortis

Caesar Salad

6 tablespoons olive oil
1 garlic clove, crushed
1 cup French bread cubes
2 large heads romaine
¼ cup salad oil
½ cup grated Parmesan cheese
¾ teaspoon salt
freshly ground pepper
1 raw egg
1 large lemon (or 3 tablespoons lemon juice)

Combine olive oil and garlic. Let stand overnight. Toast bread cubes until golden. Wash salad greens, dry on a towel. Break into bite sized pieces and chill (about 2 quarts). Put greens in large salad bowl with plenty of room for tossing. Sprinkle with salad oil and a ¼ cup of the garlic oil. Toss gently until greens are glistening. Sprinkle with cheese, salt and pepper. Break egg on top. Squeeze lemon juice over all. Toss until egg is blended completely. Taste and adjust seasoning if needed. Toss croutons in the remaining garlic oil. Add to salad. Toss lightly and serve at once. Serves 4 to 6.

Bonnie Venn

Pickled Cucumbers

2 cups white sugar
1 cup white vinegar
1 teaspoon turmeric
1 teaspoon celery seed
1 teaspoon mustard seed
7 cups cucumbers, thinly sliced (4-5 regular size)
1 cup onions, thinly sliced

Use a large bowl with a cover. Mix liquid, sugar and spices. Pour over cucumbers and onions. Mix well. Cover and store in refrigerator. Stir once or twice daily. Use after 48 hours. No cooking required.

Alberta Dieter

Tomato Cucumber Salad

3 large tomatoes
1 large cucumber
2 green onions
1 teaspoon oregano
2 tablespoons olive oil
juice of ½ lemon
salt, to taste
freshly ground pepper, to taste
pinch of sugar

Rinse vegetables. Cut tomatoes in wedges. Score the cucumber skin with tines of a fork, then cut cucumber into thin slices. Slice onions, including most of the green tops. In a salad bowl, combine vegetables with oregano. In a small bowl, mix together olive oil, lemon juice, salt, pepper and sugar. Pour over salad and toss to mix. Serves 4.

Jeanene Procopis

Carrot Salad

1½ pounds carrots, sliced thinly
1 medium red onion
½ cup chopped green pepper
1 can tomato soup
¾ cup sugar
½ cup vegetable oil
½ cup red wine vinegar
1 teaspoon Worcestershire sauce
½ teaspoon salt

Cook carrots, keeping crisp. Mix everything together. Refrigerate 24 hours.

Merrie Edgar
Alice Asadourian
Madonna Lovett Repeta

Moroccan Salad

2 green peppers
2 tomatoes
1 large or 2 small cucumbers
¼ cup oil
½ cup wine vinegar
pinch salt

Roast green peppers on grill or range top, turning until blackened and soft. Holding under running water, discard seeds and most of charred skin. Coarsely chop peppers, tomatoes and cucumbers. Mix all in a bowl with oil, vinegar and salt. Let chill for 1 hour or more. Serves 8.

Barbara Fox Friedman

24 Hour Salad

2 eggs, well beaten
4 tablespoons sugar
4 tablespoons apple cider vinegar
2 tablespoons butter
1 cup whipping cream
2 cups crushed pineapple
2 cups dark sweet cherries
2 oranges, diced, or 1 can mandarin oranges, drained
2 cups mini marshmallows

Put well beaten eggs in top of double boiler. Add sugar and vinegar. Cook until thick and smooth. Remove from heat and add butter. Cool (or it will curdle). Whip cream and fold into egg mixture. Add well-drained fruit. Chill 24 hours.

Note: Good for Thanksgiving or Christmas salad.

Barbara Weigold

Cucumber Salad

1 large cucumber
1 large onion
⅓ cup cider vinegar
5 tablespoons water
3 tablespoons sugar
½ teaspoon salt
1 tablespoon oil
pepper to taste
dried parsley

Partially peel and score one cucumber. Slice as thin as possible. Slice onion as thin as possible. Alternate slices. Add next 5 ingredients. Sprinkle with pepper and dried parsley. Keep mixture covered with liquid about 3 hours.

Priscilla Van Wagner

Betty Ober's 24 Hour Salad

1 large head lettuce shredded
¼ cup finely chopped green onions
¼ cup finely chopped celery
1 can sliced water chestnuts, drained
1 to 2 packages frozen peas, not thawed
2 cups mayonnaise
1 tablespoon sugar
¾ pound bacon, crumbled
3 grated hard cooked eggs
sliced tomatoes to cover
Parmesan or Romano cheese

In order, layer the above seven ingredients in a clear glass bowl. Cover with foil or Saran wrap, refrigerate for approximately 24 hours. Before serving, layer the salad with bacon, eggs and tomatoes. Sprinkle cheese to taste. Serves 8 to 10.

Martha Dollen

Salad with Nuts and Seeds

1 large head Boston lettuce
1 head Romaine lettuce
1 cup grated carrots
¾ cup freshly shredded Parmesan cheese
¼ cup sesame seeds
¼ cup sunflower seeds (kernels)
¼ cup pine nuts
¼ cup sliced almond
1 cup Paul Newman's Italian Salad Dressing (olive oil and vinegar)
1 tablespoon Dijon mustard

Prepare lettuce (wash, spin dry and break into small pieces). Toast seeds and nuts on a cookie sheet in 400 degree oven until brown, 4-6 minutes. Watch closely. Cool. This may all be done early and refrigerated. Mix lettuce, carrots and cheese in a large salad bowl. Add Dijon mustard to the salad dressing and shake well. Toss salad with dressing mixture just before serving. Add toasted seeds and nuts. Serves 8-10.

Anne C. Hoffman

Glass Bowl Salad

iceberg lettuce
spinach leaves
1 cup chopped parsley
1 green pepper, chopped
1 red pepper, chopped
½ head cauliflower, coarsely chopped
½ bunch broccoli florets, separated
1 bag sliced radishes
2 carrots, julienned
1 zucchini, julienned
1 cup peas
shredded cheese to sprinkle on top
¼ cup chopped green onions for on top

Layer the ingredients in the bowl. Starting with the bottom layer of lettuce and spinach. Next layer of chopped parsley. Layer 3, chopped green and red peppers. Layer 4, cauliflower and broccoli. Layer 5, radishes. Layer 6, carrots and zucchini. Layer 7, peas.

Dressing:
1 cup mayonnaise
1 cup sour cream
2 tablespoons Dijon mustard
2 teaspoons garlic
1 teaspoon rosemary
1 teaspoon basil
1 teaspoon oregano

Combine dressing ingredients. For layer 8, spread dressing over all sealing edges. Layer 9, sprinkle cheese and ¼ cup chopped green onion on top. Seal with plastic wrap and refrigerate 24 hours before serving.

Note: For variety, layer of red onions, sliced cucumbers or other nuts may be used.

JoAnn P. Goulet
wife of Maurice Goulet, NH State Representative

Do not store carrots alongside apples (carrots will turn bitter).

Chicken Tortellini Salad with Honey-Mustard Vinaigrette

3 boneless chicken breast halves, julienned
1 cup olive oil
2 cloves garlic
2 (15 ounce) packages frozen cheese tortellini
1 green pepper, diced
3 stalks celery, diced
1 small red onion, thinly sliced
⅓ pound smoked Gouda cheese, julienned
2 tablespoons Dijon mustard
½ teaspoon dry mustard
¾ cup cider vinegar
¼ cup honey
3 ounces Canadian bacon, cooked and julienned

Heat 2 teaspoons olive oil (out of 1 cup oil) in a skillet. Add garlic and sauté until brown. Remove. Add chicken to hot oil and stir fry for 3-4 minutes, until chicken is cooked thoroughly. Drain and reserve.

Cook tortellini according to package directions. Drain and toss with 2 tablespoons olive oil (out of the 1 cup). Cool. In salad bowl, combine chicken, tortellini, green pepper, celery, onion and Gouda cheese. In a small bowl, combine remaining olive oil with mustards, vinegar and honey to make vinaigrette. Pour over salad and toss well to combine. Top with Canadian bacon and serve. Serves 6.

Pat Lauer

Use baking soda and a dry cloth to remove sticky residue on plastic items left from labels.

Taco Salad and Puff Bowl

Puff Bowl:
¼ cup margarine or butter
⅔ cup water
1 cup Bisquick baking mix
¼ cup yellow cornmeal
1 teaspoon dried oregano leaves
4 eggs

Heat oven to 400 degrees. Grease a 9 x 1½ inch pie plate. Heat margarine and water to boiling in a 2 quart saucepan. Add baking mix, cornmeal and oregano, all at once. Stir vigorously over low heat until mixture forms a ball, about 1½ minutes. Remove from heat. Beat in eggs, one at a time. Beat until smooth. Spread in pie plate bottom (not up sides). Bake until puffed and dry in the center, 35 to 40 minutes. Cool.

Taco Salad:
1 pound ground beef
½ cup chopped onion
1 cup water
1¼ ounces dry taco seasoning mix
4 ounces (1 cup) Cheddar or Monterey Jack cheese
¼ head lettuce, shredded
1 medium tomato, chopped
dairy sour cream
sliced ripe olives

Cook and stir ground beef and onion, until beef is browned. Drain. Stir in water and seasoning mix (dry). Heat to boiling. Reduce heat, simmer and stir for 10 minutes. Place puff bowl on serving plate. Fill with beef mixture. Top with remaining ingredients. Cut into wedges. Serve immediately.

Note: Puff bowl may be frozen up to 3 months. Heat unwrapped, on ungreased cookie sheet in a 400 degree oven for 10 minutes until crisp.

Margaret K. Rooney

Shrimp and Red Onion Salad

½ pound cooked and cleaned shrimp
lemon juice, to taste
2 heaping tablespoons mayonnaise
1 medium red onion, sliced thinly
1 heaping tablespoon sour cream

Sprinkle shrimp with lemon. Mix mayonnaise, onion and sour cream with the shrimp. Chill overnight. Can be made two days ahead.

Bonnie Venn

Curried Rice Salad

2 boxes Chicken Rice-A-Roni
1 jar artichoke hearts, packed in oil
20 pimento olives
8 green onions, chopped
1 green pepper, chopped
⅔ cup mayonnaise plus the artichoke oil
2 teaspoons curry powder

Cook Rice-A-Roni. Cool. Add other ingredients. Chill and serve.

Madonna Lovett Repeta

Hot Potato Salad

8-10 medium potatoes
¼ cup onions, chopped
½ pound Velveeta or Monterey Jack cheese, cubed
1 to 1½ cups mayonnaise
salt and pepper, to taste
dash of accent, to taste
Herb salt, to taste
6-7 slices bacon (cooked, drained and crumbled)

Preheat oven to 350 degrees. Boil potatoes in skins. Cool, peel and dice. Mix all ingredients, except bacon, and place in a casserole dish. Put crumbled bacon on top. Bake for 30 minutes, or until cheese melts.

Pat Korcuba

Orange-Almond Salad

¼ cup salad oil
2 tablespoons sugar
2 tablespoons cider vinegar
¼ teaspoon salt
¼ teaspoon almond extract
6 cups torn mixed greens
1 cup mandarin oranges, drained
1 cup thinly sliced celery
2 tablespoons chopped green onion
⅓ cup sliced or slivered almonds (can be toasted)

In a jar, shake the oil, sugar, vinegar, salt and extract, until sugar and salt are dissolved. Chill. At serving time, combine mixed greens and add clumps of oranges, onion, and celery. Toss almonds over all. Pour in chilled dressing. Gently toss all ingredients and serve at once. Salad serves 8.

Note: for Healthy Heart dressing, use ½ cup olive oil and ½ cup water.

Eunice Brine

Strawberry-Pineapple Jello Salad

1 large package raspberry jello
1 package strawberries
1 small can crushed pineapple
1 cup boiling water
1 pint sour cream
2 mashed bananas

Mix jello and water together until completely dissolved. Add bananas, pineapple and strawberries. Set until jelled. Pour half of the mixture into a mold, then make a layer of the sour cream. Pour the rest of the mixture on top. Chill and serve.

Martha H. Gaudes

Cool Whip Salad (Ambrosia)

1 package any flavor jello
1 small carton cottage cheese
1 small can fruit cocktail
1 can mandarin oranges
1 carton cool whip

Mix jello with cottage cheese. Stir in remaining ingredients. Chill.

Martha H. Gaudes

Waldorf Salad

2-3 large apples
1 tablespoon lemon juice
½ cup halved grapes
¼ cup chopped celery
¼ cup raisins
¼ cup chopped walnuts
¼ cup mayonnaise
lettuce leaves

Core unpeeled apples and chop coarsely. Toss with lemon juice to prevent them from turning brown. Mix next 5 ingredients and add apples. Chill. Serve on a bed of lettuce leaves. Serves 4-6.

Janet Jespersen

Frozen Cranberry Layer Salad

1 (1 pound) can jellied cranberry sauce
2 tablespoons lemon juice
1 cup heavy cream, whipped
¼ cup mayonnaise
¼ cup powdered sugar
½ cup chopped walnuts or pecans

Beat cranberry sauce with a rotary beater until saucy. Combine with lemon juice. Spread in the bottom of the mold. Layer with a mixture of whipped cream, mayonnaise, powdered sugar and nuts. Place in the freezer for at least 3 hours to become firmly frozen. Remove from freezer just before serving. Unmold and serve on lettuce.

Note: For Christmas, the whipped cream can be tinted with green for a striking effect.

Rose Marie Borelli

Cranberry Jello Mold

1 large package cherry jello
1 cup hot water
1 can whole cranberry sauce
½ cup chopped nuts
1 pint sour cream

Mix jello, water and cranberry sauce. Let set slightly (30 to 45 minutes). Add nuts and sour cream. Pour into mold and chill to set.

Jacquelin Lavoie

Lime Gelatin with Cottage Cheese

2 small boxes lime jello
1 cup boiling water
12 ounces cottage cheese
1 cup mayonnaise
½ cup chopped walnuts
¼ cup chopped green pepper
¼ cup finely chopped onion
¼ cup grated carrots

Dissolve gelatin in boiling water. Blend in the remaining ingredients and pour into a ring mold. Chill until set (at least 3 hours). Unmold onto a platter and fill center with cucumber slices. Serves 8.

Janet Jespersen

Lime and Cucumber Salad

1 (3 ounce) package lime jello
1 cup boiling water
1 cup grated fresh cucumber
1 teaspoon vinegar
¼ teaspoon onion juice
½ teaspoon salt
Dash cayenne pepper

Dissolve jello in boiling water and chill. When partly set, add remaining ingredients which have been blended together. Turn into moistened jello mold. Chill. Garnish with mayonnaise and serve with a salmon loaf or other fish dishes.

Eunice C. Brine

Lime Salad For A Crowd

2 small packages of lime jello
1 (20 ounce) can of crushed pineapple, partially drained
1 small can of mandarin orange slices, drained
1 pint of sour cream
½ cup chopped walnuts

Dissolve the jello in 1 cup of boiling hot water. Add fruit, sour cream and walnuts. Blend well and turn into a 9 x 13 inch pan. Refrigerate until fully chilled and set. May be served on a bed of lettuce, topping with sliced cherries.

Christina Barley

Madrigal Of Molded Mandarin Orange Salad

2 small packages orange jello
2 cups hot water
1 envelope plain gelatin
¼ cup cold water
1 can (small) frozen orange juice
2 pints orange sherbet
2 small cans mandarin orange slices, drained

Dissolve orange gelatin in hot water. Soften plain gelatin in cold water and combine with orange. Add frozen orange juice and stir until dissolved. With electric beaters, beat in sherbet. When thickened, stir in mandarin oranges. Pour into 2 quart container and refrigerate to set. Overnight is best.

Priscilla Van Wagner

Mandarin Salad

½ cup sliced almonds
3 tablespoons sugar
½ head iceberg lettuce
½ head romaine lettuce
1 cup chopped celery
2 whole green onions, chopped
1 (11 ounce) can mandarin oranges, drained

In a small pan over medium heat, cook almonds and sugar, stirring constantly until almonds are coated and sugar dissolved. Watch carefully as they will burn easily. Cool and store in air-tight container.

Dressing:
½ teaspoon salt
dash of pepper
¼ cup vegetable oil
1 tablespoon chopped parsley
2 tablespoons sugar
2 tablespoons vinegar
dash of Tabasco sauce

Mix all dressing ingredients and chill. Combine lettuces, celery and onions. Just before serving, add almonds and oranges. Toss with the dressing.

Note: Make double batch of almonds and dressing. Keep to add to any type of salad to dress it up.

Bonnie Venn

Strawberry Gelatin Salad

1 small package strawberry gelatin
1 cup boiling water
1 small package frozen, sliced strawberries
1 small can crushed pineapple, drained
1 mashed banana
½ pint sour cream

Dissolve gelatin in boiling water. Add frozen strawberries, pineapple and banana. Put half of the mixture in a 1½ quart mold and let set up. Spread with sour cream. Add remaining gelatin mixture. Chill for 3 hours. Serves 6.

Jacqueline Aiken

Presidential Seal Salad

1 (6 ounce) package cherry flavored gelatin
1 cup boiling water
1 (10 ounce) package frozen strawberries, thawed
1 (20 ounce) can crushed pineapple, undrained
½ cup sour cream
1 (3 ounce) package softened cream cheese
2 cups blueberries
1 slice pasteurized American cheese

Dissolve gelatin in water. Stir in strawberries and pineapple. Pour half the gelatin mixture into a lightly oiled 6 cup mold. Chill until almost set. Combine sour cream and cream cheese, mixing until well blended. Spread over molded layer. Gradually spoon remaining gelatin mixture over sour cream layer. Chill until firm. Unmold onto serving plate. Fill the center with blueberries. Top with process cheese cut into eagle shape. Serves 8 to 10.

Amanda Ober
WMUR-TV

Raspberry Mold Salad

First Layer:
1 (3 ounce) package raspberry jello
1 cup hot water
1 package frozen raspberries, thawed

Mix together ingredients for the first layer. Let set.

Second layer:
1 (3 ounce) package raspberry jello
1 cup hot water
½ pint sour cream

For second layer, dissolve jello in hot water. Stir in sour cream. Pour over layer one. Chill overnight.

Fran Wiggin
Bedford Librarian

Tuna with Mango Salsa

1 ripe mango, peeled and cut into bite-sized pieces
½ pound fresh tuna, grilled, or 2 (12 ounce) cans tuna
1-2 jalapeño peppers, diced
tortilla chips
1 tablespoon cilantro

Mix the mango, tuna and diced peppers together. Put on top of tortilla chips.

Salsa:
1 (16 ounce) can black beans, drained and rinsed
1 medium red onion
2 tablespoons lime juice
1 tablespoon oil

Mix the salsa ingredients and let flavors blend. Pour salsa over the tortilla chips and mango mixture. Garnish with cilantro. Yield: 2 servings.

Note: The amounts of seasonings (peppers, onions and lime juice) are your choice and depend upon how much spice you want in your life!

Hannah Perutz

Tuna Mousse

1 envelope gelatin
2 tablespoons lemon juice
½ cup boiling chicken broth
½ cup mayonnaise
¼ cup milk
2 tablespoons chopped fresh parsley
1 tablespoon minced green onions
1 teaspoon dry dill weed
¼ teaspoon pepper
1 (7 ounce) can white tuna, drained and flaked
½ cup finely shredded cucumber

Softened gelatin in lemon juice in a large bowl. Add broth. Stir to dissolve gelatin. Add next 6 ingredients. Beat until well mixed. Chill 30 minutes or until slightly thickened. Beat again until frothy. Fold in tuna and cucumber. Turn into 2 cup mold. Chill at least 3 hours. Turn out of mold and garnish with greens and sliced cucumbers. For lunch, serve on bed of greens. For appetizer, serve with crackers. Serves 4.

Anne C. Hoffman

Tomato Aspic

4 packets unflavored gelatin
1 cup cold water
5 cups tomato juice
1¼ teaspoons sugar
pinch salt
4 tablespoons lemon juice
10 drops Tabasco sauce
3-4 drops Worcestershire sauce (optional)
sliced black or green olives for garnish

In large bowl, stir gelatin into water and set aside to soften. Heat tomato juice in medium saucepan until hot, not boiling. Add to gelatin mixture and stir until dissolved and well mixed. Add sugar, salt, lemon juice, Tabasco sauce and Worcestershire sauce. Pour into a 6 cup mold or individual serving molds. Refrigerate at least 2 hours, until aspic is firm. To unmold put mold into hot water for 1 second and then cut around the edge of mold with a knife. Aspic can be prepared 1 day ahead. Serve on a bed of greens and garnish with olive slices. Serves: 8-10.

Anne C. Hoffman

Sauces and Dressings

Dunlap Furniture

In the eighteenth and nineteenth centuries, Bedford was the home of several members of the Dunlap circle of cabinetmakers. Major John, his brother Samuel, and their sons and nephews are nationally recognized as skilled craftsmen. Bedford, with its abundance of cherry, walnut, and maple trees, provided the setting for their creation of various types of furniture. These range from simple kitchen chairs to desks and chests superbly proportioned and elegantly crafted with artistically carved S scrolls and fans and sharply curved cabriole legs.

The fine chest-on-chest and desks they made are collected by museums and private collectors. Several homes in Bedford have moldings, fireplaces and other decorative detailing done by the Dunlap family. The Dunlaps produced graceful, well-balanced furnishings.

Trim the Tree Buffet Supper

beverages

Christmas Fruit Punch   Egg Nog

salad

24 Hour Salad   Orange-Almond Salad

entrées

Mousaka   Special Times Chicken Casserole

Medley of Western Vegetables

bread

Jalapeño Cheese Biscuits

desserts

Walnut Raspberry Brownies   Gingerbread

Creme de Menthe Bars   Cherry Berries in Snow

SAUCES AND DRESSINGS

Cranberry Sauce

12 ounces fresh cranberries
½ cup port wine
½ cup orange juice
½ cup brown sugar
½ cup white sugar
1 cup dried apricots, diced
½ cup toasted pecan pieces

Combine all ingredients in a medium size saucepan. Cook on medium heat, stirring occasionally, until sauce has thickened slightly and many of the cranberries have popped open (about 15-20 minutes). Makes 2½ cups. Chill for several hours or overnight. Bring to room temperature to serve.

Anne C. Hoffman

Fruit Dip

1 large carton plain low fat yogurt
1 small package vanilla instant pudding

Mix together. May thin with orange juice, if desired.

Barbara Weigold

Fruit Salad Dressing

1 cup sugar
2 tablespoons cornstarch
zest of 1 lemon
1 cup boiling water
juice of 1 orange
juice of 1 lemon

In small saucepan, mix sugar, cornstarch, and lemon zest. Add the liquid and cook over medium heat until it thickens slightly. Transfer to container to cool. Use desired amount for fresh fruit salad. This is excellent for preventing apples, pears and peaches from turning brown. The remaining dressing will keep for a week in the refrigerator and it also freezes well. Serves: 12.

Anne C. Hoffman

Chocolate Peanut Butter Fondue Fruit Dip

1 (6 ounce) package semi-sweet chocolate bits
½ cup sugar
½ cup milk
½ cup peanut butter (smooth or chunky)

Combine chocolate bits, sugar, and milk. Stir constantly over low heat until melted. Add peanut butter and stir until smooth. Pour into fondue pot.

Note: This can be made ahead, add a little more milk and re-heat very slowly. Tart fresh fruits are best for dipping, such as apples, fresh pineapple, strawberries and seedless green grapes. It's also good as an ice cream topping.

Bonnie Venn

Teriyaki Marinade

½ cup soy sauce
½ cup orange juice
¼ cup cooking sherry
3 tablespoons oil
2 tablespoons fresh ginger (peel, then put in cuisinart)
2 tablespoons sugar
1 clove garlic

Mix all ingredients together. Marinate meats 2 to 3 hours. Good for boneless chicken breasts, flank steak, sirloin tips and London Broil.

Barbara Weigold

Mexican Sauce for Hot Dogs and Hamburgers

1 (15 ounce) jar plain spaghetti sauce
¼ cup instant onions
1 teaspoon celery flakes
1 teaspoon sage
1 teaspoon marjoram
black pepper to taste
¼ pound fried hamburger

Mix first 6 ingredients in a saucepan and simmer for 5 minutes. Add the cooked hamburger until you like the consistency. The more pepper, the hotter the sauce. Serve warm on hot dogs and hamburgers. Good with chopped onions on the side.

Carol Molitoris

Mock Hollandaise Sauce

1 tablespoon cornstarch
1 cup chicken broth
4 teaspoons freshly squeezed lemon juice
2 tablespoons margarine
¼ cup grated low fat cheese

Mix cornstarch with a little broth to make a smooth paste. Add remaining broth, lemon juice and margarine. Heat slowly to boiling, stirring constantly. Add cheese and stir until melted. Makes one cup.

Note: Can be re-heated. Good on asparagus.

Margaret K. Rooney

Margaret's Mustard

8 tablespoons dry mustard
2 cups cider vinegar
6 eggs
2 cups granulated sugar
½ cup white wine
2 tablespoons Old Bay seasoning
2 tablespoons cornstarch

Combine mustard and vinegar in bowl and let set overnight. Combine all ingredients in a saucepan and mix well. Cook over low heat. Stir and cook until thick. Place mustard in a glass jar and refrigerate. Makes ¾ cup.

Margaret K. Rooney

Poppyseed Dressing

1½ cups sugar
2 teaspoons dry mustard
2 teaspoons salt
⅔ cup vinegar
3 tablespoons onion juice
2 cups salad oil
3 tablespoons poppy seeds

Put sugar, dry mustard and salt in blender. Mix on medium speed. Add onion juice and blend thoroughly. Slowly add oil and beat until thick. Add poppy seeds. Store in refrigerator for use with fruit salads.

Bonnie Venn

Red Sauce

1 to 2 cloves garlic, chopped
2 tablespoons oil
½ cup ground tomatoes
1 teaspoon salt
1 teaspoon oregano
½ teaspoon black pepper
1 cup water

Sauté garlic and oil in frying pan. Add tomatoes, salt, oregano and black pepper. Sauté for a few minutes and add water a little at a time. Simmer for 5 minutes (be sure sauce is thin). Pour over steak or chicken.

You will love dipping your Italian bread in this sauce.

Dorothy Czopek

Shaker Village Salad Dressing

1½ cups olive oil
½ cup white wine vinegar
½ cup maple syrup
½ cup chopped onion
1½ teaspoons minced basil
1½ teaspoons minced oregano
1 teaspoon marjoram

Place all in a blender. Add salt and pepper to taste. Blend well. Refrigerate at least 3 hours.

Alice Asadourian

Spinach Salad Dressing

½ cup olive oil
¼ cup vinegar
2 to 3 tablespoons sugar to taste
½ teaspoon salt
½ teaspoon paprika
½ teaspoon dry mustard
⅛ teaspoon black pepper
¼ teaspoon celery salt
½ medium onion chopped

Blend well in blender. Serves 6 to 8.

Martha Dollen

Soups and Sandwiches

Stone Bridges

The first bridge in Bedford was built in 1743. As roads were constructed, almost each one had to bridge a stream or brook. This presented real problems, for in the early days every task was accomplished by hand labor. Heavy storms would wash away all the results.

Bridge repairs cost the town so much that in 1835 a very practical ordinance was passed: "That any highway district build their bridges with stone abutments, and cover the water courses with good substantial stone arches, so that the town will not here after be called upon to furnish timber and plank for their repair. Any district following that directive shall receive from the town treasurer the amount of money the bridge would cost for (repair) for 20 years." As a result the town saved a great deal as stone arches and stone stringers were put over most of the bridges in town.

Bride's Luncheon

beverage

Sparkling Cranberry Punch

salad

Mandarin Salad

entrée

Grilled Salmon with a Raspberry Coulis

Lemony Asparagus & New Potatoes

dessert

Hawaiian Wedding Cake

SOUPS AND SANDWICHES

Quick and Tasty Bean Soup

¾ pound bulk Italian sausage
½ cup onion, chopped
2 cloves garlic, minced
1 tablespoon chopped fresh basil or 1 teaspoon dried
1 (14.5 or 16 ounce) can whole tomatoes, undrained, cut up
1 (14.5 ounce) can beef broth
1 (15 ounce) can black beans, drained
1 (15.5 ounce) can butter beans or lima beans, drained
2 tablespoons grated Parmesan cheese

In large saucepan or Dutch oven, combine sausage, onion, garlic and basil. Cook over medium-high heat until sausage is well browned and onion tender, stirring occasionally. Drain. Add tomatoes with their juice, beef broth, black beans and butter beans. Stir. Cover and cook over medium heat 10-15 minutes or until thoroughly heated. Sprinkle Parmesan cheese on top.

Note: Do not use crushed tomatoes.

Bonnie Venn

Parsnip & Apple Soup

1 ounce butter
1 medium onion
2 parsnips
1 cooking apple
1 tablespoon or 1 cube vegetable stock
2 tablespoons parsley, chopped
½ teaspoon mixed herbs
1 pint milk
salt
pepper

Peel and chop vegetables and fruit. Sauté in melted butter until onion is transparent. Add stock, parsley and herbs and bring to a boil. Reduce heat, cover and simmer for 30 minutes. Cool slightly, add milk and blend in a blender. Reheat and adjust seasoning to taste. Preparation time: 15 minutes. Cooking time: 45-60 minutes. Serves 4-6.

Doris Guimont

Dibby's Ground Beef Soup

½ pound extra-lean ground beef
1 large onion, chopped
1 clove garlic, crushed
2 carrots, sliced
1 (16 ounce) can pinto beans
1 (16 ounce) can plum tomatoes with juice, coarsely chopped
2 (14½ ounce) cans beef broth
1½ cups water
¾ cup red wine
1 bay leaf
1 teaspoon salt
½ teaspoon basil
¼ teaspoon pepper
fresh parsley, chopped (optional)
½ cup elbow macaroni
9 ounces frozen cut green or Italian beans
grated Parmesan cheese

In Dutch oven, brown beef, stirring occasionally. Add onion and garlic and sauté for 5 minutes. Pour off fat. Add all but last 3 ingredients, heat to boiling and cover. Simmer for 45 minutes. Stir occasionally to break up tomatoes. Add macaroni and cook for 10 minutes. Add green beans and cook for 10 minutes more. Serve with grated Parmesan cheese. Serves 4.

Note: Each serving provides 325 calories with the cheese. The soup preparation may be stopped prior to adding the macaroni and green beans. Simply reheat to boiling and proceed. This recipe may be doubled or tripled.

Anne C. Hoffman

Danish Cold Buttermilk Soup

4 cups buttermilk
2 eggs
4 tablespoons sugar
1 teaspoon vanilla
juice of 1 lemon

Beat eggs, sugar, lemon juice and vanilla together. Separately beat buttermilk. Gradually fold all ingredients together and serve. Preparation time: 10 minutes. Serves 4.

Note: May top with whipped cream, if desired.

Janet Jespersen

Cream of Broccoli Soup

2 pounds fresh broccoli
3 teaspoons butter
¼ cup onion, finely chopped
2 tablespoons flour
1 quart whole milk
1½ cups grated Cheddar or Swiss cheese
¼ teaspoon salt
sour cream or plain yogurt (optional)

Trim tough stems and leaves from broccoli. Split and soak in cold salted water for 1 hour, and then drain. Reserve 8 small florets. Place broccoli in a soup kettle with just enough water to cover. Cook for 15 minutes or until broccoli is tender, then drain. Puree the broccoli in a blender or food processor and set aside.

Over medium-low heat, melt butter in the soup kettle, and sauté onions until tender. Whisk in flour, then gradually whisk in milk, 1 cup at a time. Whisk in pureed broccoli. When hot, stir in the cheese until melted. Add salt. Garnish with florets and sour cream. Serves 6.

Donna Joas

Simply Soupier Vichyssoise

1 can Campbell's Cream of Potato Soup
1 cup sour cream
1 chicken bouillon cube, dissolved in small amount of water
1 fistful of 6 inch chive stalks
whole milk
chopped chives for garnish
grated nutmeg for garnish

Place potato soup, sour cream, dissolved bouillon cube and chive stalks in blender. Fill rest of space in blender with whole milk. Run blender for 1 minute or less. Serve chilled with garnish of finely chopped chives and grated nutmeg. Serves 4.

Note: May adjust amounts of sour cream and chives to taste.

Barbara A. Upton

Cure-All Chicken Soup

1 whole chicken
1 cup onion, chopped
1 onion, whole, peeled and studded with 2 whole cloves
1 stalk celery with leaves
½ cup celery, thinly sliced
1 cup carrots, peeled and sliced
3 cloves garlic, peeled
1 bay leaf
⅛ teaspoon thyme
¼ teaspoon dill
⅛ teaspoon red pepper flakes
pinch saffron (optional)
salt
freshly ground pepper
1 cup peas, fresh or frozen
½ cup uncooked white rice or 1 cup uncooked small pasta or orzo

Place the chicken in a large stock pot. Add the whole onion with cloves and the whole celery stalk. Cover the chicken with water and bring to a boil over high heat, then reduce heat. Simmer for 1 hour or until chicken is tender. Skim off any residue that forms on top of the soup. Discard the onion and celery stalk. Remove the chicken from the broth and cool slightly. Discard the skin and bones. Cut the meat into bite-sized pieces.

Pour the broth into a container and allow to cool, then skim off excess fat. Return skimmed broth to the stock pot. Add the chicken pieces and all other ingredients except for the peas and rice or pasta. Partially cover. Simmer for 20 minutes. Add the peas and rice or pasta. Simmer for an additional 20 minutes. Serves 6-8.

Louise Langley

Dill - Both leaves and seeds of dill are used. Leaves may be used as a garnish or to cook with fish. Leaves or the whole plant may be used to flavor dill pickles.

Cabbage Soup

1 tablespoon olive oil
1 large onion, diced
3 cloves garlic, minced
1 head cabbage, cored and chopped
⅓ cup flour
⅓ cup dry vermouth or white wine
6 cups beef stock
⅓ cup bottled chili sauce
1 (28 ounce) can whole Italian-style tomatoes, crushed
1 teaspoon sugar
juice of 1 lemon
1 tablespoon paprika
dash pepper

In a large soup kettle, sauté onions and garlic in olive oil until onions are clear. Add cabbage and stir-sauté. Cover and cook until cabbage wilts. Sprinkle flour over cabbage and stir in thoroughly. Add vermouth or wine and stir until mixture begins to thicken. Add beef stock, crushed tomatoes, chili sauce, pepper, sugar and paprika. Simmer for 30 minutes. Adjust seasonings to taste, add lemon juice and serve.

Note: Do not use crushed or pureed canned tomatoes as a substitute for the Italian-style whole tomatoes. May add celery, carrots, 1 can pinto beans and/or cooked elbow macaroni (about 1 dry cup).

Jeanene Procopis

Easy Clam Chowder

1 (10½ ounce) can cream of celery soup
1 (10½ ounce) can cream of potato soup
1 (10½ ounce) can cream of onion soup
2 (10½ ounce) cans New England clam chowder soup
½ can water
1 pint heavy whipping cream
pepper

Add all ingredients to a crockpot and gently simmer or put ingredients into a pot and heat until warm, then simmer to blend flavors. Preparation time: 10 minutes. Serves 4-6.

Note: May add corn.

Madonna Lovett Repeta

Arlene's Crab Soup

1 can cream of asparagus soup
1 can cream of mushroom soup
1 package of crab meat, drained
1 cup cream

Heat gently and top with fresh grated black pepper.

Note: Serve with French bread.

Wesley Maloney

Bedford Fish Chowder

1 onion, diced
6 potatoes, peeled and cut into small chunks
1½ pounds haddock, cut into 1 inch cubes
1 (16 ounce) can whole kernel corn, drained
6 scallions, trimmed and minced
6 slices bacon, cooked crisp and crumbled
2 bottles clam juice
1 (15 ounce) can Snows clam chowder, undiluted
2 (12 ounce) cans evaporated milk
1 tablespoon fresh hot pepper, ground
1 (15 ounce) can salmon, picked for bones and broken into small pieces

Sauté onions in butter until clear. Boil potatoes until cooked. Simmer haddock in water until cooked through. Reserve the liquid to put into the soup. Combine all ingredients in a large soup pot, warm and stir. Refrigerate overnight to thoroughly blend flavors. Reheat but do not let soup come to a boil. Serves 10.

Note: This recipe may be frozen, but is best when 1-2 days old! May be thinned with skimmed milk, if necessary. This is an original recipe that was well received at a luncheon given in 1995.

Margaret K. Rooney

New England Fish Chowder

¼ pound salt pork
½ pound diced onion
2 pounds haddock or cod
salt and pepper
½ bay leaf
pinch of thyme
4 potatoes, peeled and diced
1½ quarts half and half or milk

Remove the rind from the salt pork and dice. In a heavy kettle, slowly sauté salt pork, until it is crisp and brown. Remove from kettle. Sauté onions in pork fat. In a separate pot, sprinkle fish with salt and pepper, and cover with water. Add bay leaf and thyme to fish. Simmer on low heat for 25 minutes or until fish flakes easily. Lift fish out of pan and remove skin and bones and break fish into small pieces. Strain the fish stock and add to the onions. Cook the potatoes in the stock until tender, but not mushy. Add the fish, milk and salt pork. Season to taste. Reheat making sure soup does not boil. Serves 6.

Christina Barley

Creamy Onion Soup

3 teaspoons butter or margarine
3 cups thinly sliced onions
2 cloves garlic, minced
¼ cup flour
4½ cups water
⅓ cup sherry
4½ packages instant beef broth
1½ cups milk
¾ cup sour cream
⅛ teaspoon white pepper

In a large saucepan, sauté onions and garlic in butter until onions are transparent. Sprinkle in flour and cook for 1 minute, stirring constantly. Gradually add water while stirring. Add sherry and instant beef broth, stirring until broth crystals are dissolved. Bring to a boil. Reduce heat to low, stir in milk. Cook for 15 to 20 minutes, stirring occasionally until soup thickens slightly. In a bowl, mix 2 cups soup with sour cream. Add mixture to soup and season with pepper. Continue cooking until thoroughly heated, stirring occasionally. Do not let soup boil. Serves 6.

Pat Lauer

Creamy French Onion Soup

¼ cup (½ stick) butter or margarine
7 cups sliced onions (about 2 pounds)
2 tablespoons flour
4 cups water
12 beef bouillon cubes
4 cups milk

Melt butter in 4-quart saucepan. Sauté onions until tender, about 15 minutes. Stir in flour. Add water and beef bouillon cubes and bring to a boil. Reduce heat and cover. Simmer for 30-40 minutes. Stir in milk. Reheat to serving temperature without letting soup boil.

Croutes (Croutons):
½ cup (1 stick) butter or margarine
1 clove garlic, crushed
8 slices French bread, cut 1 inch thick
1 (8 ounce) cup shredded Swiss cheese

Preheat oven to 325 degrees. Melt butter in pan and stir in garlic. Dip both sides of bread in butter, and place bread on a baking sheet. Toast for 15 minutes until lightly browned, turning bread once.

Place cup of soup in oven proof soup bowls. Top each bowl with 1 croute and ¼ cup Swiss cheese. Place soup bowls in oven for 10 minutes or until cheese melts. Preparation time: about 1½ hours. Serves 8-9.

Sharlene Genest

To remove marker writing on plastic storage containers, bags and canning jar lids, just spray with hair spray and wipe clean.

Nouvelle French Onion Soup

2 tablespoons margarine
4 large onions, thinly sliced
4 cups chicken stock or beef broth
1 clove garlic, minced
1 bay leaf
French bread
mozzarella cheese

Melt margarine in a soup kettle, and sauté separated onion rings until tender. Add stock or broth, garlic and bay leaf. Cover and bring to a boil, then reduce heat. Simmer for 35-40 minutes. Remove and discard bay leaf. Top each serving with a small piece of toasted French bread. Top French bread with mozzarella cheese. Microwave individual servings on medium just long enough to melt cheese. Preparation time: 10 minutes. Serves 6.

Jacquelin Lavoie

Lentil Soup

1½ cups lentils
4 slices bacon
3 tablespoons butter or margarine
3 tablespoons flour
1 cup leeks, chopped (white part only)
6 cups beef broth
½ cup onions, chopped
¼ cup carrots, chopped
2 tablespoons vinegar
1 can stewed tomatoes, chopped

Place lentils and 5 cups beef broth in a large kettle and bring to a boil. Reduce heat, cover and simmer for 1 hour, stirring occasionally. Cut bacon into small pieces and sauté until crisp. Add the leeks, onions and carrots. Continue to sauté over low heat for about 5 minutes. Add the sautéed mixture to the lentils. Stir in the stewed tomatoes. Melt butter in the sauté skillet and remove from heat. Stir in flour until smooth. Gradually stir in remaining cup of beef broth. Add vinegar, return to heat and bring to boiling point, stirring constantly. Add to soup. Cook over low heat for 30 minutes, stirring occasionally. Preparation time: 1½ hours. Serves 10-12.

Note: If using salt free broth, add salt to taste.

Barbara Weigold

Ham and Split Pea Soup

1 (16 ounce) package green split peas
1 medium onion, chopped
1-2 stalks celery
1-2 pounds ham, diced
4 cups water
1 clove garlic, chopped
1 tablespoon salt (optional)
dash pepper

Combine all ingredients and bring to a boil. Reduce heat and simmer for 1½ hours or until peas are soft. Stir occasionally. Put through strainer, if desired. Preparation time: 10 minutes. Serves 8.

Note: May use ham hocks in place of diced ham. This soup is hearty and delicious!

Caroline Williams

Prize Winning Split Pea Soup

3 cans condensed split pea soup
2½ cups stewed tomatoes
1 package frozen potatoes, "O'Brien" or hash browns
1 package frozen mixed peas and carrots
1 package frozen corn
1 green pepper, chopped fine
½-1 package spinach, fresh with stems removed or frozen

Combine all ingredients. Cover and simmer for 30 minutes.

Note: This recipe once won a $100.00 prize, though not for me!

Wesley Maloney

Pumpkin Soup

2 pounds diced pumpkin
1 cup diced onion
1 cup diced celery
3 tablespoon butter
2 bay leaves
3 tablespoons flour
5 cups chicken broth or bouillon
½ teaspoon salt
⅛ teaspoon pepper
⅛ teaspoon nutmeg
⅛ teaspoon mace
¼ teaspoon cinnamon
half-and-half or cream

Melt butter in large pot and sauté the pumpkin, onion and celery. Add the bay leaves and cook for 15 minutes. Add 3 tablespoons of flour and cook. Add the chicken broth and simmer for 30 minutes. Place the above soup mixture in a blender or food processor. Add all of the spices and puree. Add the half-and-half (or cream) until desired flavor is achieved. Serves 4-6.

Note: May use acorn squash or butternut squash in place of pumpkin.

Doris Guimont

Sausage Soup

½ pound Italian sausage, removed from casing
1 large onion, chopped
1 (2 pound 3 ounce) can Italian tomatoes
2 (13¾ ounce) cans chicken broth
1 teaspoon leaf basil, crumbled
½ cup orzo macaroni
¼ teaspoon salt
dash pepper

Cook sausage in soup kettle, breaking up meat, until all pink color is gone. Remove sausage from kettle. Sauté onions in kettle until soft, and then return sausage to kettle. Add tomatoes, broth and basil, and bring to a boil. Stir in macaroni, salt and pepper, and lower heat. Simmer for 20 minutes. Preparation time: 15 minutes. Serves 4-6.

Note: May run tomatoes through blender before adding, if desired.

Pat Cobb

Curried Butternut Squash Soup

4 tablespoons butter or margarine
2 cups yellow onion, finely chopped
1½ teaspoons curry powder
3 pounds butternut squash (about 2 medium sized squash)
2 Macintosh apples, peeled, cored and chopped
3 cups chicken stock
1 cup apple cider
salt
pepper

Melt butter in a soup pot, add onions and curry. Cover and cook on low for 25 minutes or until onions are tender. While onions are cooking, peel squash, scraping out seeds and cut into pieces. When the onions are ready, add the squash, apples and stock. Bring to a boil. Reduce heat and partially cover. Simmer for 25 minutes or until squash and apples are very tender. Pour soup through a strainer, reserving liquid, and transfer the solids to a food processor fitted with a steel blade. Add 1 cup stock and process until smooth. Return pureed soup to the pot adding the cider and just enough of the reserved liquid, (about 2 cups) until the soup is at a desired consistency. Season to taste with salt and pepper and additional curry, if desired. Simmer briefly to heat through. Serve immediately, garnished with shredded apple or sliced chives floated on top. Preparation time: 1½ hours. Serves 8.

Barbara Weigold

Curry Powder - A number of spices combined in proper proportions to give a distinct flavor to such dishes as vegetables of all kinds, meat, poultry, and fish.

Tortellini Soup

1 tablespoon butter
4 cloves garlic, minced
2 (14½ ounce) cans chicken broth
1 (9 ounce) package cheese Tortellini
1 (14½ ounce) can stewed tomatoes
½ bunch spinach, stems removed
6 fresh basil leaves, chopped, or 1 teaspoon dried basil leaves, crushed
salt
pepper
grated Parmesan cheese

Melt butter in large soup kettle over medium heat. Add garlic and sauté for 2 minutes. Stir in chicken broth and Tortellini and bring to a boil. Season with salt and pepper. Reduce heat, and simmer about 5 minutes or until Tortellini are just tender. Add stewed tomatoes, spinach and basil, and simmer for 2 minutes. Serve with grated Parmesan cheese. Preparation time: 30 minutes. Serves 4-6.

Note: May use 3-cheese Tortellini or spinach Tortellini in place of cheese Tortellini. This recipe doubles easily and freezes well.

Louise Langley

Zucchini Spaghetti Soup

1 medium onion, minced
1 clove garlic, minced
¼ cup olive oil
4-4½ cups zucchini, sliced thin
1 tomato, chopped (or ¼ cup tomato sauce)
½ teaspoon basil
¼ teaspoon pepper
6 cups chicken broth (or 6 bouillon cubes and 6 cups water)
1¼ cups uncooked spaghetti, broken in thirds

In large saucepan sauté onion and garlic in olive oil. Add zucchini, tomato, seasonings and chicken broth. Cover, simmer over low heat 1½ hours. Add short lengths of spaghetti and continue simmering another 10 minutes, or until spaghetti is done. Serves 6-8.

Catherine Liotta

Chicken Salad

1 cup cooked chicken, finely chopped
½ cup celery, finely chopped
½ cup apple, finely chopped
⅓ cup crushed pineapple, well drained
3 tablespoons mayonnaise
salt to taste
pepper to taste
1 teaspoon fresh lemon juice

Combine chicken, celery, apple and pineapple in a bowl. Stir in mayonnaise, salt, pepper and lemon juice. Refrigerate several hours or overnight. Spread salad on buttered bread, with or without a top slice. Cut in desired serving size and garnish with apple slices or pineapple. Yields enough for 8 sandwiches.

Bess Morrison

Crab Luncheon Supreme

6 ounces cream cheese
2 cans crabmeat (save liquid, use to thin the cream cheese)
1 teaspoon grated onion
1 teaspoon Worcestershire sauce
3 English muffins
6 thick slices tomato
6 slices American cheese

Preheat oven to 325 degrees. Put the cream cheese in a bowl and thin with the crabmeat juice. Add onion and Worcestershire sauce and mix. Fold in the crabmeat and let stand. Toast the English muffin halves. Put a scoop of the mixture on each muffin. Add a slice of tomato and a slice of cheese on top. Bake on a cookie sheet for 20-25 minutes. Serves 6.

Betty Gollihue

Ham and Spinach Wheels

1 (10 ounce) package frozen chopped spinach, thawed
8 ounces light or regular cream cheese
2 teaspoons prepared horseradish
1/8 teaspoon allspice
1/8 teaspoon ground pepper
6 flour tortillas (7 inch wide)
3/4 pound thinly sliced cooked ham
1/4 cup thinly sliced green onions (optional)

Press spinach firmly in a sieve to remove excess moisture. In a bowl, mix spinach, cream cheese, horseradish, allspice and pepper. Divide the spinach mixture evenly among the 6 tortillas. Spread the mixture to cover the tortilla. Divide ham in 6 equal portions. Place one portion of ham on each tortilla, covering the spinach mixture. Sprinkle with green onions. Roll each tortilla tightly to encase the filling. If made ahead, cover in an airtight container and chill overnight. With a sharp knife cut each tortilla diagonally into 4 equal slices. Serves 6.

Barbara Weigold

Hot Pockets

1 pound hamburger
1 small onion, chopped
salt to taste
pepper to taste
Frank's Hot Sauce
2 packages Hungry Jack Refrigerated Biscuits
shredded sharp Cheddar cheese

Preheat oven to 350 degrees. In a frying pan, brown hamburger and onions. Drain grease. Add salt and pepper. Sprinkle mixture with hot sauce to taste. Open biscuits, using 2 for each sandwich. Flatten 1 biscuit and spoon the hamburger mixture on it. Add cheese. Take the other biscuit and flatten for the top. Seal the edges and set on an ungreased cookie sheet. Repeat for the rest of the biscuits. Bake in the oven for 15 to 20 minutes. Remove when brown.

Carol Molitoris

Ribbon Sandwich Loaf

1 loaf unsliced bread
soft butter or margarine
3 different fillings
8 ounces cream cheese
garnishes for decoration

Taking the loaf of unsliced bread, cut off the crust. Slice horizontally 4 even layers. Spread 3 slices with soft butter or margarine. Spread each layer with a different filling such as: crabmeat salad, tuna salad, egg salad, chicken salad, ham salad or cream cheese with olive or pineapple.

Assemble the layers back into a loaf shape. Cover the loaf completely with cream cheese. Decorate with garnish of your choice (olives, radish slices, green pepper slices, parsley, etc.). To serve cut vertically into 8-10 slices.

Janet Jespersen

Ham Luncheon for 100

3 dozen cans soup

3 quarts water or milk to dilute soup

15 pounds sliced ham

20 pounds potato salad

10 dozen rolls

4 pounds butter

2 quarts cream

3 pounds coffee

12 sponge cakes

15 quarts ice cream

1 gallon chocolate sauce

Meat Entrées

Presbyterian Church

The Bedford Presbyterian Church was organized in 1749, one year before the incorporation of the town. The community was settled by Scotch-Irish Presbyterians. The first meetinghouse was erected on the site of the present Town Hall and was used for worship and town meetings for 75 years, when it became too small.

The forefathers planned well by purchasing a prominent site on a hill in the center of town for $100.00. The building was constructed between July 20 - Sept. 20th, 1832, at a cost of $3,700.00. Interesting to note that this church remained the only one in town until 1964.

In 1894, the large "Longfellow porch" replaced the small entry. The architect for this addition was Wadsworth Longfellow, a nephew of the poet.

Sweet Sunrise

beverages

Flavored coffees

Assorted teas

breads and muffins

Cream Cheese Braids

Pumpkin Apple Bread

Banana Nut Bread

Cranberry-Corn Muffins

Morning Glory Muffins

lighter fare

Fruit Salad

MEAT ENTRÉES

Delicious Brisket

4 tablespoons brown sugar
12 ounces unsweetened pineapple juice
4 tablespoons soy sauce
1 package dry onion soup mix
3½ pounds beef brisket

Start preparation early in day. Brisket will be ready to serve the following day. Mix sugar, juice, soy sauce and soup mix. Pour over meat. Seal roasting pan tightly with foil. Refrigerate. Do not open again. In evening, bake at 325 degrees for 2½ hours. Turn oven off. Do not open oven door. The next morning slice meat across the grain. Return to sauce and refrigerate. Before serving, seal pan tightly with foil and heat at 350 degrees for 30 minutes. Yield: 6 servings.

Note: The broth is very good with rice or noodles. The leftover meat makes wonderful sandwiches. This brisket is easy and delicious for entertaining.

Tish Smith

Beef Bourguignonne For Golfers

2 pounds beef chuck, cut up
1 can mushroom soup, undiluted
½ package onion soup mix
1 can mushrooms
1 cup Burgundy (optional)

Preheat oven to 250 degrees (can use crock pot). Cook first 3 ingredients for 3½ hours in covered casserole dish. Add mushrooms 10 minutes before end of cooking time. Pour Burgundy into casserole before serving. Serve over cooked egg noodles. Yield: 6-8 servings.

Note: Can be prepared ahead of time. I have used this recipe many times, and people think you have slaved over a hot stove all day instead of playing golf, tennis, or just shopping.

Eunice Brine

Boeuf Bourguignonne

6 ounces thin stripped bacon
1 tablespoon oil
3 pounds lean stewing beef, cut-up
1 carrot, sliced
1 onion, sliced
1 teaspoon salt
¼ teaspoon pepper
2 tablespoons flour
3 cups red wine
2-3 cups beef bouillon (or beef broth)
1 tablespoon tomato paste
2 cloves garlic, mashed
½ teaspoon thyme
1 bay leaf, crumbled
1 pound mushrooms, sliced
18-24 small white onions
½ cup red wine
3 tablespoons cornstarch
3 tablespoons warm water

Preheat oven to 450 degrees. In Dutch oven that can be used on top of range and in oven, sauté bacon until light brown. Remove bacon and add 1 tablespoon oil. (Dry pieces of beef on paper towel.) Sauté meat a few pieces at a time until brown. Remove as they brown. Sauté carrot and onion. Pour out any fat and return beef and bacon. Add salt, pepper and flour. Toss beef until lightly coated. Set mixture uncovered in middle of oven for 4 minutes. Toss again and put in oven for another 4 minutes. Reduce heat to 325 degrees. Add wine, bouillon, tomato paste, garlic, thyme and bay leaf. Bring to boil on stove top. (At this time, the mixture can be transferred to a crock pot.) Cook in covered casserole/Dutch oven for 3-4 hours. Regulate heat so liquid is slowly simmering. In separate pan, sauté mushrooms in a butter and oil mixture. Remove. Sauté onions for 10 minutes (for braised onions). Add to Dutch oven mixture the sautéed mushrooms, onions, ½ cup red wine, salt and pepper. Mix together cornstarch and warm water and add to Dutch oven. Stir so no lumps form.

Herb bouquet:
4 parsley sprigs
½ bay leaf
¼ teaspoon thyme

Add herb bouquet wrapped in cheesecloth or coffee filter. Cover and simmer 40-50 minutes. Serve over egg noodles. Yield: 6-8 servings.

Anne C. Hoffman

Beef in Beer

1 tablespoon olive oil
2 pounds stewing steak, cut into 2-inch squares
¾ pound onions, chopped
1 heaping tablespoon flour
½ pint beer
½ teaspoon dried thyme or small sprig of fresh thyme
1 bay leaf
1 clove garlic, crushed
salt and fresh milled black pepper

Preheat oven to 275 degrees. Heat oil in heat resistant casserole dish. Sear meat in it, a few pieces at a time, until they are dark brown all over. As pieces brown, remove them to a plate. Then add onions to the casserole and, with the heat still high, toss them around until brown at the edges. Return the meat to the casserole with any juices. Add the flour, turn heat down and stir. Next gradually stir in beer and while everything slowly comes to a simmering point, add the thyme, bay leaf, garlic, salt and pepper. As soon as it begins to simmer, stir thoroughly. Put on a tight fitting lid and transfer casserole to middle shelf of oven. Cook at a gentle simmer for 2½ hours. Do not take lid off during this time. Delicious served with fresh crusty bread.

Gillian Jukes

Carbonade Beef Stew

½ cup flour (or more)
1 teaspoon salt
1 teaspoon pepper
2-3 pounds cubed beef (stew)
⅓ cup oil
4 large onions, thin sliced
1 teaspoon dry garlic chips
1 teaspoon thyme
1 can beer

Place flour, salt and pepper in bag. Add meat and shake. Brown meat in hot oil in heavy Dutch oven. Remove meat and add onions. Cook until limp. Return meat and add everything else. Cover and simmer 2½ - 3 hours with lid on. Yield: 4 servings.

Note: Excellent the next day. Serve with broad egg noodles or rice and vegetables on the side.

Wesley Maloney

One Pot No-Fail Beef Stew

2 pounds stew meat, cubed
2-3 onions, quartered
3 stalks celery, cut in inch pieces
3-4 carrots, cut in inch pieces
3-4 potatoes, quartered
salt and pepper
¼ cup tapioca
1 (16 ounce) can whole tomatoes, cut up
½-1 cup wine, red or white (if dry, add 1 tablespoon sugar)
1 can beef gravy

Preheat oven to 275 degrees. Put all ingredients except gravy in pot or casserole. Cover. Bake 5 hours at 275 degrees or 3½ hours at 325 degrees. Add can of beef gravy before serving.

Tish Smith

Special Beef Stew

2 pounds stew beef
½ cup tomato sauce
1 cup unsweetened grape juice
1 medium onion, diced
3 tablespoons vinegar
2 tablespoons oil
1 bay leaf
1 teaspoon oregano
salt and pepper to taste

Put all ingredients in large skillet. Bring to boil, cover and simmer 1½ to 2 hours. Yield: 4-6 servings.

Pat Cobb

Oven Stroganoff

3 pounds beef chuck, cubed
1 package onion soup mix
½ cup mushroom soup (undiluted)
½ cup red wine
¾ cup sour cream

Preheat oven to 350 degrees. Put all ingredients but sour cream in casserole. Bake 3 hours in oven. When ready to serve stir in sour cream. Yield: 6 servings.

Janis Galeucia

Ropa Vieja (Old Clothes)

1½ pound flank steak
2 medium onions
2 green peppers
1 head garlic
1 tomato
6-8 cups water
½ cup white dry wine
olive oil
1 can tomato sauce

Boil meat, 1 whole onion with skin, 1 whole green pepper, 1 whole tomato, 1 whole (less 3 cloves) head of garlic in 6-8 cups of water for 1 hour. Reserve 1 cup of broth. Into this 1 cup of broth, strain and press through a colander the tomato, onion, pepper and garlic from the soup. Cut flank across grain in 1½ inch strips, pound and shred. Sauté in olive oil 1 onion chopped fine and 1 chopped green pepper, until soft. Add 3 cloves garlic chopped fine, sauté ½ minute. Add can of tomato sauce, wine and broth. Simmer for 5 minutes. Add meat and simmer for 20 minutes. Serve over white rice. By-product: make a soup with broth.

Bonnie Venn

Colorful Fresh Pepper Steak

3 packages gravy mix
1 red bell pepper, cut in 1-2 inch squares
1 green bell pepper, cut in 1-2 inch squares
1 large onion, cut in eighths
1-2 inch thick London Broil

Prepare gravy mix according to package directions in frying pan. Let sit while cutting peppers and onions. Start broiling steak. Add peppers and onions to gravy mix. They should be warmed but still crisp. Slice steak diagonally. Arrange slices on plates. Cover with gravy mix.

Note: Serve with whipped potatoes. The potato water, when added to gravy mix, makes a super gravy.

Artie Roberson
Bedford Town Manager

Broiled Bracciole

top of round steak
Crisco

Cut round steak into 2x3 inch pieces. Place between layers of waxed paper and pound thin with mallet. Spread Crisco on slice of meat.

Bread Crumb Mixturc:
1 cup bread crumbs
½ cup grated cheese
½ teaspoon salt
parsley, basil and black pepper, to taste
1 teaspoon oil

Sprinkle with bread crumb mixture. Roll like jelly roll. Hold every 2 pieces together with 2 toothpicks. Place bracciole on foil lined broiler pan.

Marinade:
1 cup water
½ teaspoon salt
½ teaspoon pepper
1 tablespoon oregano
2 tablespoons oil
celery leaves

Mix water, salt, pepper, oregano and oil together for marinade. Brush both sides of meat with marinade using celery leaves as a brush. Cook until meat starts to turn brown. Turn (about 5 minutes on each side). Baste meat with marinade as meat cooks. Pour remaining marinade over cooked meat and serve.

Dorothy Czopek

Spicy Roast

2 cans beer
2 small jars Heinz Chili Sauce
1 package onion soup mix
8 pound sirloin tip roast

Preheat oven 300 degrees. Mix beer, sauce and soup together. Pour over roast in roasting pan. Cover pan and roast 5 hours. Cool. Slice or shave roast into very thin slices. Serve room temperature. Yield: 16 servings.

Note: Can do ahead. Very tasty.

Margaret K. Rooney

Gourmet Sirloin Tips

2 tablespoons oil
1 clove garlic, minced
1½ pounds sirloin tips
1 cup ketchup
3 tablespoons Worcestershire sauce
½ cup margarine, melted
1 tablespoon lemon juice
½ teaspoon salt
⅛ teaspoon pepper

Sauté garlic in hot oil. Add meat and brown on all sides. Mix remaining ingredients and add to meat. Cover and simmer over low heat or bake in 350 degree oven for 1 hour. Serve over hot fluffy rice.

Donna Joas

Stuffed Grape Leaves

1½ pounds chopped meat
3 large onions, chopped
1 cup rice
salt and pepper to taste
dried mint leaves
water
1 pound jar grape vine leaves
3 bouillon cubes
1 tablespoon butter

Combine meat, onions, uncooked rinsed rice, salt, pepper and dried mint leaves. Add 1 cup water to meat mixture. Mix well. Drain brine from jar of grape vine leaves. Remove leaves and wash well with clear water to remove all traces of brine. Put heaping tablespoon of meat and rice mixture in center of each leaf. Roll leaf carefully, folding edges over and rolling tightly towards point of leaf. Arrange in layers in greased Dutch oven or casserole which has been lined with broken leaves. Cover with water. Add dissolved bouillon cubes and butter. Cover with heavy plate to keep rolls from opening as rice puffs. Cover and steam. Simmer slowly for one hour. Add water if needed. Yield: 6 servings.

Bonnie Venn

Spicy Beef Pie

2 tablespoons vegetable oil
1 cup (4 ounces) mushrooms, chopped
1 large onion, chopped
½ cup carrot, grated
1 small rib celery, chopped
½ teaspoon salt (optional)
4 tablespoons Dijon mustard
1 (10 ounce) package frozen patty shells, thawed (6 shells)
1 pound rare roast beef, sliced
½ cup (2 ounces) grated Monterey Jack cheese
1 large egg
1 tablespoon water

In 10-inch skillet, heat oil over medium heat. Add mushrooms, onion, carrot and celery. Cook about 10 minutes, stirring occasionally until tender. Remove from heat. Stir in salt and 1 tablespoon mustard. Heat oven to 425 degrees. On lightly floured surface, roll each patty shell into 7-inch circle. Lightly spread each pastry circle with mustard to within 1-inch of edge. Cover mustard with sliced roast beef, dividing evenly. Spoon vegetables over beef. Sprinkle with cheese. In small bowl, beat egg with 1 tablespoon water. Brush edge of each pastry circle with mixture. Bring edges of pastry up and over filling to form package. Press edges firmly to seal. Crimp edges decoratively. Brush meat pies with beaten egg mixture. Place in ungreased jelly roll pan. Bake 15 minutes until golden brown. Serve hot, with tossed green salad. Yield: 6 servings.

Note: This makes a hot sandwich something really special.

Rita Fitzgerald

Sage - Used fresh and dried. May be used in poultry and meat stuffings; in sausage and practically all meat combinations; in cheese and vegetable combinations, as in vegetable loaf, or curry. The flowers are sometimes used in salads.

Hamburg Meat Pie

1 pound lean hamburger
1-2 medium onions, chopped
2 beef bouillon cubes
½ teaspoon sage
2 cups water
Bisquick (double crust)

Preheat oven to 425 degrees. Combine all ingredients except Bisquick. Cook until well done. Make dough from Bisquick according to package directions. Roll out double pie crusts. Put one crust at bottom of pie plate. Drain liquid from meat mixture and add to pie. Add upper crust and seal edges. Make several slits in upper crust. Bake 30 minutes.

Mrs. Donald A. Skelly
(Mother of Carol Skelly)

Lemon Meat Loaf

2 slices stale bread (at least 2 days old)
⅛ cup beef bouillon
⅛ cup lemon juice
1½ pounds ground beef
¼ cup minced onion
5 pieces raw bacon
pinch herb seasonings of your choice
¼ teaspoon salt
¼ teaspoon pepper
1 egg, beaten

Preheat oven to 325 degrees. Place stale bread in bowl, cover with the bouillon and lemon juice until saturated. In separate bowl, combine meat, onion, bacon, seasonings and beaten egg. Add bread to meat mixture. Mix well and put in loaf pan.

Topping:
½ cup brown sugar
½ cup ketchup
⅛ teaspoon dry mustard
⅛ teaspoon allspice
⅛ teaspoon ground cloves
1 lemon, thinly sliced

Mix topping ingredients together. Spread topping over meat loaf. Place thin slices of lemon on top. Bake 1 hour 15 minutes. Serve hot. Yield: 4-6 servings.

Note: A California recipe from the early 1960's. Always receives rave reviews because it is that good.

Virginia Larson

Mushroom and Veal Ragout

2 pounds veal, cut into thin strips
½ cup butter
1 medium onion, sliced thin
1 pint boiling water
2 chicken bouillon cubes
½ teaspoon salt
¼ teaspoon pepper
paprika, to taste
½ pound fresh mushrooms, sliced
¼ cup dry white wine

Coat veal strips lightly with flour. Melt ¼ cup butter in skillet. Add onion. Cook slowly until onion is soft and yellow. Add veal to skillet, brown stirring constantly. Pour water and seasonings over mixture. Cover tightly, reduce heat and simmer gently for 30 minutes. While meat mixture is simmering, melt remaining ¼ cup butter in second skillet. Add mushrooms. Cook about 10 minutes. After meat has cooked for 30 minutes, add mushrooms and wine to it. Stir well. Cook 2 minutes more. Serve over noodles or white rice. Yield: 4 servings.

Christina Barley

Veal Spizzato

2 pounds veal stew meat
¼ cup oil
3 cloves garlic, chopped
parsley, to taste
basil, to taste
salt and pepper
2 cups water
4-6 potatoes, cubed
oil
angel hair pasta

Cut veal in cubes (not too small). Brown lightly in oil small amounts at a time. Remove from pan. Set aside. Add garlic, brown lightly. Add veal, parsley, basil, salt and pepper to taste. Add water. Cook over medium heat for 30 minutes. Peel and cube potatoes, add to kettle and cook for 45 minutes. Serve sauce over angel hair pasta or can use as a stew. Yield: 6 servings.

Dorothy Czopek

Lamb Curry

2 cups leftover lamb
1 tablespoon fat
3 tablespoons onion
1 tablespoon curry powder
1 tablespoon flour
2 bouillon cubes
2 cups hot water
¼ cup ketchup
½ teaspoon salt
½ cup chopped apple
1 cup diced celery

Brown meat in fat. Add onion and cook until yellow. Add curry mixed with flour. Allow to bubble. Add bouillon cubes dissolved in water, ketchup, salt, apple and celery. Simmer 1¼ hours over low heat. Serve over hot rice. Yield: 4 servings.

Note: In 1988 the GFWC published a hard cover book of recipes. This was the only recipe published by a member of The Bedford Woman's Club.

Jean Rice

Shish-Kebab

3 cups olive oil
1 cup red wine
3 cloves garlic, chopped
1 medium onion, diced
2 tablespoons oregano
juice of 2 lemons
5-6 pounds boned lamb leg

Mix together all ingredients except lamb. Cut lamb into 1 inch cubes leaving some fat on. Marinate lamb in mixture (refrigerated) turning frequently if desired that day, otherwise, every 2-3 hours until the next day. Skewer lamb and broil 12-15 minutes turning skewers once or twice during broiling. Yield: 16-18 servings.

Doris Guimont

Mousaka

1 pound minced lamb
1 medium onion
1 ounce butter
1 tablespoon flour
salt and pepper to taste
2 tablespoons tomato paste
2 tablespoons water
1 clove garlic, crushed
2 medium eggplants
3 tablespoons olive oil
3 medium potatoes, cooked, peeled and sliced
3 medium tomatoes, peeled and sliced

Cook meat and onion in butter for about 5 minutes. Blend in flour, salt and pepper. Add tomato paste, water and garlic. Cover and cook gently for 30 minutes. Cut unpeeled eggplant into half inch slices and sprinkle liberally with salt. Set aside for ½ hour. Drain, dry and fry in oil until brown on both sides. In lightly greased casserole, arrange alternating layers of meat, potatoes, tomatoes and eggplants. Season each layer with salt and pepper.

Sauce:
1 ounce butter
3 tablespoons flour
salt and pepper to taste
pinch nutmeg
pinch mustard
1 cup milk
1 egg, separated
2 tablespoons grated cheese

Melt butter. Blend in flour, salt, pepper, nutmeg and mustard. Cook one minute. Add milk. Cook, stirring until thick. Cook two minutes. Blend in beaten egg yolk. Beat egg white until frothy, fold into the sauce with the cheese. Spoon over casserole. Bake at 400 degrees for about 20 minutes to heat through and lightly brown the top. Yield: 6 servings.

Note: This takes a while to prepare, but well worth the effort.

Caroline Williams

Valentine Lamb Shank

4 tablespoons lite olive oil
5 meaty lamb shanks
flour
salt and pepper
1 cup onion, chopped
1 cup carrot, chopped
1 tablespoon basil
1 tablespoon thyme
1 tablespoon minced garlic
3 tablespoons pine nuts (optional)
½ bottle dry red wine
1 can chicken broth
½ large can crushed tomatoes with puree
18 dried figs, quartered (or dried fruit), or Paul Newman's Diavolo/Spicy Simmer Sauce

Preheat oven to 325 degrees. Heat 2 tablespoons oil in Dutch oven or heavy pot. Shake lamb shanks in bag with flour, salt and pepper. Brown on all sides, about 8 minutes. Transfer to platter. Add 2 tablespoons more oil to pot. Sauté onions, carrots and seasonings, about 7 minutes. Return lamb to pot. Pour in wine, chicken broth, tomatoes and figs. Cover tightly. Cook in oven 1 hour 45 minutes, stirring occasionally. Remove lamb from pot. Reduce sauce. Skim off fat. Can cook night before — refrigerate, remove fat and re-heat. Yield: 5 servings.

Note: Serve with rice or noodles. Awesome!

Wesley Maloney

Pork Tenderloin

pork tenderloin, sliced in rounds
1 tablespoon olive oil
1 onion, sliced round
3 Granny Smith apples, sliced round, seeds removed
2 yams, sliced half inch thick
2 parsnips, sliced
4 carrots, sliced
1 cup chicken stock or white wine (or half of each)

In skillet sauté pork in oil. Place 1 slice each of onion, apple and yam on each tenderloin. Arrange rest of vegetables around the pork. Add stock. Cook on low heat until done, about an hour.

Note: Can use pork chops.

Alice Asadourian

Barbecued Spareribs

2 pounds pork spareribs
2 medium onions, chopped
2½ tablespoons oil
¼ cup lemon juice
2 tablespoons vinegar
1 tablespoon honey
1 tablespoon Worcestershire sauce
4 tablespoons brown sugar
½ cup water
1 cup chili sauce
¾ cup tomato ketchup
salt and pepper

Preheat oven to 350 degrees. Cut ribs into serving portions. Place in baking pan. Bake 30 minutes. Drain fat from pan. In separate pan, brown onions in oil. Add lemon juice, vinegar, honey, Worcestershire sauce, brown sugar, water, chili sauce, ketchup, salt and pepper. Cook slowly 20 minutes. Pour over spareribs and continue baking 1 hour. Yield: 4 servings.

Alice Asadourian

French Pork Pie (Tortier)

5 pounds ground pork
5 pounds ground beef
2 pounds onions, chopped
4 tablespoons ground cloves
4 tablespoons ground cinnamon
1 tablespoon black pepper
2 tablespoons salt
1 cup water
5 pounds potatoes
3 (9 inch) top and bottom pie crusts

Combine meat, onion, spices and water in large pan. Cook over low to medium heat for about 1 hour. Stir often for first few minutes until water comes out of meat and starts to bubble. This will prevent meat from catching on bottom. Peel and boil potatoes while meat is cooking. After meat is cooked, place meat in colander over large pan so juices will drip into pan. Use fat separator to remove fat. Discard fat, return juices and meat to pan. Hand mash potatoes into meat mixture. Put ⅓ mixture into each of three 9-inch pie pans lined with crust. Place crust on top. Bake in 350 degree oven for 1 hour. Yield: 18 servings.

Note: May be frozen.

Doris Guimont

Pork Chops

6 (2 inch thick) pork chops

Marinating Sauce:
2 cups soy sauce
1 cup water
½ cup brown sugar
1 tablespoon dark molasses
1 teaspoon salt

Mix together soy sauce, water, brown sugar, molasses, and salt in pan. Bring to a boil. Let cool. Put 6 chops in pan. Pour sauce over chops. Let stand overnight in refrigerator.

Red Sauce:
1 (14 ounce) bottle ketchup
1 (12 ounce) bottle chili sauce
½ cup brown sugar
1 tablespoon dry mustard

Next day: Preheat oven to 375 degrees. Take chops out of sauce, place in baking pan. Cover tightly with foil. Bake until tender about 2 hours. While chops are baking, combine all red sauce ingredients in heavy saucepan or double boiler. Dilute dry mustard, sugar and water together leaving no lumps. Bring to slight boil. The red sauce is finished after chops are tender. After removing chops from oven, dip each chop in red sauce. Place dipped chops in baking pan. Bake in 350 degree oven 30 minutes or until slightly glazed. Both sauces can be reused if frozen.

Note: This is an outstanding Michigan Restaurant Specialty.

Bonnie Venn

Pork Tenderloin with Raspberry Sauce

1 pound pork tenderloin
cayenne pepper, to taste
2 teaspoons butter
6 tablespoons red raspberry preserves
2 tablespoons red wine vinegar
1 tablespoon ketchup
½ teaspoon horseradish
½ teaspoon soy sauce
1 clove garlic, minced
2 kiwi fruit, peeled and thinly sliced
fresh raspberries for garnish

Flatten 8 crosswise slices of pork to 1 inch thickness. Lightly season with cayenne pepper. In non-stick skillet heat butter on medium high heat. Add pork, cook 4 minutes on each side. Meanwhile in small saucepan combine preserves, vinegar, ketchup, horseradish, soy sauce, and garlic. Simmer over low heat about 3 minutes, stirring occasionally. Keep warm. Spoon sauce over pork. Garnish each piece with a slice of kiwi and garnish platter with fresh raspberries. Yield: 4 servings.

Merrie Edgar

Pork Tenderloin with Stilton and Port

2 tablespoons vegetable oil
2 (1 pound) pork tenderloins
2 cups Port wine
1 cup chicken stock
1 cup heavy cream
6-8 ounces Stilton cheese

Preheat oven to 450 degrees. Heat oil in large skillet. Add pork and brown on all sides. Transfer pork to covered roasting pan. Deglaze skillet with Port and reduce by half. Add chicken stock and bring to a boil. Pour over pork and bake until done, approximately 15 minutes. Remove pork and keep warm. Reduce liquid by half. Slowly stir in cream. Cook over medium heat until sauce thickens. Add Stilton and stir to blend. Spoon sauce over sliced tenderloin. Yield: 6-8 servings.

Note: This dramatic sauce may also accompany a beef tenderloin. It is also delicious without the Stilton.

Jane Charlesworth

Poultry Entrées

Presbyterian Church Steeple

The church steeple contains many of Bedford's treasures. The church bell dates 1844 and was purchased from the sale of pews. The first one cracked and fell to the ground. The bell rings the time every hour on the hour.

The weathervane is unique in that it was designed by a local blacksmith, Nathan Kendall in 1832. It rests on his crowbar for its axis. It represents the sun, the moon and seven stars for each day.

The clock in the tower was given by the Ladies Circle to the town in 1895. The town pays for its maintenance. It is wound once a week by hand through the use of a lever that raises a wooden box of crushed stones, which have been carefully selected by weight so that the clock will not run down for seven days. Mr. Wiggin has been doing this task for the last forty years. The tower dome and the clocks' faces are gilded in gold leaf.

Bridge Luncheon for 8

salad

Glass Bowl Salad

entrée

Ribbon Sandwich Loaf

Lime & Cucumber Salad

Fresh Fruit Kabob with Fruit Dip

dessert

Lemon Torte

Brown Sugar Cookies

POULTRY ENTRÉES

Chicken and Asparagus Casserole

2 whole broiler-fryer chicken breasts, skinned, boned and cut into 2x4¾ inch pieces
1½ teaspoons Accent (optional)
¼ teaspoon pepper
½ cup corn oil
2 (10 ounce) packages frozen asparagus
1 can condensed cream of chicken soup
½ cup mayonnaise
1 teaspoon lemon juice
½ teaspoon curry powder
1 cup shredded sharp Cheddar cheese

Preheat oven to 375 degrees. Sprinkle Accent and pepper over chicken. Pour oil into 10-inch skillet. Heat over medium heat. Add chicken. Sauté slowly about 6 minutes or until white and opaque. Remove from skillet. Drain on paper towels. Cook asparagus as package directs, 4-5 minutes. Drain. Place asparagus on bottom of 9x9x2 inch baking pan. Place chicken over asparagus. Mix together soup, mayonnaise, lemon juice and curry powder. Pour over chicken and asparagus. Sprinkle cheese over top. Cover with aluminum foil. Bake 30 minutes or until done. Yield: 4 servings.

Sharlene Genest

Wild Rice and Chicken

1 can cream of chicken or mushroom soup
3 cups water
1 cup wild rice
1 package onion soup mix
6-8 pieces chicken

Preheat oven to 350 degrees. Butter a 9x13 inch baking dish. Mix one can of cream soup with three cups water. Sprinkle rice in bottom of baking dish. Sprinkle with onion soup mix. Pour soup mixture over rice. Lay chicken on top. Bake two hours. Yield: 6 servings.

Martha Glasheen

Chicken and Wild Rice Casserole

1 (6 ounce) package long grain and wild rice
¼ cup butter or margarine
¼ cup flour
1 (13 ounce) can evaporated milk
½ cup chicken broth
2½ cups cooked chicken, chopped
1 large can sliced mushrooms, drained
⅓ cup green pepper, chopped
¼ cup pimento, chopped
¼ cup slivered almonds, lightly toasted

Preheat oven to 350 degrees. Prepare rice according to package directions. Set aside. Melt butter, add flour, stir until smooth. Cook 1 minute, stirring constantly. Gradually add milk and broth. Cook over medium heat. Stir constantly until thick and bubbly. Add remaining ingredients except almonds to sauce. Pour into lightly greased 9x13 inch dish. Sprinkle with almonds. Bake uncovered for 30 minutes. Yield: 6-8 servings.

Note: This is the recipe for the casserole served at the 1994 Holly House Luncheon. Can be prepared ahead. Cover, refrigerate overnight and bake the following day.

Rita Fitzgerald

Chicken Breasts a la Smitane

4 salted chicken breasts
2 tablespoons butter
¼ cup dry white wine
dash cayenne
1 onion, sliced
several scallions
⅓ cup white wine
⅔ cup sour cream
1 tablespoon lemon juice
blanched toasted almonds

Cook chicken in butter, ¼ cup wine and dash of cayenne. In separate pan, sauté onion and scallions. Add ⅓ cup wine, sour cream and lemon juice. Pour over chicken and simmer, uncovered until the sauce is thick. Strain sauce and serve over chicken. Sprinkle blanched, toasted almonds over the top. Yield: 4 servings.

Gary A. Howard
Chairman, Bedford Planning Board

Chicken Cacciatore

4 boneless, skinless chicken breasts
1 can tomatoes, minced in blender
1 red or yellow pepper, chopped
1 white Bermuda onion, chopped
1-2 cloves of garlic, minced
1 teaspoon dried oregano or 1 tablespoon fresh
½ teaspoon thyme or 2 teaspoons fresh
¼ teaspoon black pepper
salt to taste

In crock pot place all the ingredients, except salt, in the above order. Set to low and cook all day. Stir to break up chicken. Salt to taste about twenty minutes before serving. Serve over cooked pasta. Yield: 4-6 servings. Recipe may be doubled.

Note: To serve at a potluck dinner, cut fresh angel hair pasta into 2-inch sections, cook the pasta al dente, drain it and add to the crock pot.

Anne C. Hoffman

Chicken Casserole

4 chicken breasts, cooked
1 can mushroom soup
¾ cup mayonnaise
1 cup chopped onion
1½ cups chopped celery
1 can water chestnuts, rinsed
½ cup margarine, melted
7 or 8 ounces dry stuffing

Preheat oven to 350 degrees. Mix soup and mayonnaise. Add to chicken. Add onion, celery and water chestnuts. Spoon into slightly greased 9x13 inch baking dish. Mix melted margarine with dry stuffing. Sprinkle over top of casserole. Cover with tinfoil (shiny side down). Bake for 40 minutes. Yield: 4 servings.

Bonnie Venn

Chicken Cordon Bleu

3 full boneless chicken breasts (6 halves)
6 slices boiled ham, thinly sliced
6 slices Swiss cheese
1 stick margarine or butter, melted
½ cup dry bread crumbs
½ teaspoon seasoned salt
½ teaspoon pepper
½ teaspoon thyme

Preheat oven to 350 degrees. Place each breast between two pieces of waxed paper. Flatten with meat hammer. Peel off top layer of waxed paper. Layer breast with a piece of ham and then cheese. Roll up breasts and set aside. Place melted butter in a shallow bowl. Place bread crumbs in another bowl. Mix in salt, pepper, thyme. Roll breasts in butter, then in bread crumbs. Place breasts on a greased baking pan. Bake for 30 minutes. Yield: 6 servings.

Serve with mushroom sauce.

Mushroom Sauce:
6 ounces fresh mushrooms, sliced
½ cup onion, chopped
¼ cup butter
2 tablespoons flour
1 cup light cream
1 teaspoon salt
½ teaspoon pepper
1 cup sour cream

Mushroom sauce: Sauté mushrooms and onions in butter until tender. Add flour, mix well. Stir in cream slowly, add salt and pepper. Heat to boiling, stirring constantly. Stir in sour cream just before serving, heat through. Makes 3 cups.

Sharlene Genest

Chicken Cordon Bleu

8 pieces boneless chicken breast
1 egg
fine bread crumbs
8 pieces boiled ham, thinly sliced
8 slices mozzarella cheese
1 cup sliced mushrooms
¼ pound margarine
¼ cup white cooking sherry

Dip chicken in beaten egg then in bread crumbs. Fry in cooking oil until evenly brown. Place chicken in baking dish. Layer each piece of chicken with a slice of boiled ham folded over evenly to cover size of chicken breast. Top with mozzarella cheese. Sauté mushrooms in several tablespoons of margarine and place on top of chicken. Melt remaining margarine and add cooking wine. Pour over chicken. Bake at 325 degrees for 35 to 40 minutes. Yield: 8 servings.

Jacquelin Lavoie

Chicken Divan

2 packages frozen broccoli spears, thawed
3 whole chicken breasts, boned and cooked
2 cans cream of chicken soup
1 cup mayonnaise
½ teaspoon curry powder
1 teaspoon lemon juice
½ cup sharp Cheddar cheese, grated
½ cup bread crumbs
1 tablespoon butter, melted

Preheat oven to 350 degrees. Arrange broccoli and chicken in buttered 9x13 inch baking dish. Mix soup, mayonnaise, curry powder and juice together. Pour mixture over chicken and broccoli. Add cheese and bread crumbs to butter. Mix together and pour on top of casserole. Bake 30 minutes. Yield: 4 servings.

Ann Marie Patterson

Chicken Easy

6 boneless chicken thighs
1 jar spaghetti sauce
Parmesan cheese
1 (8 ounce) package of mozzarella cheese

Preheat oven to 350 degrees. Trim fat off chicken and flatten out. Lightly brown, either in oil or Pam. Season with salt and pepper. Pour a little sauce in bottom of glass baking pan. Add chicken and rest of sauce. Sprinkle Parmesan cheese on top and bake in oven about 30 minutes. Cut mozzarella into slices. Put slice on each piece of chicken. Continue baking until cheese is melted. (About 20 minutes.) Yield: 4 servings.

Note: I serve with lightly buttered linguine, a green salad, and garlic bread. It is very good with homemade sauce also.

Carol Molitoris

Chicken Jubilate

3-4 whole meaty chicken breasts, boned, skinned, cut in half
2-3 tablespoons cooking oil
1 (21 ounce) can Comstock cherry pie filling
½ cup white wine
¼ cup packed light brown sugar
¼ teaspoon ground allspice
¼ teaspoon ground cloves
¼ teaspoon ground nutmeg
salt and pepper, to taste
½ cup orange juice

Heat oil over medium heat. Brown chicken pieces in hot oil about 10 minutes. Drain off excess oil. Combine all ingredients except orange juice and pour over chicken. Cover and simmer about 20 minutes. Add orange juice and simmer another 20 minutes or until chicken is tender. Adjust time for smaller chicken breasts. Yield: 8 servings.

Priscilla VanWagner

Chicken Piccata

5 boneless/skinned chicken breasts
½ cup flour (seasoned with black pepper)
4 tablespoons butter
½ cup water
1 cube chicken bouillon
1 tablespoon lemon juice
5 lemon slices

Coat chicken with flour and brown in butter in a large skillet over medium high heat. Remove chicken from pan and keep warm in oven. Do not clean out skillet. Add water, bouillon cube and lemon juice to skillet. Stir to dissolve bouillon cube and bring to a boil. Return chicken to skillet. Top each chicken breast with a slice of lemon. Cover and simmer for 10-20 minutes. Yield: 4-5 servings.

Note: Delicious with cranberry sauce.

Madonna Lovett Repeta

Chicken Ruby

1 broiler, cut in quarters (or boneless equivalent)
1 teaspoon salt
¼ cup butter or margarine
½ medium onion, chopped
¼ teaspoon cinnamon
¼ teaspoon ginger
1 teaspoon grated orange rind
¾ cup orange juice
1½ cups cranberries
½ cup chopped walnuts
¼ cup sugar

Sprinkle chicken with salt. Brown in butter in skillet. Add onion, spices, orange rind and juice. Simmer covered for 20 minutes. (If preparing ahead of time stop here. Complete last step at the last minute. If sealed and refrigerated can be prepared the day before and reheated.) Add cranberries and walnuts. Sprinkle with sugar. Simmer uncovered 10 minutes longer. Yield: 4 servings.

Janis Galeucia

Chicken Tarragon with Asparagus

1 tablespoon vegetable oil
1 pound fresh asparagus, cut in inch pieces
1 large sweet red pepper, diced in inch pieces
1 large onion, largely diced
12 ounces boned, skinned chicken breasts, cut in inch pieces
2 cups orange juice, divided
2 teaspoons cornstarch
1½ teaspoons tarragon leaves, crushed
½ teaspoon salt
⅛ teaspoon ground black pepper

Heat oil in large non-stick skillet over medium heat. Add vegetables. Cook stirring frequently until tender crisp. Add chicken. Cook stirring frequently until chicken is opaque, about 2 minutes. In small bowl combine ¼ cup orange juice and cornstarch. Stir into skillet with remaining juice, tarragon, salt and pepper. Cook until mixture thickens and boils about 2-3 minutes, stirring constantly. Boil 1 minute longer, stirring constantly. Serve hot over angel hair pasta or fettucini. Yield: 4 servings.

Note: Low fat and low calorie.

Martha Dollen

Congressional Chicken

1 (10¾ ounce) can condensed cream of chicken soup
1 (10¾ ounce) can condensed cream of mushroom soup
½ cup milk
1 (6 ounce) package long grain and wild rice mix
4 chicken breasts, split, boned, skinned
½ cup grated Parmesan cheese

Preheat oven to 350 degrees. Combine soups and milk, mixing until blended. Combine 1½ cups soup mixture with rice mix. Spoon into 13x9 inch baking dish. Top with chicken and remaining soup mixture. Cover. Bake 1 hour and 15 minutes. Sprinkle with cheese. Continue baking, uncovered 15 minutes. Yield: 8 servings.

Amanda Ober
WMUR-TV

Chow Mein

¼ cup margarine
2-3 cups cooked chicken, turkey or pork
1 cup onion, chopped fine
1 cup celery, sliced thin
1 teaspoon salt
pinch pepper
1½ cups stock or hot water
1 can bean sprouts, drained

Thickening:
½ cup water
3 tablespoons cornstarch
3 teaspoons soy sauce
1½ teaspoons sugar

In large frying pan melt margarine. Add cooked meat, sear quickly. Add onions, fry 5 minutes. Add celery, salt, pepper, and stock or water. Cover and cook 5 minutes. Add drained bean sprouts. Mix and heat to boiling. Add the thickening. Stir lightly. Cook 5 minutes more. Serve over chow mein style noodles. Yield: 4 servings.

Note: Excellent way to make use of leftover turkey, chicken or pork.

Martha Glasheen

Chinese Chicken

3-4 pounds chicken, cut up
4 tablespoons soy sauce
¾ cup ketchup
¾ cup water
2 tablespoons cider vinegar
1 small onion, diced
dash garlic powder
dash Lawry's seasoned salt

Preheat oven to 350 degrees. Wash chicken. Place in bottom of lightly greased one-inch deep baking dish. Mix together remaining ingredients. Pour over chicken. Bake, uncovered for 1-1½ hours occasionally spooning sauce over chicken as it bakes. Yield: 4 servings.

Christina Barley

Tarragon - Leaves have a hot, pungent taste. Valuable to use in all salads and sauces. Excellent in tartar sauce. Leaves are pickled with gherkins. Used to flavor vinegar.

Coq Au Vin

4 slices bacon, cut in small pieces
2 tablespoons onion, chopped
2½-3 pounds chicken thighs
8 shallots or small whole onions
½ cup carrots, coarsely chopped
1 stalk celery, chopped
1 clove garlic, minced
2 tablespoons brandy
1 pint mushrooms
2 tablespoons butter
1 bay leaf
½ teaspoon dried thyme
3-4 sprigs parsley
2 cups red Burgundy

Preheat oven to 350 degrees. In skillet, brown bacon pieces and chopped onion. Remove. Add chicken pieces. Brown slowly in bacon drippings. Add shallots, carrots, celery, garlic and brandy. Cook 3 minutes. Cook mushrooms in butter. Place chicken in 2-quart casserole in layers with vegetables, mushrooms, herbs and parsley. Add wine to skillet. Heat to boiling and stir to loosen crusty brown bits. Pour mixture over casserole. Cover. Bake for 2 hours. Yield: 4 servings.

Note: This has always been enjoyed when made for dinner parties and served with rice. The chicken is very tender from cooking in the wine.

Caroline Williams

Sour Cream Chicken

1 pound chicken breast, cooked, boned and cut-up
2 cans cream of mushroom soup
1 large sour cream
fresh mushrooms, sliced or canned
1 small package Pepperidge Farm dressing

Preheat oven to 350 degrees. Mix chicken, soup, sour cream and mushrooms together. Put in baking dish. Mix the package of dressing according to directions and put on top of casserole. Bake 45 minutes. Yield: 6-8 servings.

Note: Double recipe for large casserole.

Mary Dambach

Healthy Chicken Linguine

1 cup good quality olive oil
5 cloves garlic, finely chopped
1 tablespoon hot pepper flakes (or less)
4 whole chicken breasts, deboned, skinned and cut into julienne strips
3 cups no fat chicken broth
juice of 3 lemons
2 pounds fresh linguine
½ cup fresh grated Parmesan cheese
¼ cup fresh parsley, chopped
1 lemon

Place olive oil, garlic and pepper flakes in a large skillet. Warm over medium heat. Add chicken strips. Stir to separate. Cook until chicken is white. Add broth and simmer 5 minutes. Add lemon juice and simmer 5 more minutes. While chicken cooks, bring a large pot of water to a boil. Add linguine and cook 1-3 minutes until done. Drain and rinse pasta with cold water. Place chicken mixture in large pot, add pasta and toss to mix. Divide onto 4 plates. Sprinkle with Parmesan and parsley. Garnish with a lemon wedge. Yield: 4 generous servings.

Madonna Lovett Repeta

Poulet

1 package stuffing mix (Pepperidge Farm)
1 stick butter or margarine, melted
1 cup water
2½ cups cooked chicken, diced
½ cup onions, chopped
½ cup celery, chopped
½ cup mayonnaise
2 eggs
½ cup milk
1 can cream of mushroom soup
Cheddar cheese, for top

Mix stuffing, butter and water. Layer half of stuffing mixture in buttered casserole dish. Mix chicken, onion, celery and mayonnaise. Spread chicken mixture over stuffing. Layer the other half of stuffing mixture over chicken. Beat eggs, add milk and put on top. Let sit in refrigerator overnight. Pour soup on top. Bake in 325 degree oven for 40 minutes. Add cheese and bake 10 minutes more. Yield: 4 servings.

Donna Ebert
(Daughter of Rose Marie Borelli)

Simon and Garfunkel Chicken

3 boned chicken breasts, skinned and halved
1 stick butter
salt and pepper
6 slices mozzarella cheese
flour
1 egg, beaten
bread crumbs
2 tablespoons parsley
¼ teaspoon sage
¼ teaspoon rosemary
¼ teaspoon thyme
½ cup white wine

Preheat oven to 350 degrees. Flatten chicken between sheets of waxed paper. Spread half of butter on chicken. Season with salt and pepper. Place one slice cheese on each piece, roll and tuck ends. Coat with flour, dip in egg, roll in bread crumbs and arrange in baking dish. Melt remaining butter, add parsley, sage, rosemary and thyme. Bake 30 minutes basting with butter mixture. Pour wine over chicken, baste. Bake 30 minutes longer. Yield: 3-4 servings.

Donna Joas

Special Times Chicken Casserole

Uncle Ben's Rice
8 boneless chicken breasts, skinned
1 can cream of chicken soup
1 can cream of mushroom soup
1 can cream of celery soup
1 pound sharp Cheddar cheese, grated
1 package slivered almonds

Preheat oven to 350 degrees. Cook enough rice to serve 8 people or to cover bottom of large baking dish. Place rice in baking dish, covering entire bottom. Cut breasts in half and roll. Place rolled chicken breasts on top of rice. Empty each can of soup, undiluted, on top of chicken. Spread over entire surface. Place grated cheese over entire surface. Place slivered almonds on top. Bake in oven for 1 hour 15 minutes. Yield: 8-10 servings.

Note: This is a great dish for large parties. Keeps well until time to serve. Reheat as needed. Good the next day also.

Virginia Larson

Sweet and Sour Chicken

4 chicken breasts, boned, skinned and cut into 2-inch long strips
1 egg, beaten
1 cup prepared bread crumbs
1 cup oil or shortening, melted and very hot

Dip chicken into beaten egg; then roll in crumbs. Fry chicken in oil until golden brown. Drain on paper towels.

Sauce:
2 tablespoons oil
2 cups pineapple juice
6 tablespoons vinegar
½ cup ketchup
2 tablespoons soy sauce
2 cups orange juice
½ cup brown sugar
2 tablespoons cornstarch, mixed with 12 tablespoons water and whisked smooth
2 green peppers, cut into chunks
1 large can chunk pineapple
1 small jar maraschino cherries, drained

Combine and heat all sauce ingredients (except peppers, pineapple and cherries) over medium heat until well blended, smooth and slightly thickened. To the heated sauce add peppers, pineapple and cherries. Heat on medium heat for 15 minutes. Place drained chicken in 9x13 inch baking pan. Pour sauce evenly over it. Bake at 350 degrees 20-25 minutes. Serve with rice. Yield: 4 servings.

Note: Recipe may be doubled.

Catherine T. Liotta

Woodchuck (Chicken)

Melt in top of large double boiler pan over hot water the following:

1 can mushroom soup, undiluted
1 jar Old English cheese
¼ pound Velveeta cheese

Thin the above with milk or chicken bouillon.

In another pan, boil in water for ten minutes the following:

½ cup celery
1 green pepper, chopped

Combine the celery and pepper with the cheese mixture.

Add the following ingredients and allow to heat thoroughly.

½ cup toasted slivered almonds
1 small jar chopped pimentos
½ cup chopped ripe olives
onion juice for seasoning
3 pounds baked and basted chicken, diced

Just before serving add:

4 boiled eggs, chopped

Serve over warmed canned Chinese fried noodles. Yield: 8 servings.

Note: A great recipe for a large group.

Virginia Larson

Quick and Easy Chicken

2 cups uncooked rice
8-10 chicken pieces
1 can chicken broth
1 can cream of chicken soup

Preheat oven to 425 degrees. Place rice in bottom of large roasting pan. Place layer of chicken over rice. Mix together the soups. Pour soups over chicken and rice. Cook approximately 25 minutes.

Jean Rice

Moist Pheasant in Sour Cream and Wine Sauce

½ teaspoon salt
½ cup flour
½ teaspoon black pepper
½ teaspoon celery salt
1 cup milk
1-2 pheasants, skinned, cut into serving pieces
4 tablespoons butter
½ cup stock (or chicken broth)
2 green onions, chopped
½ cup celery, chopped
peel of one orange
1 cup dry white wine
1 tablespoon honey
1 cup mushroom caps
1 cup sour cream

In paper bag, combine salt, flour, pepper and celery salt. Dip pheasant pieces in bowl of milk, then drop in bag and shake until pieces well coated. Melt butter in skillet. Over medium heat, lightly brown meat. Transfer browned pieces to oven to keep warm. Blend some of the flour mixture with remaining butter in skillet until thicken. Add stock, onions, celery and orange peel. Stir and cook for 3 minutes. Mix wine with honey. Add to sauce. Pour sauce over pheasant in oven. Cover and bake 2 hours at 325 degrees. Mix mushroom caps with sour cream. Add to pheasant. Stir. Cover and cook for 30-40 minutes. Serve over wild rice. Yield: 4 servings.

Note: Can substitute chicken for pheasant.

Dr. Thomas Fairchild
Interim President
University of New Hampshire

Wild Rice Stuffed Chicken Breasts

1 package Uncle Ben's Long Grain and Wild Rice
6 whole chicken breasts, boned and pounded flat
¼ cup white wine or dry vermouth
¼ cup orange juice

Preheat oven to 350 degrees. Cook rice as package directs. Cool. Place a portion of the rice in the center of each chicken breast. Roll chicken around rice, and place, seam side down, in buttered shallow casserole or baking dish. Mix wine and orange juice together. Pour over chicken breasts. Bake for 30 minutes, until lightly brown. Cover with foil and continue baking for 20 minutes. Yield: 6 servings.

Mary Hamrock

Turkey Divan

1 package frozen broccoli or asparagus
2-3 cups leftover turkey
½ cup Pepperidge Farm stuffing
½ cup grated Parmesan cheese

Preheat oven to 350 degrees. Prepare vegetable according to package directions. Spread in greased 13x9 inch dish. Add turkey cut into small pieces.

Sauce:
1 cup cream of chicken soup
¼ cup mayonnaise
¼ cup milk
½ teaspoon curry powder
½ teaspoon lemon juice

Cover with sauce. Sprinkle stuffing over sauce. Sprinkle Parmesan cheese over the top. Bake for 30 to 40 minutes. Yield: 4 servings.

Note: This is delicious served over rice.

Doris Guimont

Seafood Entrées

The Little Green House

The Little Green House, built in 1849, was formerly owned and operated as a shoemaker's shop by Oliver Kendall. Over the years it has been used as a post office, store, for tenants as a residence and was even a private laundry. It was eventually willed to the town and used by the Ladies Social Circle and other groups for small public meetings. The ladies had one room remodeled for a kitchen and did some painting and papering. At present it is operated by the Bedford Craftworkers Guild, a group of very talented craftspeople who teach a variety of courses and offer a sales outlet at specific times of the year.

Little Green House Game Night

nibbles

Spicy Bourbon Pecans

Nibblers Delight

with crackers

Nutty Cheese Ball

Hot Artichoke Dip

Crab Dip Supreme

dessert

Fudge Cake

SEAFOOD ENTRÉES

Calamari (Squid in sauce)

1 large onion, chopped
2 tablespoons oil
1 (8 ounce) can tomato sauce
parsley, to taste
basil, to taste
1 teaspoon salt
¼ teaspoon pepper
1-2 pounds squid

Sauce: Sauté onion in oil. Add tomato sauce and seasonings. Cook 15-20 minutes.

Squid: Prepare squid by cutting open and cleaning inside. Remove the colored skin on outside. Cut squid into 2-inch strips and rinse well. Can put fish in frying pan and let water dry up or drain, careful not to burn. Add squid to sauce. Cook 30-40 minutes until tender.

Dorothy Czopek

Stuffed Clams

1 cup bread crumbs
½ cup grated Romano cheese
black pepper
parsley, to taste
basil, to taste
dash salt
⅛ cup oil
2 cups cooked spaghetti sauce
2 (6½ ounce) cans minced clams, undrained
24 empty clam shells

Preheat oven to 350 degrees. Season bread crumbs with cheese, black pepper, parsley, basil, salt and oil. Add 1-1½ cups spaghetti sauce and minced clams to mixture. Mixture will be paste-like consistency. Fill shells but do not pack them. Place on cookie sheet. Drizzle 1 tablespoon sauce (diluted to watery consistency) over each shell. If sauce is thick, add a little water. You may want to put 1-2 drops oil on each filled shell. Bake 20 minutes or until slightly bronzed on top. Serve hot.

Dorothy Czopek

Lancaster County Crab Cakes

1 pound crab meat
2 tablespoons lemon juice
2 eggs, beaten
2 tablespoons mayonnaise
1 cup bread crumbs
⅛ teaspoon pepper
1 teaspoon dry mustard
1 teaspoon Worcestershire sauce

Pick over crab meat, discarding bits of shell or cartilage. Sprinkle crab meat with lemon juice.

White sauce:
1 tablespoon butter
1 tablespoon all-purpose flour
½ cup milk
salt to taste

Make a medium white sauce by melting butter, flour, milk and salt. Stir constantly until smooth and thick. Mix eggs with white sauce, mayonnaise, bread crumbs and seasonings. Stir well. Gently combine crab meat with mixture. Chill until firm. Shape into cakes.

Breading:
3 tablespoons all-purpose flour
½ cup bread crumbs
2-3 tablespoons shortening

Prepare crumbs for breading cakes by mixing flour and crumbs. Roll cakes in crumb mixture. Fry in shortening, turning a few times until all sides are brown. Yield: 10-12 servings.

Note: This recipe comes from the Central Market Cookbook. Central Market is located in Lancaster, Pennsylvania, and is the oldest farmer's market in the Nation.

Christina Barley

Crazy Crab Casserole

2 cans cream of mushroom soup
1 cup Best Foods mayonnaise
¼ cup sherry
½ cup half and half cream
1 package (3-4 cups) sea legs or shrimp and crab
3 cups seasoned croutons
2 cans sliced water chestnuts
½ cup onions, minced
1 cup grated Parmesan cheese, sprinkle on top

Preheat oven to 350 degrees. Mix everything in order listed. Bake in greased ovenproof dish. Bake at 350 degrees for 45 minutes. Yield: 6 servings.

Wesley Maloney

Seafood Debonair

1 small can shrimp
1 small can crabmeat
1 small can pimento plus liquid
1 small can mushrooms plus liquid
1 cup raw celery, chopped
1 medium onion, chopped
¼ cup green pepper, chopped (optional)
fresh ground pepper
Lawry's seasoned salt
1½ cups uncooked Minute rice
1 cup mayonnaise or salad dressing
grated cheese
paprika
buttered bread crumbs

Preheat oven to 350 degrees. Combine all ingredients, except cheese, paprika and crumbs, in 1½ quart casserole. Sprinkle grated cheese, paprika and buttered crumbs on top. Bake 30-40 minutes enough to heat thoroughly. May be mixed the day before. Yield: 4-6 servings.

Bonnie Venn

Paella Valenciana

1½ pound lobster, keep whole
1 pound shrimp
12 fresh clams
4 crab claws
1 (2 pound) chicken, cut-up in eighths
1½ teaspoons salt
pepper and garlic powder to taste
6 spoonfuls Spanish olive oil
1 clove garlic, mashed
2 medium onions, chopped
1 green pepper, chopped
4 ounces cooking ham, cut-up
1 Spanish sausage (chorizo), sliced
1 ounce salt pork, cut-up
1 teaspoon Spanish capers
1 small can tomato sauce
4-5 cups chicken broth
2¼ cups Valencia rice, uncooked
1 cup Spanish white cooking wine
1 teaspoon yellow food color, or less
1-3 cans beer
1 small can sweet peas
1 small can pimento
1 can asparagus

Clean and cut up seafood and chicken. Season with salt, pepper and garlic powder to taste. Heat olive oil in large pot. When hot, add garlic, onion and green pepper. Cook until tender. Add chicken pieces. Cook at fairly low heat, making certain onion and green pepper do not burn. Add seafood. Let cook at low heat for about 5 minutes. Add ham, Spanish sausage, pork and capers. Cook slowly for a few minutes. Add tomato sauce and chicken broth. Bring to a boil. Add rice which has already been washed. Bring to boil, then reduce heat to low. Add immediately the clams and wine.

Cooking Process: Let everything cook at low heat. Add beer as needed to maintain enough broth to keep pot from drying up but not too much as to make it soupy. Stir pot only occasionally to keep from sticking on bottom. This rice is unusually hard, so it may take 2-3 cans of beer. The dish is ready when the rice is tender, about an hour. Pour in sweet peas and stir. Garnish with pimento, asparagus and some parsley. Yield: 6 servings.

Note: Adding a teaspoon of sugar helps to neutralize any acidity. This recipe is from a Brazilian friend. We cook it on the grill outside for big parties.

Bonnie Venn

Seafood Casserole

8 ounces Ritz cracker crumbs
½ pound margarine, melted
⅓ cup milk
½ cup clam juice
dash of Tabasco sauce
salt to taste
1 pound haddock, raw, cut up
½ pound scallops, raw, cut up if large
½ pound lobster meat, cooked
½ pound shrimp, raw or frozen

Preheat oven to 325 degrees. Combine cracker crumbs and margarine. Mix and set aside. Mix milk, clam juice, Tabasco sauce and salt together. Add all seafood and mix together. Spread in 2 or 3 layers in casserole with layers of crumbs. Put last ⅓ of crumbs on top. Bake 40-45 minutes.

Doris Guimont

Shrimp Rockefeller

2 (10 ounce) packages frozen chopped spinach
6 slices crisp bacon, crumbled
¾ cup minced onion
3 tablespoons minced parsley (optional)
2 bay leaves, crumbled
dash of Tabasco
⅓ cup diced celery
1 stick butter or margarine
¼ teaspoon horseradish
¼ cup milk
¼ cup white wine (dry vermouth recommended)
¾ cup dry bread crumbs
salt and pepper
1 pound shrimp, cooked, shelled and deveined (size 30 count per pound)

Cook spinach as package directs and drain well. Mix spinach with bacon, onion, parsley, bay leaves, Tabasco and celery. Melt butter and horseradish. Add spinach mixture, cook over medium heat until thoroughly heated - about 3-4 minutes, stirring constantly - gradually adding milk and wine alternately. Stir in bread crumbs, add salt and pepper and let boil 1-2 minutes (stirring constantly). Butter 6 casseroles that hold 1 cup each or two quart baking dish. Put ⅔ of shrimp on bottom, top with mixture. Nestle remaining shrimp into top. Bake in 400 degree oven 5-10 minutes, just until heated through. Yield: 6 servings.

Mary Hamrock

Mixed Grill of Shrimp, Sausage and Mushrooms

¾ cup olive oil
2 tablespoons (packed) fresh thyme leaves or 1 tablespoon dried
2 large garlic cloves, minced
½ teaspoon dried crushed red pepper
2-3 drops Tabasco sauce
32 large uncooked shrimp, peeled and deveined
32 mushrooms, stems trimmed
8 bamboo skewers, soaked 30 minutes in water
1½ pounds cooked sausage, cut into ¾-inch thick rounds

Blend olive oil, thyme, minced garlic, crushed red pepper, and Tabasco sauce in processor for 1 minute. Pour mixture into large bowl. Add shrimp and let stand for 1 hour at room temperature. Remove shrimp from marinade. Reserve marinade. Thread a mushroom horizontally on a skewer. Hold a sausage piece in curve of a shrimp. Thread together on skewer, sliding next to mushroom. Repeat, alternating a total of 4 mushrooms, 4 shrimp and 4 sausage pieces on each skewer. (Can be prepared 1 day ahead. Cover and chill reserved marinade and skewers separately).

Prepare barbecue (medium-high heat). Bring reserved marinade to boil in heavy small saucepan. Arrange skewers on grill and brush with marinade. Grill until shrimp are cooked through, turning occasionally and basting with marinade, about 8 minutes. Yield: 8 servings.

Anne C. Hoffman

Baked Haddock

2 pounds haddock fillets
Italian bread crumbs
¼ pound butter, melted
lemon juice

Preheat oven to 350 degrees. Wash haddock fillets and place in 9x13 baking pan. Add water to cover bottom of pan approximately ¼ inch deep. Sprinkle bread crumbs generously covering all fillets. Add lemon juice to melted butter. Pour lemon butter mixture over breaded fillets. Bake for 15 minutes or until fish flakes. Yield: 4-6 servings.

Note: Can substitute scallops for the haddock but bake in smaller pan. Water keeps fish moist.

Doris Guimont

Almost Lobster

1-1½ pounds haddock or white fish
1 can frozen cream of shrimp soup or 1 can Campbell's cream of shrimp soup
¼ teaspoon garlic salt
¼ teaspoon chopped onion or instant minced onion
¼ cup butter, melted
15 Ritz crackers, crushed

Preheat oven to 375 degrees. Grease 13x9 inch pan. Place a layer of fish in pan. Add garlic salt, onion and soup. Pour melted butter over all. Bake for 20 minutes. Remove from oven. Add crackers. Bake an additional 10 minutes.

Betty Gollihue

Lemon Herbed Salmon

2½ cups fresh bread crumbs, from wheat bread
4 cloves garlic, minced
½ cup fresh parsley, chopped
6 tablespoons grated Romano cheese
2 teaspoons grated lemon peel
6 tablespoons margarine, divided and melted
½ teaspoon salt (optional)
1 (3-4 pound) salmon fillet, fresh
1 tablespoon lemon juice

Preheat oven to 350 degrees. Combine bread crumbs, garlic, parsley, cheese and lemon peel. Add 4 tablespoons melted margarine. Mix well. Pat salmon dry. Place skin side down in greased baking dish. Sprinkle with lemon juice and remaining melted margarine. Cover with crumb mixture. Bake 20-25 minutes until salmon flakes easily. Yield: 8 servings.

Phyllis Hickey

Salmon Loaf

2 cups flaked salmon (canned or fresh cooked)
2 cups soft bread crumbs
2 eggs, beaten
¾ cup milk
⅛ teaspoon pepper
½ teaspoon salt
1 tablespoon onion, finely minced
1 teaspoon lemon juice

Preheat oven to 325 degrees. Flake salmon with fork and add remaining ingredients. Mix well. Place in greased loaf pan and bake 45 minutes. Yield: 4-6 servings.

Note: This is delicious served with lime and cucumber salad. Can be prepared ahead of time and served hot or cold.

Eunice Brine

Magnificent Mussel Stew

6 pounds mussels
½ Bermuda onion, sliced
4 celery stalks, 4 inches long
40 peppercorns
10 cloves
6 bay leaves
½ pound butter
4 cups chopped mushrooms
1 quart whole milk
2 large Bermuda onions, chopped
6 scallions, chopped
4 cups chopped celery
4 cloves chopped garlic
2 cups chopped parsley
1 quart half and half
3 teaspoon curry powder
3 cups Pepperidge Farm Herb Seasoned Stuffing
1 pint heavy cream
2 tablespoons brown sugar
salt to taste

Clean and de-beard mussels. Place on steamer rack in a large pot, with 4 cups of water over ½ sliced Bermuda onion, 4 inch celery stalks, 40 peppercorns, 10 cloves, and 6 bay leaves. Cover and place on medium heat. Steam for 10-15 minutes. Mussels will open. Remove pot and set aside.

In a large skillet, sauté ¼ pound butter and mushrooms. When mushrooms are light brown add ½ cup milk, chopped onions, chopped scallions, chopped celery, chopped garlic and parsley. Simmer entire mixture for about 20 minutes, adding a little milk if necessary.

Remove cooled mussels from shells and place them in a separate bowl. Large mussels may be cut in half with scissors. Remove vegetables from broth and strain it through a fine strainer into large pitcher and set aside.

Clean mussel pot, place on large burner. Pour all simmered ingredients from skillet. Add mussels from the bowl. Then add all remaining ingredients (butter, milk, half and half, cream, brown sugar, curry and stuffing). Add reserved mussel broth to taste and desired thickness of stew. Cover and simmer over low heat for 1 hour. Let cool. Serve with oyster crackers. Yield: 20 servings.

Note: May be served hot or cold. Freezes well.

Barbara Upton

Oysters Escalloped

2½ cups bread and cracker crumbs
¼ pound oleo, melted in crumbs
1 pint oysters, rinsed
salt and pepper to taste
1½ cups milk
⅛ cup sherry
½ teaspoon Worcestershire sauce

Preheat oven to 450 degrees. Layer in casserole dish: crumbs, oysters, crumbs, oysters, and ending with crumbs. Lightly salt and pepper layers. Mix milk, sherry and Worcestershire sauce together. Pour on top. Bake 25 minutes. Yield: 4 servings.

Lee Tebbetts, Student
The Culinary Institute of America

Scallop Casserole

1 pound scallops, cut up if large
1 cup medium white sauce
1 tablespoon sherry
buttered crumbs
grated cheese

Preheat oven to 300 degrees. Place scallops in casserole dish. Mix white sauce and sherry. Pour over scallops. Sprinkle top with buttered crumbs and grated cheese. Bake 15 minutes. Yield: 2 servings.

Lee Tebbetts, Student
The Culinary Institute of America

Pasta and One-Dish Meals

Granite

New Hampshire itself is nicknamed the Granite State. The town abounds in a great variety of minerals, but the economically important one is granite. Granite quarries were worked in several locations in Bedford. They supplied the stone used as the headers and sleepers for the railroads as well as the piers and abutments of the bridge over the Merrimack River at Goffe's Falls. The underpinning for the Presbyterian Church construction in 1832 was taken from a nearby quarry owned and cut by Benjamin Riddle. Another quarry on North Amherst Road was opened about 1800 and continued successfully for more than one hundred years producing an unusually high quality of granite.

The large granite horse trough, c1870, located in the triangle at the beginning of Ministerial Road is a fine example of the art of the stone carvers of this period.

New Year's Eve Feast

beverage

Champagne

hors d'oeuvres

Cranberry Topped Brie

Soused Shrimp

Spinach Soufflé Triangles

entrée

Coq Au Vin

Wild Rice

Esther's Gourmet Spinach

salad

Caesar Salad

desserts

Kahlua Whipped Cream Pie

Chocolate Pears

PASTA AND ONE-DISH MEALS

Crusty Beef Noodles

2 pounds hamburger
1 onion, chopped
40 ounces mushroom spaghetti sauce
1 cup fresh mushrooms, sliced (optional)
salt and pepper to taste
1 pound very small noodles
1 pound grated cheddar cheese

Preheat oven to 325 degrees. Brown onion and hamburger. Add sauce. If fresh mushrooms are used, cook until tender first. Slightly under cook noodles. Layer in large casserole: half noodles, half hamburger mixture, and half cheese. Then layer other half. Bake for 1 hour if pan is shallow, 1½ hours if pan is deep. Yield: 6-8 servings.

Janis Galeucia

Noodle Bake

2 pounds ground beef
1 pound egg noodles
1 (8 ounce) container sour cream
1 (32 ounce) container small curd cottage cheese
2 (16 ounce) cans tomato sauce (use 3rd if needed)
1 small onion, chopped
½ teaspoon salt
½ teaspoon garlic powder

Crumble beef in skillet and brown (do not use oil in skillet). Spoon off fat. Add garlic powder, salt, chopped onion and tomato sauce. Simmer for one hour.

Preheat oven to 350 degrees. Boil noodles and drain. In mixing bowl stir cottage cheese and sour cream together. Add noodles to cheese mixture and transfer to 9x13 baking pan. Spoon meat on top of noodle mixture. Bake 45 minutes to 1 hour (until bubbly).

Bonnie Venn

Cherries Noodle Bake

4 eggs
1 pound cottage cheese
1 stick margarine, melted
½ cup sugar
1 teaspoon vanilla
1 pound noodles, cooked
1 can cherry pie filling

Mix together eggs, cottage cheese, margarine, sugar and vanilla. Mix with noodles, stirring carefully. Place in shallow baking dish. Bake 1 hour, less time if using glass dish. Top with cherry pie filling and bake 20 minutes. Cut into squares.

Note: Great with ham or chicken.

James Dias
Chairperson, Bedford School Board

Macaroni and Cheese Casserole

½ pound elbow macaroni
1 tablespoon butter or margarine
1 egg, beaten
1 teaspoon salt
1 teaspoon dry mustard
1 tablespoon hot water
1 cup milk
3 cups (8 ounces) grated sharp cheese

Preheat oven to 350 degrees. Boil macaroni in water until tender. Drain well. Stir in egg and butter. Mix salt and mustard with hot water and add to milk. Add cheese, leaving enough to sprinkle on top. Pour macaroni mixture into buttered casserole. Add milk mixture. Sprinkle with remaining cheese. Bake 35-45 minutes or until custard is set and top crusty.

Alberta Dieter

Bowtie Pasta with Spinach and Beans

1 pound bowtie pasta
2 teaspoons olive oil
2 tablespoons garlic, finely chopped
1 pound spinach, cleaned and cut into 1 inch pieces
1 (16 ounce) can cannellini beans, undrained
1 can pink beans (kidney or pinto), drained and rinsed
1 can no fat chicken broth
½ teaspoon salt
¼ teaspoon crushed red pepper flakes
½ teaspoon dried basil
1 large fresh tomato, chopped
Grated Parmesan cheese

Cook pasta following package directions until al dente, firm but tender. Drain well. Heat oil in large nonstick skillet over very low heat. Add garlic. Sauté until golden, about 2-3 minutes being careful not to over brown. Add spinach and sauté, stirring frequently until spinach is wilted, about 4 minutes. Add the cannellini beans with liquid, drained pink beans, ½ cup chicken broth, salt, red pepper flakes and basil. Cook for 5 minutes to blend flavors. Add tomato and cook 1 minute. Add pasta and toss to mix. If dry add a little more chicken broth. Serve immediately with grated Parmesan cheese. Yield: 6 servings.

Note: This is a very low-fat (about 4 grams/serving) high protein (about 24 grams/serving) meal.

Dianne Russell

Rice Pilaf

½ stick butter, melted
¼ cup chopped onions
1 cup sliced mushrooms
1 teaspoon oregano
1 can chicken or beef broth
¾ can water
¼ cup cooking sherry
1 cup Uncle Ben's rice

Preheat oven to 350 degrees. Simmer butter, onion, mushrooms, and oregano 10 to 12 minutes. Add broth, water and sherry. Place rice with rest of ingredients in baking dish. Cover and bake for 45 minutes.

Jacquelin Lavoie

Macaroni and Cheese Pizza

1 (7.25 ounce) package macaroni and cheese dinner
2 eggs
1 (8 ounce) can tomato sauce
1 (4 ounce) can mushrooms, drained
¼ cup chopped onions
¼ cup chopped green peppers
1 teaspoon oregano leaves
1 teaspoon basil leaves
1 cup pepperoni slices
1 cup (4 ounces) shredded mozzarella cheese

Prepare dinner as directed on package. Add eggs and mix well. Spread into well-greased 12 inch pizza pan or 13x9 inch baking pan. Bake at 375 degrees for 10 minutes.

Combine tomato sauce, mushrooms, onions, green peppers and seasonings. Spoon over dinner mixture. Top with pepperoni and cheese. Continue baking for 10 minutes more. Allow to sit for 5 minutes before serving.

Note: As with any pizza, substitute with your favorite toppings or combinations.

Robert A. Fabich, Sr.
Bedford Fire Chief

Homemade Egg Substitute

6 egg whites
¼ cup powdered non fat milk
1 tablespoon corn oil

Combine the above ingredients and blend until smooth. Store in refrigerator up to one week. May be frozen. To make scrambled eggs: fry slowly over low heat in non stick pan. Makes one cup. ¼ cup equals one whole egg. 70 Calories.

Cheaper than using the commercial products.

Margaret Rooney

Gnocchi

1 cup potato flakes
1 cup plus 2 tablespoons boiling water
1 teaspoon salt
2 cups flour

Put flakes in large dish. Pour water and salt over them. Mix well. Let set until cold. When potato mix is cold, add flour and knead about 5 minutes. Cut into small chunks. Roll out each one using enough flour on board so it is not sticky. Each roll should be about the size of your finger thickness. After all are rolled, cut into 1 inch pieces. Press 2 fingers on each piece and roll down to "open." Repeat until all are rolled. Can put cornmeal on cookie sheet and lay the gnocchi's in a single layer for freezing. The next day, remove from pan and put into a plastic bag in freezer until needed. Can use 2 pounds ricotta or left over mashed potatoes in place of potato flakes.

To Cook: Fill pan ¾ with water. Add 1 tablespoon salt. Boil water and add gnocchi. Cook 5-10 minutes, until all come to surface. Strain. Add sauce and serve.

Dorothy Czopek

Sausage and Rice

1 cup rice
6 cups water
2 packages Lipton (Soup Secrets) chicken noodle soup with real broth
1-1½ pounds hot sausage (may use sweet)
1 onion, chopped
1 medium green pepper, chopped
2 small cans mushrooms

Boil rice, water and soup for 25 minutes, until thick. Brown sausage. Add onion and pepper. When cooked, add mushrooms. (If sausage is lean add ½ stick of margarine.) Add sausage mixture to rice mixture. Mix well. Serve. Yield: 8-10 servings.

Note: Can be easily doubled or cut in half.

Marge McNamee
(Friend of Member Rose Marie Borelli)

No Fuss Lasagna

1 pound ground beef
1 (26-32 ounce) jar spaghetti sauce
1 (14 ounce) can diced tomatoes
1 (15 ounce) carton ricotta cheese
1 egg, well beaten
¼ cup grated Parmesan cheese
1 teaspoon dried basil leaves
6 uncooked lasagna noodles
2 cups shredded mozzarella cheese

Preheat oven to 375 degrees. Cook ground beef. Pour off drippings. Add spaghetti sauce and tomatoes with liquid to beef mixture. Stir and set aside. Combine Ricotta cheese, egg, Parmesan cheese and basil. Spread two cups beef sauce mixture over bottom of 11x7 inch dish. Arrange a single layer of three noodles on sauce. Press down into sauce. Spoon Ricotta cheese mixture on top. Sprinkle with one cup mozzarella cheese. Top with two cups beef sauce. Arrange remaining noodles, pressing lightly into sauce. Spread remaining beef sauce over noodles. Bake for 45 minutes or until noodles are fork tender. Sprinkle remaining mozzarella cheese on top. Tent lightly with foil. Let stand 15 minutes. Yield: 8 servings.

Tish Smith

6 Layer Dinner

1 cup sliced carrots
1½ cups sliced potatoes
1 layer of sliced onions and sliced celery
1½ pounds lean hamburger
1 can tomato soup

Preheat oven to 350 degrees. Layer ingredients in casserole. First carrots, then potatoes, then onions and celery, then hamburger. Pour tomato soup on top. Bake 1½ hours with cover on, then ½ hour uncovered and cut down through hamburger. Salt and pepper to taste. Yield: 4 servings.

Priscilla VanWagner

Ravioli

Filling:

1 pound ricotta cheese
½ cup Romano cheese
2 eggs
1 teaspoon parsley
salt and pepper

Mix filling ingredients together. Use 1 rounded teaspoon of filling for each ravioli.

Dough:

3 cups flour
3 eggs
pinch salt
2 tablespoons water

Mix dough ingredients. Knead for at least 10 minutes until dough is smooth. Test by cutting dough in middle, consistency should be smooth with no lumps. (Dough can be made the night before. Wrap in towel and refrigerate.) Roll out dough to 1⁄16 inch. Turn as you roll to make even.

On outer edge of rolled out pasta, place each teaspoon of filling about 1 inch apart, 2 inches in from edge so dough can be folded over filling. Gently press dough over filling. Cut out each ravioli using rippled edge cutter. Press ends of raviolis with fork to seal in filling. Repeat each time. Using a toothpick, puncture tops of raviolis. Allow them to set before boiling in water. Cook in boiling salted water for 10 minutes or until the edge tastes cooked. Drain. Place in platter and cover with sauce. If preparing raviolis in advance, freeze them in single layers. Then place them in freeze-lock bags until ready for cooking.

Dorothy Czopek

Carol's Baked Rigatoni

⅓ ounce dried porcini or 6 ounces fresh button mushrooms
2 tablespoons unsalted butter (if using fresh mushrooms add 6 tablespoons butter)
12 ounces rigatoni
⅓ cup all purpose flour
2½ cups milk
pinch freshly grated nutmeg
salt and freshly ground pepper, to taste
4 ounces Fontina or Swiss cheese, cut into julienne strips
6 ounces ham, roughly chopped

If using porcini, place in bowl of lukewarm water and soak about 30 minutes, until soft. Drain, squeeze out excess water and chop finely. Set aside. If using fresh mushrooms, trim and discard stems. In frying pan melt 2 tablespoons butter over medium heat. Add sliced mushrooms and sauté for 2 minutes. Remove from heat.

In large pot bring 5 quarts salted water to boil. Add rigatoni and cook approximately 6 minutes, or al dente. Drain pasta. Transfer to large bowl. Add 2½ tablespoons of butter and toss.

Preheat oven to 350 degrees. Melt 2½ tablespoons butter over medium heat in saucepan. Add flour and stir until smooth, about 2 minutes. Stirring constantly, gradually add milk. Stir until it thickens and is creamy and smooth, about 10 minutes. Remove from heat, add the porcini or fresh mushrooms, sprinkle with nutmeg and stir well. Season with salt and pepper. Grease 8x12 inch ovenproof dish with remaining butter. Arrange ⅓ of rigatoni in the dish. Sprinkle ⅓ of the cheese and ham over top. Spoon on ⅓ of the sauce. Repeat the layers in same order two more times, ending with sauce. Place in oven. Bake until thoroughly heated and bubbly, about 20 minutes. Serve at once. Yield: 6 servings.

Madonna Lovett Repeta

Shells Stuffed with Meat

½ package shell pasta
3 tablespoons butter
½ pound ground sweet Italian sausage
1 pound ground beef
⅓ cup onion, minced
¼ cup celery, minced
1 clove garlic, minced
⅓ cup sherry wine
⅓ cup grated Parmesan cheese
⅓-½ cup dry bread crumbs
2 pint jars meatless spaghetti sauce

Preheat oven to 375 degrees. Add 2 tablespoons of salt to 2 quarts rapidly boiling water. Gradually add shells so water does not stop boiling. Boil, uncovered for 15 minutes. Stir occasionally. Drain portion of water, allowing shells to remain in warm water. Melt butter in large frying pan. Add sausage and beef. Cook until lightly browned. Add onion, celery and garlic. Cover and cook 10-15 minutes, until celery is tender. Remove from heat. Stir in sherry, grated cheese and bread crumbs. Stuff each shell with slightly cooled mixture, close. Pour 1 jar of spaghetti sauce into a shallow casserole. Arrange stuffed shells in casserole. Top with second jar of sauce. Cover and bake for 30 minutes.

Bonnie Venn

Rice with Mushrooms

1 stick butter or margarine
1 green pepper, chopped
1 medium onion, chopped
1 small can mushrooms, chopped
1 (10½ ounce) can beef consommé soup
1 cup rice, long cooking

Preheat oven to 350 degrees. Sauté first four ingredients. Add consommé and bring to a boil. Place rice in baking dish. Pour boiling ingredients over rice and bake covered for 45 minutes. Yield: 4-6 servings.

Madonna Lovett Repeta

Taglione

2 green peppers, finely chopped
2 large onions, finely chopped
1 large can tomatoes
1 can tomato paste
1 large can pitted ripe olives
16 ounces Pastene macaroni shells (shells 25)
2 pounds ground beef
½ pound sharp Cheddar cheese

Preheat oven to 350 degrees. Sauté peppers and onions in oil. Add tomatoes, tomato paste and juice from olives. Simmer. In separate pan cook ground beef until brown. In separate pot, boil macaroni as package directs. Grease two 2-3 quart casseroles. Layer ingredients in casseroles in following order — macaroni, ground beef, tomato mixture and ending with cheese on top. Bake in oven 30 minutes. Add olives on top layer and bake 15 minutes. Yield: 14-16 servings.

Note: Serve with salad and Italian bread. Tastes better if made a day or so ahead. Can be frozen.

Eunice Brine

Mushroom Casserole

1 large onion, chopped
¼ cup butter or margarine
2 (8 ounce) cans mushrooms (reserve liquid)
2 eggs, beaten
½ cup cream
¾ cup mushroom liquid
½ teaspoon salt
¼ teaspoon pepper
1 cup crushed crackers
½ cup Velveeta cheese cubes

Preheat oven to 350 degrees. Sauté onions and mushrooms in butter. Mix together eggs, cream, mushroom liquid, salt, pepper, and crackers. Place all ingredients into casserole. Put cheese cubes on top. Bake 30 minutes covered, remove cover and bake 30 minutes. Yield: 4 servings.

Mary Brambilla

Frijoles Negros

1 pound black beans
½ green pepper
1 small onion
1 whole head garlic
olive oil
salt
1 large onion, chopped fine
1½ green peppers, chopped fine
4-5 cloves garlic
1 teaspoon oregano
½ teaspoon ground cumin
Dash pepper

Soak beans in cold water for 1 hour. Retain water. Bring to a boil. Add ½ green pepper, small onion, whole garlic, swig of olive oil and salt. Simmer until tender, about 1½ to 2 hours. Remove onion, garlic and green pepper. In skillet sauté large onion and 1½ green peppers in olive oil until tender. Add 4-5 cloves garlic. When garlic starts smelling (don't burn), add oregano, cumin and pepper. Add skillet contents to beans. Simmer slowly for 30 minutes.

Note: Can add olives, red wine, a little sugar, experiment! Serve over white rice. Garnish with chopped onion.

Bonnie Venn

Hutspot

6 medium potatoes, peeled and cubed
6 medium onions, chopped
6 medium carrots, cut up
Kielbasa*
salt and pepper

Boil vegetables in water. Drain when cooked. Mash vegetables in pot. Place sausage on top of vegetables. Cover and let heat from vegetables warm sausage. Salt and pepper to taste. *Can substitute Knockwurst or other cooked sausage. Yield: 4-6 servings.

Note: Hearty, good supper on a cold day. Eet smakelijk!!

Jo Fearon

Kielbasa Stew

1 pound Kielbasa or summer sausage, cut into 1-2 inch pieces
1 can sauerkraut
1 can whole potatoes
1 can mushrooms
1 can corn
1 can beer

Put all ingredients in slow cooker on low setting. Cook 6-8 hours. Great for a busy day.

Jeanne Thibault

Layered Taco Casserole (Microwave)

1 pound ground beef
2 tablespoons butter
1 medium onion, chopped
2 tablespoons diced green chilies
1 (8 ounce) can tomato sauce
1 package taco seasoning mix
½ cup water
2 eggs
1 cup dairy half and half
1 (6 ounce) package corn chips
8 ounces Monterey Jack cheese, shredded
1 cup dairy sour cream
½ cup grated Cheddar cheese

This recipe is for the microwave — high power, 25 to 30 minutes total microwave time.

In 2-quart casserole, place beef and microwave at high 5 to 6 minutes, stirring after 3 minutes. Drain beef and remove from casserole. In 1-quart glass measure, place butter, onions and chilies. Microwave at high 2 to 2½ minutes, stirring after 1 minute. Add tomato sauce, taco seasoning mix and water. Microwave at high 1½ to 2 minutes more. Beat eggs, blend in half and half. Add to tomato sauce mix, stirring constantly. Place half of corn chips in same 2-quart casserole. Top with half of ground beef, half of cheese and half of sauce. Repeat layers. Microwave at high 15 minutes, rotating dish after 8 minutes. Top with sour cream and grated cheese. Microwave at high 2 to 4 minutes until cheese is melted. Yield: 6 servings.

Priscilla VanWagner

Primavera Pie

6 ounces linguini or capellini
4 tablespoons butter or margarine
3 eggs
⅔ cup grated Parmesan cheese
1 small sweet pepper, sliced into thin strips
1 medium onion sliced into rings
2 cups broccoli florets, drained
½ cup cooked chicken, chopped
1 tablespoon Italian seasoning
3 tablespoons heavy cream

Preheat oven to 350 degrees. Cook pasta according to package directions. Drain well. Stir 2 tablespoons butter into hot pasta. Stir in 2 beaten eggs and ⅓ cup Parmesan cheese. Form pasta mixture into a crust in well greased 9 inch pie plate. Set aside.

For filling: In 10-inch skillet cook pepper and onion in remaining butter until vegetables are just tender. Stir in broccoli, chicken, 3 tablespoons of cheese and Italian seasoning. Remove from heat. Combine cream and remaining egg. Stir into vegetable mixture. Spoon vegetable mixture onto pasta crust. Cover pie with foil. Bake for 25 minutes. Uncover and sprinkle remaining cheese over filling. Bake 5 minutes more. Let pie stand 5 minutes before serving. Yield: 6 servings.

Merrie Edgar

Pineapple Stuffing

¼ pound margarine, melted
1 cup sugar
4 eggs
5 slices bread, cubed
1 can crushed pineapple, drained

Preheat oven to 350 degrees. Mix together margarine and sugar. Add eggs and pineapple. Mix together with bread. Put in ungreased loaf pan. Bake 1 hour.

Note: Excellent with ham.

James Dias
Chairperson, Bedford School Board

Sesame Noodles with or without Chicken

½ pound angel hair pasta (or linguini)
4 tablespoons vegetable oil
1 teaspoon minced garlic
6 scallions, sliced
¼ cup soy sauce
2 tablespoons white vinegar
1 tablespoon sesame oil
hot oil to taste (scant ½ tablespoon)
pinch of sugar
½ boneless chicken breast, slivered
2 tablespoons soy sauce
1 tablespoon arrowroot or cornstarch
1 tablespoon vegetable oil

Cook pasta according to package directions. Add 1 tablespoon vegetable oil. Set aside. Heat the remaining 3 tablespoons vegetable oil, add garlic and scallions. Stir 30 seconds. Add ¼ cup soy sauce, vinegar, sesame oil, hot oil and sugar. Pour over pasta. Serve chilled.

To add chicken: Mix 2 tablespoons soy sauce, arrowroot and 1 tablespoon oil to make marinade for chicken. Marinate 15-20 minutes. Using a bit of oil in bottom of wok, stir fry chicken until done. Add to the pasta salad. Serve chilled.

Evelyn S. Letendre
Bedford Representative
NH State Legislature

Thelma's Rice Casserole

1 stick margarine, melted
1 can beef stock
1 can onion soup
1 large can mushrooms
1 cup raw rice

Preheat oven to 350 degrees. Stir all ingredients together. Place in casserole dish. Bake uncovered 45-60 minutes.

James Dias
Chairperson, Bedford School Board

Vegetable Chili

1 medium eggplant, unpeeled, cut into ½-inch cubes
1 tablespoon salt
½ cup best quality olive oil
2 medium yellow onions, chopped
4 cloves garlic, finely chopped
2 large green bell peppers, cored, seeded and diced
2 (28 ounce) cans Italian plum tomatoes
1 cup celery, cut-up
½ cup carrots, cut-up
1 tablespoon chili powder
1 tablespoon ground cumin
1 tablespoon dried oregano
1 tablespoon dried basil
2 teaspoons freshly ground black pepper
1 teaspoon salt
¼ cup fresh parsley, chopped
1 cup canned dark red kidney beans, drained
1 cup canned chick peas (garbanzos), drained
1 tablespoon dry dill
2 tablespoons lemon juice
shredded Cheddar cheese

Place eggplant in colander and sprinkle with 1 tablespoon salt. Let stand for one hour. Pat dry with paper towel. Heat ¼ cup oil in large skillet over medium heat. Add eggplant and sauté until almost tender, adding more oil if necessary. Remove eggplant to a casserole or Dutch oven. Heat the remaining ¼ cup oil in same skillet over low heat. Add the onions, garlic and green peppers. Sauté just until softened, about 10 minutes. Add to the casserole with any oil. Place the casserole over low heat. Add canned tomatoes with their liquid, celery, carrots, chili powder, cumin, oregano, basil, pepper, salt and parsley. Cook uncovered, stirring frequently, for 30 minutes. Stir in kidney beans, chick peas, dill and lemon juice. Cook another 15 minutes. The eggplant peel should be tender. Stir well, taste and adjust seasonings. Serve immediately with (or over) brown rice and lots of shredded Cheddar cheese. Yield: 8 servings.

Barbara Weigold

Yalanchi

1 cup olive oil
5 cups onions, chopped
salt to taste
½ cup parsley leaves
½ cup bleached raisins, optional
1 cup whole grain rice, washed
⅛ cup minced dill
2 lemons
1½ cups water
2 (8 ounce) jars grape leaves

Heat oil in saucepan. Add onions and sauté until limp. Add salt, parsley, raisins, rice and dill. Mix thoroughly with fork. Add juice of one lemon and ½ cup water. Bring to boil, then cover and simmer until liquid is absorbed by rice, about 15 minutes. Boil grape leaves and rinse thoroughly in cold water. Squeeze excess water from leaves. Line bottom of pan with double layer of grape leaves. Trim stems of remaining grape leaves. Place leaf on plate, shiny side down. Spoon a heaping teaspoon near base of leaf. Roll one turn, then fold left and right edges toward center, finish roll. Layer rolls in pan. Slice one lemon paper-thin and arrange on top of Yalanchi. Add 1 cup water. Cover, bring to boil, then simmer for 30 minutes until lemon is soft and limp. Rice should be tender.

Alice Asadourian

Zucchini Quiche

3 cups unpared, grated zucchini
1 cup Bisquick
½ cup grated Parmesan or Cheddar cheese
½ cup onion, finely minced
½ teaspoon salt
½ teaspoon seasoned salt
½ teaspoon oregano
dash pepper
½ cup oil
4 eggs, beaten

Preheat oven to 350 degrees. Mix all ingredients together. Place in greased 13x9 inch pan. Bake 25 minutes.

Martha Harris Gaudes
Executive Assistant to Bedford Town Manager

Crustless Quiche

¼ cup oil
1 eggplant, cut in ½-inch cubes
1 onion, chopped
1 clove garlic, minced
3 large mushrooms, sliced
1 small zucchini, sliced
½ teaspoon sweet basil
½ teaspoon oregano
pinch thyme
salt and pepper
3 large tomatoes, peel, seed and chop
½ cup grated Parmesan cheese
8 ounces mozzarella cheese
8 ounces Swiss cheese
1 whole egg
4 egg whites
paprika

Heat oil in skillet. Add eggplant, onion and garlic. Cook for ten minutes, stirring often. Add mushrooms, zucchini and seasonings. Cook until mushrooms are soft, about 5 minutes. Add tomatoes and simmer 15 minutes or until liquid has evaporated. Beat egg and whites with ¼ cup Parmesan cheese. Stir into vegetable mixture. Pour half the mixture in well buttered quiche dish or a 9-inch deep dish pie plate. Mix together mozzarella and Swiss cheese and sprinkle on top. Add remainder of vegetable mixture. Sprinkle with ¼ cup Parmesan cheese and paprika. Bake 35-45 minutes, until puffed and golden brown. Let stand 5-10 minutes before cutting into wedges. Yield: 6-8 servings.

Alice Asadourian

Rice Pilaf

1 cup Uncle Ben's rice
¼ cup Orzo
1 onion
½ stick margarine
1 can chicken broth
1 teaspoon salt
½ teaspoon pepper

Sauté orzo and onion. Cook rice in chicken broth. Add onion and orzo right away. Cook together 30 minutes.

Sheila Roberge

Zucchini Parmigiana

1 large zucchini
salt
2 eggs
2 tablespoons water
1 cup flour
1 cup bread crumbs
black pepper to taste
basil to taste
parsley to taste
oil

Slice zucchini ⅛ inch thick. Salt lightly and set on waxed paper. Beat 2 eggs with 2 tablespoons water. Mix together flour, bread crumbs and pepper, basil and parsley. Dip zucchini in flour mixture then in egg batter. Let excess drip off. Add enough oil to fry pan to cover bottom. Fry zucchini until lightly brown. Set aside.

Sauce:
1 small clove garlic, chopped
1 (8 ounce) can tomato sauce
1½ cups water
pepper to taste
parsley to taste
basil to taste
grated Parmesan cheese
1 egg, beaten

Sauce: Put oil in small pan. Sauté garlic. Add tomato sauce and water. Add seasonings. Cook 10-15 minutes. In pie plate, layer sauce, zucchini, grated cheese and drizzle with beaten egg. Repeat until desired thickness. Four rows is ample. Bake at 350 degrees for 30 minutes.

Dorothy Czopek

Vegetables

Schoolhouse

By 1800 church and school had been firmly established. At least six schoolhouses had been erected, probably by people in the vicinity, as there were no records of monies being appropriated by the towns. Boundaries of school districts were not fixed, and people were free to join any district they wished. Thus schools where the teacher was known to be "good" were often overcrowded while a less popular teacher had few pupils.

Horace Greeley (1811-1872) attended school in the western district and No. 6 in the northeastern district. But more often he went to "the school at the center of town, which was much larger, and generally better taught." (probably No. 1)

The Bedford Historical Society presently has an office in a restored One-Room Schoolhouse located in the center of Bedford.

Super Bowl Half-time Buffet

hors d'oeuvres

Jane's Dip with blanched fresh vegetables

Cocktail Meatballs in Italian Tomato Sauce

entrées

Honey Baked Ham

Heidi's Cranberry Chutney

Variety of Mustards

Primavera Pie

salad

Carrot Salad

dessert

Anne's Viennese Apple Cobbler

VEGETABLES

Dark Beans with Rum

1 pound navy pea beans
1 onion
5 whole cloves
1 pound salt pork, cut in inch cubes
salt and pepper
¾ cup molasses
⅓ cup dark rum
¼ teaspoon dry mustard
pinch powdered thyme
hot water

Soak beans overnight in water. Insert cloves into onion. Place in bottom of ceramic pot. Layer the soaked beans and salt pork in pot. Sprinkle each layer with salt and pepper. Mix molasses, rum, dry mustard and thyme. Pour over beans and salt pork. Add hot water to just cover the beans. Cover and bake for at least eight hours at 250 degrees. Check periodically to make certain liquid has not dried out. Add water as necessary.

Artie Roberson
Bedford Town Manager

My Dad's Easy Pickled Beets

2 cups sliced beets (1 pound can)
½ cup vinegar
¼ cup sugar
1 teaspoon pickling spices

Drain beets. Measure ¼ cup beets into saucepan. Add remaining ingredients and bring to boil. Add rest of beets and simmer five minutes.

Christina Barley

Broccoli Casserole

½ cup mayonnaise
1 can cream of mushroom soup
2 eggs, slightly beaten
1 bag broccoli, chopped
½ cup sharp Cheddar cheese, grated
½ cup butter
½ cup stuffing mix or bread crumbs

Preheat oven to 350 degrees. Mix together mayonnaise, soup and eggs. Add broccoli to mixture. Spread broccoli mixture in casserole dish. Sprinkle cheese on top of broccoli mixture. In pan melt butter and mix in bread crumbs. Sprinkle bread crumb mixture on top of cheese. Bake 45 minutes.

Alberta Dieter

Broccoli Casserole

2 (10 ounce) boxes frozen chopped broccoli, thawed
1 can cream of mushroom soup
1 can cream of chicken soup
¼ teaspoon garlic powder
1 large can mushroom pieces, drained
½ cup grated Velveeta cheese
1 teaspoon parsley
1 small onion, chopped
salt and pepper to taste

Preheat oven to 350 degrees. Mix all ingredients together except margarine and stuffing mix. Put in 2-quart casserole dish.

Topping:
1 stick margarine, melted
2 cups Pepperidge Farm herb stuffing mix

Mix together margarine and stuffing mix and sprinkle on top. Bake uncovered until top is brown and bubbly. Yield: serves large crowd.

Priscilla VanWagner

Evye's Broccoli Casserole

2 (10 ounce) boxes frozen chopped broccoli or 2 bunches fresh
1 can cream of mushroom soup
1 cup mayonnaise
2 eggs, well beaten
1½ cups sharp Cheddar cheese, grated
4 tablespoons chopped onion or dry chips
pepper to taste
½ cup Ritz crackers, crushed
butter

Preheat oven to 350 degrees. Parboil and drain broccoli. Put into 13x9 inch greased Pyrex dish. In a bowl combine soup, mayonnaise, eggs, cheese, onion and pepper. Pour on top of broccoli. Cover with crackers and dot with butter. Bake 30 minutes.

Wesley Maloney

Broccoli Casserole

1 bunch fresh broccoli (or frozen)
1 can cream of mushroom soup or Cheddar cheese soup
2 small packages grated Cheddar cheese
bread crumbs

Preheat oven to 350 degrees. Cook broccoli just until slightly tender. Drain. Butter round casserole or small square pan. Put small amount of soup on bottom of dish. Add layer of broccoli and pour more soup over it. Add layer of Cheddar cheese. Repeat layer of broccoli, soup and cheese. Top with bread crumbs. Cover. Bake 20-30 minutes until cheese mixture is bubbly. Can be put together the night or morning before.

Sally Balog

Curried Carrots

12 medium carrots, peeled, cut into inch lengths, or 2 pounds baby carrots
6 teaspoons unsalted butter, room temperature
2 tablespoons best quality curry powder
¼ teaspoon salt
¼ teaspoon freshly ground black pepper
¼ cup fresh lemon juice
2 tablespoons brown sugar
1 cup pecans, toasted and chopped

Place carrots in large heavy saucepan and add cold water to cover. Cook over medium-high heat just until tender, 15-20 minutes. Drain and return to pan. Mix butter, curry powder, salt and pepper and add to the carrots. Heat over very low heat, tossing to coat carrots with butter mixture. Add lemon juice and brown sugar. Heat, tossing occasionally, until carrots are glazed. Sprinkle with chopped pecans. Serve immediately. Yield: 6-8 servings.

Jacqueline Aiken

Lemon Glazed Carrots

2 pounds carrots, scraped and diagonally sliced
¼ cup butter or margarine
½ cup brown sugar, firmly packed
¼ cup lemon juice
½ teaspoon salt

Cook carrots in small amount of boiling water 12-15 minutes or until crisp-tender. Drain. Melt butter in small saucepan. Add remaining ingredients. Bring mixture to a boil, stirring constantly. Pour over carrots and toss gently.

Fran Wiggin
Bedford Librarian

Green Bean and Onion Ring Casserole

1 (2.8 ounce) can French fried onions
2 tablespoons Dijon style mustard
2 tablespoons cider vinegar
2 shallots, minced
½ cup olive oil
salt and freshly ground pepper to taste
2 pounds fresh green beans, ends trimmed

Preheat oven to 350 degrees. Crisp onions on baking sheet for 7-10 minutes. Turn oven off but leave onions inside to keep warm. Whisk together mustard and vinegar in small saucepan. Mix in shallots and slowly whisk in olive oil. Season to taste with salt and pepper. Bring the mixture to a boil, whisking constantly and then cook for 2 minutes. Keep warm over low heat. Cook beans in large pot of boiling water just until crisp tender, 4-5 minutes. Drain and immediately transfer to mixing bowl. Toss with warm dressing and then mix in toasted onions. Serve immediately. Yield: 8-10 servings.

Doris Guimont

Mushroom Cutlets

1 cup fresh mushrooms, finely chopped
1 green onion, minced
2 eggs
½ cup bread crumbs
¾ cup grated mild Cheddar cheese

Do not mix until ready to fry and serve. Mix all ingredients but do not turn into a mush. Form into 8 patties. Fry in butter over low heat on both sides about 10 minutes. The cutlets should be crisp and brown on outside and moist on inside. Serve with any beef dish.

Note: These should be cooked just before serving.

Joan Hetland

Short N Sweet Onions

3-4 medium to large onions, sliced
2 tablespoons butter
2 tablespoons brown sugar (light or dark)
1 teaspoon paprika

Fry sliced onions in butter. When soft, add brown sugar and mix thoroughly until all onions are coated. Stir in paprika. Serve hot. Yield: 3-4 servings.

Artie Robersen
Bedford Town Manager

Barbecue Potatoes

¼ cup butter or margarine, melted
3 tablespoons ketchup
1 teaspoon chili powder
1 teaspoon light brown sugar
⅛ teaspoon salt
⅛ teaspoon ground red pepper
4 medium baking potatoes

Preheat oven to 425 degrees. Grease a baking pan. Set aside. In small bowl, combine butter, ketchup, chili powder, brown sugar, salt and red pepper. Cut each potato lengthwise into 8 wedges. Place in pan. Brush with some of the sauce. Bake 30 minutes, brushing occasionally with remaining sauce, until potatoes are tender.

Carol Molitoris

Crisp Onion Roasted Potatoes

1 envelope onion soup mix
½ cup oil
¼ cup butter, melted
1 teaspoon marjoram
1 teaspoon thyme
¼ teaspoon pepper
2 pounds potatoes, quartered

Preheat oven to 450 degrees. Mix all ingredients together in shallow baking pan. Bake for 60 minutes or until tender. Yield: 8 servings.

Jacqueline Aiken

Healthy Home Fries

1 pound (3½ cups) small red potatoes, cubed and cooked
1 small onion, chopped
1 small red or green pepper, diced
¼ teaspoon thyme or rosemary
¼ teaspoon salt
⅛ teaspoon pepper

Spray 10-inch skillet with cooking spray. Heat over medium heat. Add all ingredients. Stir occasionally and cook 8-10 minutes, until lightly browned and tender. Yield: 6 servings.

Margaret Rooney

Irish Mashed Potato Casserole

8-10 medium potatoes, peeled
1 (8 ounce) package cream cheese, softened
1 (8 ounce) container sour cream
½ cup butter, melted
¼ cup chopped chives
1 garlic clove, minced
2 teaspoons salt
paprika

Cook potatoes in boiling water for 30 minutes or until tender. Drain and mash. Beat cream cheese with electric mixer until smooth. Add potatoes and remaining ingredients except paprika. Beat just until combined. Spoon mixture into lightly buttered 2-quart casserole. Sprinkle with paprika. Cover and store in refrigerator overnight. Uncover and bake at 350 degrees for 30 minutes or until thoroughly heated. Yield: 8-12 servings.

Bonnie Venn

Paprika - A Hungarian red pepper. Bright red in color. May be used in all meat, vegetables and salads. In soups, both cream and stock. As a garnish for potatoes, cream cheese and salads.

Potato Casserole

2 pounds frozen hash browns
1 can cream of chicken soup
1 cup onions, chopped
16 ounces sour cream
8 ounces shredded sharp Cheddar cheese
1 teaspoon salt
1 teaspoon pepper

Thaw hash browns for 20 minutes. Preheat oven to 375 degrees. Mix the remaining ingredients together (except cornflakes and butter) and add hash browns. Pour into a 13x9 inch dish.

Topping:
2 cups cornflakes, crushed
½ cup butter, melted

Mix cornflakes and butter, spread on top. Bake for 1 hour.

Priscilla VanWagner

Pumpkin Casserole

1 medium pumpkin
6 cups apples, peeled and chopped
1 cup raisins
½ cup dates
1 cup nuts, chopped
1 cup sugar
1 teaspoon juice
¼ teaspoon cinnamon
¼ teaspoon nutmeg

Preheat oven to 350 degrees. Cut top off pumpkin. Clean out inside. Wash and dry pumpkin. Mix all ingredients and put mixture inside pumpkin. Place filled pumpkin on cookie sheet. Put top on sheet also. Bake for 2 hours or until everything (including inside of pumpkin) is done. Top with sour cream and cinnamon, if desired.

Note: Great for fall or Thanksgiving centerpiece.

Betty Gollihue

Sweet Potato South

4 pounds sweet potatoes
1 teaspoon salt
boiling water
6 medium bananas (2½ pounds)
¼ cup orange juice
½ cup light brown sugar, firmly packed
½ teaspoon ground cinnamon
4 tablespoons butter or margarine

Clean potatoes. Place in large saucepan with salt. Cover with boiling water. Cover pot. Reduce heat to low. Simmer 30-35 minutes, until potatoes are tender. Drain, peel and cut crosswise into ¼ inch thick slices.

Preheat oven to 375 degrees. Grease 2-quart casserole dish. Peel bananas, cut crosswise into ¼ inch slices. Place in bowl and toss with orange juice. Mix brown sugar with ground cinnamon in another bowl. Set aside.

Arrange ⅓ of potato slices overlapping in bottom of casserole dish. Top with ½ of banana slices and sprinkle with ⅓ of sugar mixture. Dot with ⅓ of the butter. Repeat with ⅓ of potatoes and bananas. Reserve 12 banana slices for the top. Sprinkle with ⅓ of the sugar mixture and dot with ⅓ of the butter. Top with remaining potatoes. Arrange reserved banana slices on top. Sprinkle with remaining butter and pour on remaining orange juice. Bake 45 minutes until very hot. Yield: 12 servings.

Note: May add ¼ cup honey to orange juice and layer shredded coconut between other layers.

Margaret K. Rooney

Apricot-glazed Sweet Potatoes

3 pounds sweet potatoes
1 cup firmly packed brown sugar
1 tablespoon plus 1½ teaspoons cornstarch
¼ teaspoon salt
⅛ teaspoon ground cinnamon
1 cup apricot nectar
½ cup hot water
2 tablespoons butter or oleo
½ cup chopped pecans

Cook sweet potatoes in boiling salted water about 10 minutes or until fork-tender. Cool to touch. Peel and cut into ½ inch slices. Arrange potato slices in 2-quart casserole. Combine brown sugar, cornstarch, salt and cinnamon in saucepan. Stir well. Add nectar and water. Cook over medium heat, stirring constantly, until thick and bubbly. Stir in butter and pecans. Pour sauce over sweet potato slices. Bake in 350 degree oven 25 minutes. Yield: 6 servings.

Note: Different kind of sweet potato dish for the holidays. Very good!

Marge McNamee

Sauerkraut To Die For

1 pound bacon, cut in 1½ inch strips
½ pound carrots, sliced very thin
3 large onions, sliced thin
4 large cans sauerkraut, washed and drained
2 cans beef bouillon
2 cans water
1 tablespoon black pepper, fresh ground
1 tablespoon parsley
2 bay leaves
1 cup gin
1 cup white wine

Preheat oven to 325 degrees. Cook bacon, carrots and onions in big Dutch oven several minutes—but not brown. Add everything else and bring to a boil. Bake in oven for 4 hours. Check about halfway and add more water if necessary, not broth. Serve with ham and/or sausages.

Note: Men love this.

Wesley Maloney

Esther's Gourmet Spinach

3 packages frozen chopped spinach, cooked and well drained
1 small can sliced mushrooms, chopped
1 envelope Lipton onion soup mix
½ pint sour cream
1 small can water chestnuts, chopped
Parmesan cheese

Preheat oven to 350 degrees. Mix all ingredients together well, and put in baking dish. Sprinkle with Parmesan cheese. Heat 25 minutes. Yield: 8 servings.

Christina Barley

Spinach-Artichoke Casserole

1 can artichoke hearts, cut in half
2 boxes frozen chopped spinach, cooked and drained
1 can cream of mushroom soup
¼ teaspoon garlic salt
1 large can mushrooms, drained
½ cup sour cream
½ cup mayonnaise
½ teaspoon lemon juice

Preheat oven to 350 degrees. Drain artichokes. Place in bottom of 9x9 inch baking dish. Mix together the cooked spinach, soup, garlic salt and drained mushrooms. Spread mixture over artichokes. Mix together the sour cream, mayonnaise and lemon juice. Spread over spinach. Bake 30 minutes. Yield: 6-8 servings.

Note: This can be made early in the day, refrigerated and baked later. It is wonderful with steak.

Betty Gollihue

Spinach Casserole

2 boxes frozen chopped spinach
2 small cans fried onion rings
2 small containers sour cream
¼ cup bread crumbs

Preheat oven to 350 degrees. Cook spinach as stated on the box. Drain and press out additional water. Combine spinach with fried onion rings and sour cream. Top with bread crumbs. Bake for 30 minutes. Serve hot. Yield: 4 servings.

Note: This recipe has been used for Thanksgiving and Christmas dinner for over fifty years in the Rhodes family tree. No one has ever said, "not me, thank you" to this dish, even those who do not like spinach.

Virginia Larson

Butternut Squash Casserole

3 cups cooked butternut squash, mashed
¼ cup (½ stick) butter or margarine
2 tablespoons brown sugar
¼ teaspoon salt
¼ teaspoon pepper
1½ tablespoons butter
6 cups sliced apples (about 2 pounds)
¼ cup sugar
1½ cups cornflakes, coarsely crushed
½ cup chopped pecans
½ cup brown sugar
2 tablespoons butter, melted

Preheat oven to 350 degrees. Season squash with ¼ cup butter, brown sugar, salt and pepper. Heat 1½ tablespoons butter in skillet, add apples and sprinkle on ¼ cup sugar. Cover and simmer until barely tender, about 5 minutes. Spread apples in a 3-quart casserole. Spoon squash evenly over apples. Mix everything else and sprinkle over squash. Bake for 15 minutes. Yield: 4-6 servings.

Wesley Maloney

Squash Casserole

2-2½ pounds fresh yellow squash
½ cup margarine, butter or bacon drippings
¾ cup chopped onions
15 Ritz crackers, crumbled
2 eggs, beaten
salt and pepper to taste
½ teaspoon Tabasco sauce
½ cup grated sharp cheese
1½ cups additional Ritz cracker crumbs
½ cup additional butter or margarine, melted

Slice and cook squash until tender, then drain. Sauté onions in margarine. Mix with squash. Add crackers, eggs, seasonings and cheese. Put in 2-quart casserole dish. Cover with additional cracker crumbs and melted butter. Bake at 350 degrees for 35 minutes. Serve hot. Yield: 8-10 servings.

Virginia Larson

Squash and Pecan Casserole

3½ cups acorn or butternut squash, cooked and mashed
½ cup pecans, coarsely chopped
⅓ cup honey
¼ cup butter or margarine, melted
2 tablespoons grated lemon rind (one lemon)
½ tablespoon lemon juice
1 teaspoon salt
⅛ teaspoon nutmeg
¼ teaspoon ground cloves
⅛ teaspoon pepper
whole pecans for garnish

Preheat oven to 375 degrees. Combine all ingredients except whole pecans. Blend thoroughly. Spoon into greased 1½-quart casserole dish. Top with whole pecans. Bake 20-30 minutes. Yield: 6-8 servings.

Mrs. Lester J. Grant

Tata Squash

5 medium to large potatoes, cut in half
5 medium to large sweet potatoes, cut in half
1 large butternut squash, cut in fourths
1 large carnival squash, cut in fourths
2 large onions, finely chopped
2 tablespoons butter
½ cup brown sugar
2 tablespoons honey
1 (16 ounce) can crushed pineapple
½ cup chopped walnuts, optional

Preheat oven to 350 degrees. Spray one or two cookie sheets with Pam. Place potatoes and squash cut side down on cookie sheets. Bake for one hour or until done. Cool. Scoop meat out of shells. Discard seeds and shells. Sauté onions in butter. Add onions, 2 tablespoons butter, brown sugar and honey to potatoes and squash. Place in food processor and blend—leaving some lumps of the vegetables. Add pineapple. Place mixture in 3-quart, 2 inch deep Pyrex dish or divide into two smaller dishes. Sprinkle top with walnuts. Bake at 350 degrees 20-25 minutes. Yield: 12 servings.

Note: Recipe may be frozen, thaw before reheating. Carnival squash is available in the fall for a short period. It has a wonderful flavor. Can substitute butternut or acorn squash.

Margaret K. Rooney

Zucchini in Almond Wine Sauce

6 small zucchini, sliced thin
¼ cup butter or margarine
½ cup toasted slivered almonds
⅓ cup white wine

Cook zucchini in boiling salted water until crisply tender (very short time) check with fork. Drain. Melt butter in small pan and add almonds. Cook over low heat until butter browns lightly. Remove from heat and add wine. Pour over zucchini. Yield: 6 servings.

Wesley Maloney

Cheese Fried Zucchini

¼ cup dry bread crumbs
2 tablespoons grated Parmesan cheese
2 tablespoons flour
1 teaspoon salt
2 medium zucchini
1 egg, well beaten
olive oil

Combine bread crumbs, Parmesan cheese, flour and salt in a plastic bag. Thinly slice (¼ inch to ½ inch) zucchini and dip into the egg. Coat with mixture in the plastic bag. Fry in hot olive oil until golden brown and crispy, turning occasionally. Drain on paper towels. Serve at once. Yield: 4-6 servings.

Barbara Weigold

Turnip Soufflé

2 medium turnips, peeled and diced (about 6 cups)
¼ cup fine dry bread crumbs
¼ cup cream
½ teaspoon nutmeg
1 teaspoon salt
2 eggs, beaten
3 tablespoons margarine

Cook turnips until soft, about 20 minutes. Drain and mash. Soak crumbs in cream. Stir nutmeg, salt and eggs into soaked crumbs. Combine with mashed turnips. Spread in buttered 2-quart casserole dish. Dot with margarine and bake at 350 degrees for 60 minutes or until lightly brown.

Jacquelin Lavoie

Medley of Western Vegetables

2 cups broccoli florets
1 cup cauliflower florets
1 cup zucchini, sliced
1 cup crookneck squash, sliced
3 large mushrooms, sliced
1 red pepper, cut into strips
1 green pepper, cut into strips
¼ pound butter
garlic powder
salt
pepper

Select a large round platter that will fill the entire microwave cavity (12 inch round). Arrange broccoli florets around the outside of the platter. Arrange other vegetables in center, alternating for color. Melt butter in small measuring cup and pour over vegetables. Season vegetables. Cover well with plastic wrap and cook on high for 5 minutes. Let stand 5 minutes before serving. Vegetables should be fork tender. When using fresh vegetables add 2 tablespoons of water per 2 cups of vegetables.

Merrie Edgar

Combo-Veggie Casserole

1 (16 ounce) package frozen broccoli, cauliflower and carrots
1 can cream of mushroom soup
½ cup sour cream
¼ teaspoon pepper
1 can Durkee onion rings
4 ounces shredded Swiss cheese

Preheat oven to 350 degrees. Mix together vegetables, soup, sour cream, pepper, ½ can onion rings and 2 ounces Swiss cheese. Bake 30 minutes or more. Last 5 minutes, top with remainder of onion rings and cheese. Bake 5 minutes more.

Mary Dambach
Madonna Lovett Repeta

Healthier Cooking

Pulpit Rock

Bedford's Pulpit Rock Conservation Area consists of 143.6 acres of unique geological, historical and multiple-use open space. Mixed strands of hardwood, pine and hemlock cover much of the property. The wetlands forms the headwaters of the Pulpit Brook which cascade over small picturesque waterfalls leading toward the vast rock formation known as Pulpit Rock. At the bottom there is always a small pool of water, where the warmth of the sun rarely penetrates.

Another interesting curiosity is a large granite boulder about half a mile below the Pulpit, called Indian Rock. It is fifteen feet high and forty feet in circumference, and is nicely balanced on three flat stones. On the southern side is an opening leading to a cave. On the inside of the cave is a stone seat, with arms at the sides and a hollow for the head rest. Legend has it that this stone chair was a favorite place for the Indian Medicine Men to fast and listen to the Great Spirit.

Pulpit Pasta Night

soup

Dibby's Ground Beef Soup

entrée

Shells Stuffed with Meat

Tossed Salad

Dinner Rolls

dessert

Italian Rum Cake

Bisquoti

Anise Slices

HEALTHIER COOKING

Bean Salad

1 (15 ounce) can red kidney beans
1 (15 ounce) can chick peas
1 box frozen green beans, cooked
1 box frozen wax beans, cooked
1 medium onion, chopped
1 green pepper, chopped

Drain beans and peas. Mix together in a large bowl with onion and pepper.

Dressing:
½ cup sugar
⅔ cup wine vinegar
½ cup canola oil
1 teaspoon salt
½ teaspoon pepper
½ teaspoon Worcestershire sauce
½ cup chopped parsley

Mix all dressing ingredients together and pour over the bean mixture. Let marinate in refrigerator for at least 24 hours, stirring a few times. Serve with a slotted spoon.

Note: Do ahead to marinate.

Phyllis Hickey

Cucumber Salad

3 large cucumbers
1 large Spanish onion
¾ cup sugar
¾ cup vinegar

Slice cucumbers and onions. Dissolve sugar in vinegar and pour over cucumbers and onions. Add enough water to cover. Marinate for 24 hours.

Note: Do ahead. This is Heart Healthy.

Phyllis Hickey

Hot Chicken Salad Casserole

2 cups cubed cooked chicken
1 small green pepper, diced
1 (4 ounce) can mushrooms, drained
1 (8 ounce) can sliced water chestnuts, drained
1 (2 ounce) jar sliced pimentos, drained
½ teaspoon salt (optional)
¼ cup light or no cholesterol mayonnaise*
¼ cup skim milk*
1 can French fried onions

Preheat oven to 350 degrees. Combine milk and mayonnaise in a quart casserole. Add all other ingredients except French fried onions. Mix lightly. Top with onions. Cover and bake 15 minutes or until bubbly. Remove cover and bake 5 minutes longer to crisp onions. Yield: 4 servings.

*May be increased a bit for a saucier dish.

Note: Good served with rice. Quick and easy.

Phyllis Hickey

Mock Sour Cream

2 tablespoons skim milk
1 tablespoon lemon juice
1 cup cottage cheese, 1 percent milkfat
¼ teaspoon salt

Place all ingredients in a blender and mix on medium high speed until smooth and creamy. Use as a sour cream substitute. Makes 1¼ cups.

Note: Add to hot dishes at the last moment. May also be served cold with the addition of flavoring or herbs. Also as a dressing for salad or sauce for a mousse.

Phyllis Hickey

Carrot-Apple Sauté

3 cups diagonally sliced carrots
1 tablespoon margarine
⅓ cup finely chopped onion
1 large Granny Smith apple, peeled and thinly sliced
⅓ cup unsweetened apple juice
1½ teaspoons sugar
1 teaspoon lemon juice
¼ teaspoon salt
Dash of ground nutmeg

Boil carrots 6 minutes (until tender). Drain and set aside. Melt margarine in a large skillet over medium heat. Add onion, sauté 3 minutes. Add apple, sauté 4 minutes. Add carrots, apple juice and remaining ingredients. Cover. Reduce heat and simmer 3 minutes. Serve warm. Preparation time 20 minutes. Cooking time total 16 minutes. Serves 8.

Note: Calories 59 per ½ cup serving, Protein 0.6g, Fat 1.6g, Carbohydrate 11.2g, Cholesterol 0mg, Iron 0.3g, Sodium 108mg, Calcium 18g.

Suzanne Hyman

Lemony Asparagus and New Potatoes

12 ounces asparagus spears
8 whole tiny new potatoes, unpeeled and cut into quarters
2 teaspoons olive oil
½ teaspoon finely shredded lemon peel
¼ teaspoon salt
¼ teaspoon dried thyme, crushed

Snap off and discard woody base from fresh asparagus. Scrape off scales. Cut into 2 inch pieces and set aside. Cook potatoes, covered in a small amount of boiling water for 10 minutes. Add asparagus. Cook covered 8 more minutes. Drain. Transfer vegetables to a serving dish.

For the dressing combine olive oil, shredded lemon peel, salt and thyme. Add to the vegetables. Toss gently to coat. May garnish with lemon peel curl and fresh thyme. Serves 4.

Note: Calories per serving 105, Total Fat 3g, Sodium 141mg, Carbohydrate 19g, Fiber 2g, Protein 3g.

Doris Guimont

Stir Fried Broccoli and Mushrooms

2 tablespoons corn oil
1 small onion, cut in thin wedges
1 garlic clove, minced
2 cups broccoli florets
2 cups sliced mushrooms
½ teaspoon salt
⅛ teaspoon pepper

In large skillet heat corn oil. Add onion and garlic. Stir fry 30 seconds. Add broccoli, mushrooms, salt and pepper. Stir fry 5 minutes until tender-crisp. Serves 4.

Note: Calories per serving 90, Protein 2g, Carbohydrate 5g, Fat 7g, Cholesterol 0mg, Sodium 280mg.

Doris Guimont

Green Beans with Red Peppers

1 tablespoon corn oil
1 large red pepper, cut into thin strips
1 large onion, thinly sliced
1 pound green beans, cooked
2 tablespoons cider vinegar
⅛ teaspoon crushed red pepper

Heat corn oil in medium skillet. Add red pepper strips and onion. Sauté 3 minutes. Add beans. Heat through. Toss with vinegar and crushed red pepper. Serves 4.

Note: Calories per serving 70, Protein 3g, Carbohydrate 12g, Total Fat 4g, Cholesterol 0mg, Sodium 10mg.

Doris Guimont

Scalloped Potatoes with Smoked Ham

5 small leeks (1 pound)
¼ cup water
1 tablespoon light corn-oil spread
1 cup sliced onions
½ pound smoked low-fat ham, coarsely chopped
¾ teaspoon salt
½ teaspoon pepper
½ teaspoon thyme
3 pounds baking potatoes, peeled
⅔ cup all-purpose flour
1 quart 1 percent milk
1 tablespoon chopped fresh parsley

Preheat oven to 350 degrees. Coat 13x9 inch baking dish with vegetable cooking spray. Discard green portion from leeks. Slice white portions lengthwise in half, then crosswise into slices. Rinse leeks well to remove all sand. Drain. Heat water in a Dutch oven over high heat. Add leeks, sliced onions and ½ teaspoon salt. Toss to coat well. Reduce heat to low; cover and simmer, stirring until leeks and onions are tender, about 10 minutes.

Stir in ham, salt, pepper and thyme. Cook uncovered, stirring over medium heat until liquid is evaporated and leeks and onions are golden.

Slice potatoes thin. Place flour in large bowl. Gradually whisk in milk until smooth. Gradually add to leek-onion mixture. Bring to boil, stirring until thickened, about 1 minute. Spoon ½ cup milk mixture into bottom of prepared pan. Top with half the sliced potatoes. Spoon half the remaining sauce over potatoes. Arrange the remaining potatoes. Cover with remaining sauce. Cover dish with foil and bake 1¼ hours. Sprinkle with parsley and bake uncovered 15 more minutes, until potatoes are tender. Serves 8. Preparation time 35 minutes.

Note: Calories per serving 310, Total Fat 4g, Saturated Fat 1g, Cholesterol 18mg, Sodium 841mg, Carbohydrate 54g, Protein 15g.

Suzanne Hyman

Roasted Garlic Potatoes

2 tablespoons corn oil
1 garlic clove
1 teaspoon dried rosemary, crushed
4 medium potatoes, unpeeled and sliced ⅛ inch thick
2 tablespoons grated Parmesan cheese
¼ teaspoon pepper
no-stick cooking spray

Preheat oven to 400 degrees. Spray cookie sheet with cooking spray. In small bowl combine corn oil, garlic and rosemary. Arrange potato slices on the cookie sheet. Brush with corn oil mixture. Sprinkle with Parmesan and pepper. Bake for 30 minutes, until lightly browned and crisp. Serves 4.

Note: Each serving provides Calories 200, Protein 4g, Carbohydrate 29g, Total Fat 8g, Cholesterol 5mg, Sodium 55mg.

Doris Guimont

Fettucini Alfredo

½ pound fettucini noodles
2 tablespoons margarine
2 tablespoons flour
1½ cups skim milk
⅓ cup plus 2 tablespoons Parmesan cheese
1 teaspoon fresh lemon juice
⅛ teaspoon ground white pepper
2 tablespoons chopped fresh parsley

Cook fettucini noodles. Drain and set aside. Melt margarine in medium saucepan. Add flour. Cook 1 to 2 minutes, stirring constantly. Whisk in milk and bring to a boil. Reduce heat to low and add more milk if thinner consistency is desired. Add ⅓ cup Parmesan cheese. Pour warm sauce over warm fettucini noodles and garnish with parsley and remaining 2 tablespoons Parmesan cheese.

Note: This is heart healthy. For a more complete meal, top noodles with steamed vegetables and then pour sauce over all.

Phyllis Hickey

Vegetable Lasagna

1½ cups chopped onion
2 teaspoons minced garlic
6 ounces chopped mushrooms
3 tablespoons sherry
1 tablespoon margarine
4 cups chopped broccoli
½ pound spinach, washed well and chopped
½ teaspoon salt
16 ounces low-fat cottage cheese
4 ounces part-skim mozzarella cheese, shredded
3 tablespoons grated Parmesan cheese
¼ cup chopped fresh parsley
2 eggs
¼ teaspoon salt
¼ teaspoon black pepper
3 cups tomato sauce
8 ounces lasagna noodles, cooked

Preheat oven to 375 degrees. In large skillet, sauté onion, garlic and mushrooms in sherry and butter until vegetables are soft. Add chopped broccoli, spinach and salt. Stir to combine ingredients, reduce heat, cover and simmer for 5 minutes, until broccoli is tender. In medium bowl, combine cottage cheese, mozzarella, Parmesan, parsley, eggs, salt and pepper.

In a 13x9 inch baking dish, spread ½ cup tomato sauce on the bottom. Layer the ingredients with 3 strips cooked lasagna noodles on the bottom. Spread half the cheese mixture on noodles, ½ vegetable mixture on top, and the 1 cup of tomato sauce. Repeat layering, ending with noodles on top with tomato sauce over all. Sprinkle top with additional Parmesan cheese. Bake for 25 minutes. Let stand 10 minutes before serving. Preparation time: 1 hour.

Suzanne Hyman

Baked Ziti with Roasted Vegetables

1 pound eggplant, cut into 1 inch dices
1 large red onion, cut into 1 inch dices
2 yellow peppers, chopped
1 tablespoon olive oil
½ teaspoon salt

Preheat oven to 450 degrees. Toss eggplant, red onion, peppers, oil and salt in pan. Roast for 30 minutes, stirring twice until vegetables begin to brown.

Tomato Sauce:
1 teaspoon olive oil
1 cup finely chopped onions
2 teaspoons minced garlic
¼ teaspoon crushed red pepper
¼ teaspoon crushed fennel seeds
1 (28 ounce) can crushed tomatoes
¾ teaspoon salt
½ teaspoon ground pepper
¼ teaspoon sugar
pinch thyme
2 tablespoons chopped fresh parsley
1 (16 ounce) package cooked ziti
10 ounces chopped spinach
1 cup shredded part-skim mozzarella cheese

Make sauce by heating oil in saucepan. Add onions and cook covered over medium heat 10 minutes. Stir in garlic, red pepper and fennel. Cook 30 seconds then add tomatoes, salt, pepper, sugar and thyme. Bring to a boil. Reduce heat and simmer 15 minutes. Stir in parsley. Makes 3 cups.

Reduce oven heat to 400 degrees. Toss cooked ziti with vegetables, sauce and spinach in bowl. Spread into shallow 3 quart baking dish, Sprinkle mozzarella over top. Bake 20 minutes. Serves 6.

Note: Calories per serving 445, Total Fat 8g, Saturated Fat 3g, Cholesterol 11mg, Sodium 819mg, Carbohydrate 77g, Protein 19g.

Suzanne Hyman

Spaghetti with Turkey Tomato Sauce

2 tablespoons corn oil
1 large onion, chopped
2 garlic cloves, minced
1 pound ground turkey
2 (28 ounce) cans crushed tomatoes
¼ cup chopped fresh basil leaves or 1 teaspoon dried basil
2 teaspoons sugar
1 teaspoon salt
1 teaspoon oregano
¼ teaspoon pepper
1 pound spaghetti, cooked and drained

Heat corn oil in large pan. Add onion and garlic. Sauté 1 minute. Add turkey. Cook 10 minutes, stirring frequently. Remove from heat, drain excess liquid. Stir in tomatoes, basil, sugar, salt, oregano and pepper. Simmer, stirring occasionally, 45 minutes. Serve over cooked spaghetti. Serves 8.

Note: Each serving - Calories 240, Protein 17g, Carbohydrate 29g, Fat 6g, Cholesterol 40mg, Sodium 630mg.

Doris Guimont

Cajun Rice

2 tablespoons corn oil
1 cup uncooked rice
1 large onion, chopped
1 large green pepper, chopped
1 tablespoon minced garlic
1 (14 ounce) can stewed tomatoes, undrained
1½ cups water
½ teaspoon hot pepper sauce

Heat corn oil in skillet over medium-high heat. Add rice, onion, pepper and garlic. Sauté 3 minutes. Stir in tomatoes, water and hot pepper sauce, breaking tomatoes with a spoon. Bring to a boil. Reduce heat. Cover and simmer for 20 minutes until liquid is absorbed and rice is tender. Stir occasionally. Serves 4.

Note: Each serving provides Calories 140, Protein 3g, Carbohydrate 24g, Total Fat 4g, Cholesterol 0mg, Sodium 135mg.

Doris Guimont

Fajita Rice

1½ cups instant brown rice
¾ pound flank steak, cut into strips
1 medium onion, sliced
1 green pepper, sliced
1 red pepper, sliced
1½ teaspoons garlic powder
1 tablespoon oil
½ cup water
¼ cup lime juice
1 teaspoon hot pepper sauce
¼ teaspoon black pepper

Prepare rice as directed on package, omitting margarine and salt.

Cook and stir meat, vegetables and garlic powder in hot oil in large skillet until browned. Add remaining ingredients. Bring to a boil. Reduce heat and simmer 5 minutes. Serve over rice. Serves 4. Preparation time 30 minutes.

Note: Calories per serving 330, Protein 21g, Carbohydrate 35g, Fat 13g, Cholesterol 45mg, Sodium 75mg, Dietary Fiber 3g.

Suzanne Hyman

Curried Chicken with Water Chestnuts

¼ cup olive or canola oil
1 bunch green onions, sliced diagonally
1 stalk celery, sliced diagonally
1 green pepper, sliced
2 tablespoons slivered almonds
2 cups thinly sliced water chestnuts
5 cups diced cooked chicken
3 tablespoons flour
1 teaspoon curry powder
1 teaspoon paprika
½ teaspoon basil
1½ cups chicken broth
¼ cup chopped pimento
1 cup drained pineapple tidbits

Heat oil in skillet and sauté onions, celery and peppers until tender. Remove from skillet. Blend flour, paprika, curry powder and basil into the oil in the skillet and gradually add chicken broth. Stir constantly until smooth and slightly thick. Return onions, celery and peppers to the skillet. Add almonds, water chestnuts, chicken, pimento and pineapple. Cover and let steam briefly. Season with salt and pepper to taste. Serve on rice. Serves 4-6.

Phyllis Hickey

Arroz Con Pollo

4 chicken breast halves
salt
½ teaspoon ground pepper
½ teaspoon paprika
2 teaspoons olive oil
1 large green pepper, chopped
¾ cup chopped onions
1½ teaspoons minced garlic
1 cup long-grain rice
1 (14 ounce) can chicken broth, defatted
⅓ cup dry white wine
⅛ teaspoon saffron powder
1 (14-16 ounce) can stewed tomatoes
1 tablespoon chopped fresh parsley

Remove all skin and fat from chicken. Combine ¼ teaspoon each of salt, pepper and paprika. Rub over chicken. Heat oil in non-stick skillet over high heat. Add chicken. Cook until golden on all sides (10 minutes). Remove chicken. Add green pepper, onions and garlic to skillet. Cook, stirring until vegetables are tender. Add rice. Cook, stirring until rice is opaque, 1-2 minutes. Stir in broth, white wine, ½ teaspoon salt, ¼ teaspoon each paprika, pepper and saffron powder. Bring to a boil over high heat. Reduce heat to low. Cover and simmer 15 minutes. Stir in chicken and stewed tomatoes with their liquid. Boil. Break tomatoes into small pieces. Cover and simmer 20 minutes more, stirring once, until chicken and rice are tender and liquid is absorbed. Stir in parsley. Spoon onto platter. Serves 4. Preparation time 25 minutes. Cooking time 50 minutes.

Note: Calories per serving 420, Total Fat 6g, Saturated Fat 1g, Cholesterol 86mg, Sodium 1299mg, Carbohydrate 50g, Protein 40g.

Suzanne Hyman

Poaching Chicken Breasts

Fill a large saucepan with water and add a few splashes of white wine or dry vermouth. Add:

2¼ cup onion slices or ¼ cup carrot slices
3 tablespoons chopped celery leaves
2 tablespoons parsley sprigs
salt and pepper to taste

Add chicken breasts. Bring pan to a full boil then turn it off, (let heat of liquid finish the cooking) to keep breasts moist and tender. When cool, remove chicken breasts and use in salad. Save poaching liquid (strained) for stock in soup or sauce recipes. Left over strained stock may be used over again to poach more batches of chicken breasts, thus making stock more flavorful. May freeze in ice cube tray. When frozen place cubes in plastic ziplock bags and place back in freezer. Good to know when doing large batches of chicken.

Margaret Rooney

Remember when health foods were whatever your mother said to eat or else?

Chicken and Mushrooms Dijon

2 tablespoons margarine
2 cups sliced mushrooms
1 small onion, chopped
1 pound boneless, skinless chicken breasts
⅔ cup chicken broth
1 teaspoon cornstarch
1 tablespoon Dijon mustard

Melt margarine in large skillet. Sauté mushrooms and onion, 5-7 minutes. Add chicken, turning frequently. In small bowl stir chicken broth and cornstarch until smooth. Add mustard. Combine with chicken mixture. Bring to a boil, stirring constantly. Boil for 1 minute. Serve over chicken. Serves 4.

Note: Calories per serving 210, Protein 29g, Carbohydrate 5g, Total Fat 8g, Cholesterol 65mg, Sodium 410mg.

Doris Guimont

Roasted Lemon Chicken

1 whole chicken
¼ cup hot water
2 teaspoons instant chicken bouillon
3 tablespoons Mrs. Dash lemon pepper seasoning
1 tablespoon dried oregano

Preheat oven 400 degrees. Place chicken in roasting pan. Combine hot water and bouillon. Pour over chicken. Combine Mrs. Dash seasoning and oregano. Coat chicken with mixture. Bake covered with aluminum foil for 50 minutes. Remove foil and baste. Bake uncovered for another 15 minutes, until chicken is done and golden brown. Serves 4.

Note: With skin, Calories per serving 210, Protein 18g, Carbohydrate 1g, Sodium 160mg, Cholesterol 70mg.

Doris Guimont

Beef Stroganoff

1 pound lean beef round or sirloin
½ pound mushrooms, sliced
1 onion, sliced
3 tablespoons olive or canola oil
3 tablespoons flour
2 cups beef broth
2 tablespoons tomato paste
1 teaspoon dry mustard
pinch of oregano
pinch of dill weed
2 tablespoons sherry
⅓ cup low-fat yogurt

Cut meat into thin strips 2 inches long. Sprinkle with salt and pepper. In a heavy skillet, sauté mushrooms in oil until tender. Remove mushrooms and sauté onion in the same oil. Remove onion. Brown meat quickly on all sides until rare. Remove and set aside.

Blend the flour into the oil in the skillet and gradually add beef broth. Stir constantly until smooth and slightly thick. Add tomato paste, dry mustard, oregano, dill weed and sherry. Blend all previously cooked ingredients well. Cook until thoroughly heated. Add yogurt five minutes before serving. Serves 4.

Phyllis Hickey

French Onion Roast

4 pound beef sirloin-tip roast
2 tablespoons instant beef bouillon
¼ cup hot water
⅓ cup Mrs. Dash onion and herb seasoning

Preheat oven to 450 degrees. Place roast in 13x9x2 inch baking dish. Combine bouillon, water and Mrs. Dash. Spread evenly over roast. Reduce oven temperature to 350 degrees. Bake uncovered 30 minutes. Cover and bake 50 minutes more or until done. Serve thinly sliced. Top with pan juices. Serves 10-12.

Note: Calories per serving 180, Fat 6g, Protein 26g, Carbohydrate 3g, Sodium 60mg, Cholesterol 70mg.

Doris Guimont

Texas Meatloaf

2 tablespoons corn oil
1 chopped green pepper
1 large chopped onion
2 garlic cloves, minced
1½ pounds lean ground beef
2 egg whites
¾ cup old fashion oats
¾ cup barbecue sauce, divided
1 (4 ounce) can chopped green chilies, undrained

Preheat oven to 350 degrees. Spray loaf pan with cooking spray. Heat corn oil in large skillet. Add green pepper, onion and garlic. Sauté 4 minutes. Remove from heat. In large bowl, combine ground beef, egg whites, oats, ½ cup barbecue sauce and chilies. Stir in cooked vegetables. Spoon mixture into loaf pan. Bake for 1 hour. Drain excess liquid. Invert loaf onto serving platter. Spoon remaining ¼ cup barbecue sauce over top. Let stand 10 minutes before slicing. Serves 8.

Note: Use ground round or 90 percent lean ground beef. Calories per serving 260, Protein 23g, Carbohydrate 14g, Fat 12g, Cholesterol 55mg, Sodium 410mg.

Doris Guimont

Toaster Trout for Two

2 whole trout (9 inch size, dressed)
2 tablespoons oil or melted butter
4 ounces sliced mushrooms
2 tablespoons Parmesan cheese, freshly grated
1 small onion, thinly sliced and buttered
salt
pepper

Coat trout inside and out with some of the oil or melted butter. Fill the cavities with mushrooms and sprinkle with Parmesan cheese. Place trout on broiler pan to fit into a toaster oven and set on broil. Cook until you see small spots of burnt skin. Turn trout over and place buttered onion slices, seasoned with salt and pepper, on the body of the fish. Continue to broil until small spots of burn appear. Serves 2.

Note: This recipe would be considered especially quick and easy. It is designed for a counter-top toaster oven with a broiler.

Suzanne Hyman

Spicy Marinated Salmon with Avocado Salsa

Marinade:

1 cup sweet vermouth
¾ cup olive oil
1 tablespoon minced fresh garlic
1 jalapeño pepper, seeded and finely chopped (1 tablespoon)
1 tablespoon fresh lemon or lime juice
1½ teaspoons freshly ground pepper
4 teaspoons red pepper sauce (Tabasco)
1¼ teaspoons salt
6 (8 ounce) salmon steaks, or substitute 1 inch thick

In 11x7 inch baking dish, combine marinade ingredients or prepare in food processor and then put in baking dish. Arrange steaks in single layer in baking dish, turning to coat. Cover with plastic wrap. Chill 2 hours, turning steaks over occasionally.

Salsa:

2 tablespoons olive oil
2 tablespoons rice wine vinegar
1 tablespoon snipped fresh cilantro leaves
¼ teaspoon salt
1 jalapeño
¼ cup coarsely chopped red onion
2 ripe avocados, peeled and seeded

In food processor bowl, combine the first five salsa ingredients and process until finely chopped. Add onion and avocado and process until coarsely chopped. Put into serving dish and cover with plastic wrap. Chill 2 hours. Bring to room temperature before serving.

Spray cooking grate with nonstick vegetable cooking spray. Prepare grill for medium direct heat. Drain and discard marinade from steaks. Arrange steaks on prepared cooking grate. Grill, covered, for 8 to 10 minutes, or until fish is firm and opaque and just begins to flake, turning over once. Serves: 6.

Note: Calories per serving 400, Protein 26g, Carbohydrate 6g, Fat 30g, Cholesterol 67mg, Sodium 282mg.

Exchanges: 3 lean meat, 1¼ vegetable, 4 fat

Anne C. Hoffman

Shrimp Scampi over Linguini

2 teaspoons cornstarch
1 (8 ounce) bottle clam juice
2 teaspoons olive oil
1 pound shrimp, peeled and deveined
1 tablespoon minced garlic
½ teaspoon crushed red pepper
¼ teaspoon salt
¼ cup white wine
pinch thyme
1 pound linguini, cooked
¼ cup chopped flat-leaf parsley
¼ teaspoon grated lemon peel
1 cup seeded, sliced plum tomatoes

Stir cornstarch into ¼ cup clam juice in cup. Set aside. Heat oil in nonstick skillet over medium heat until simmering. Add shrimp, garlic, red pepper and salt. Cook, stirring until shrimp begins to turn pink (2 to 3 minutes). Remove shrimp. Add wine, remaining clam juice and thyme to skillet. Bring to boil. Stir in cornstarch mixture and return to boil, stirring constantly. Return shrimp to skillet. Cook until heated through. Toss with linguini, parsley and lemon peel in bowl. Top with tomatoes. Serves 4. Preparation time 20 minutes. Cooking time 11 minutes.

Note: Calories per serving 570, Total Fat 6g, Saturated Fat 1g, Cholesterol 140mg, Sodium 415mg, Carbohydrate 90g, Protein 34g.

Suzanne Hyman

Baked Salmon Fillets with Spinach

4 small fillets of fresh salmon
1 package frozen spinach
minced garlic (optional)
1 medium carton cream
8 ounces white wine

Preheat oven to 400 degrees. Cook spinach with garlic and drain thoroughly. In an oven proof casserole dish, make 4 separate squares of spinach. Place a salmon fillet on each square. Pour wine over salmon and then the cream. Cook for 12 to 15 minutes. Can be prepared in advance. Serves 4.

Finola Murphy
wife of D. Patrick Murphy, Senior Executive Vice President for Bank of Ireland/First New Hampshire Bank

Vegetable Stuffed Sole with Vermouth Sauce

2 pounds sole fillets
½ teaspoon dill
¼ teaspoon salt
¼ teaspoon black pepper
2 medium carrots, cut into thin strips
1 large green pepper, cut into thin strips

Place sole fillets on a work space. Sprinkle fish with the seasoning mixture of dill, salt and pepper. Divide the carrot and pepper strips among the fillets and roll each piece of fish into a bundle. Place seam down on an ungreased 9x13 inch baking dish. Pour ¼ cup wine over fish. Cover with foil and bake for 20-25 minutes, until fish flakes easily with a fork.

Sauce:
½ cup vermouth or dry white wine
2 tablespoons butter
2 tablespoons flour
1 cup milk
½ teaspoon paprika
1 tablespoon freshly chopped parsley
salt and pepper to taste

Meanwhile, melt butter in a 1½ quart saucepan. Add flour and cook 1 minute, stirring constantly. Remove pan from heat. Whisk in the milk and remaining ¼ cup wine. Return to heat. Add paprika, chopped parsley, salt and pepper. Cook over low heat for 3 minutes until thick and creamy. Arrange fish on serving platter. Add any remaining pan juices to the sauce. Pour the hot sauce over the fish rolls and garnish with additional parsley. Serves 6. Preparation time 30 minutes.

Note: Makes an eye appealing, low calorie dinner.

Suzanne Hyman

Wacky Cake

1½ cups flour
1 cup sugar
1 teaspoon baking soda
¼ cup cocoa
1 teaspoon vanilla
1 teaspoon vinegar
6 tablespoons melted margarine
1 cup water

Preheat oven to 350 degrees. Use an ungreased 8 inch pan. Sift and mix into the pan the flour, sugar, soda and cocoa. Make 3 wells in the flour mixture. Put 1 teaspoon vanilla in the first, 1 teaspoon vinegar in the second and 6 tablespoons of melted margarine in the third well. Pour 1 cup of water over all and mix with a fork until ingredients are entirely moist. Bake for 30 minutes. Serves 6-8.

Note: This is a very moist cake and does not need frosting. It does not flip out of the pan, but must be cut into pieces and lifted out with a spatula.

Phyllis Hickey

Ambrosia Parfait

1½ cups cold milk
1 (8 ounce) can crushed pineapple, drained, reserving juice
1 small package vanilla flavored sugar free instant pudding
1 small banana, diced
1 cup sliced strawberries, fresh or unsweetened frozen
¼ cup flaked coconut (optional)

Pour milk and reserved pineapple juice into medium bowl. Add pudding mix. Beat with wire whisk 2 minutes. Stir in banana. Spoon ½ pudding mixture evenly into 6 dessert glasses. Layer with strawberries, pineapple and coconut. Spoon remaining pudding mix over fruit. Refrigerate until ready to serve. Garnish with strawberry slices. Serves 6.

Note: Calories per serving 110, Fat 2.5mg, Cholesterol 5mg, Carbohydrate 20g, Dietary Fiber 2g, Protein 3g, Sodium 260mg.

Doris Guimont

Canterbury Farm Blueberry Muffins

2 cups all-purpose flour
½ cup sugar
1 tablespoon baking powder
½ teaspoon salt
½ cup sour cream
1 egg, slightly beaten
½ cup milk
6 tablespoons butter, melted
1 teaspoon grated lemon rind
2 teaspoons lemon juice
1½ cups blueberries

Preheat oven to 400 degrees. Lightly grease a 12 cup muffin pan. Sift together the flour, sugar, baking powder and salt. Reserve 2 tablespoons of the flour mixture. In a large bowl, whisk sour cream until smooth. Stir in egg, milk, melted butter, lemon rind and lemon juice. Add dry ingredients to liquid ingredients and stir until moistened, batter will not be smooth. Toss blueberries with the reserved 2 tablespoons of flour mixture. Gently fold blueberries into the batter. Spoon the batter into the prepared muffin pan cups, using a level ⅓ cup measure for each. Bake for 25 minutes. Cool in pan for 5 minutes. Remove to a wire rack. Serve warm.

Note: Calories 203, Protein 3g, Fat 9g, Carbohydrate 28g, Sodium 274mg, Cholesterol 44mg.

Rita Fitzgerald

Raisin Cinnamon Cookies

2½ cups flour
1 teaspoon baking soda
1 teaspoon ground cinnamon
1 teaspoon salt
2 eggs
8 ounces diet margarine
¾ cup brown sugar
2 teaspoons vanilla
¾ cup raisins

Preheat oven to 375 degrees. Sift together flour, baking soda, cinnamon and salt. Set aside. Beat eggs and margarine together until fluffy. Beat in flour mixture, brown sugar and vanilla. Fold in raisins. Drop by teaspoonful, 1 inch apart, onto an ungreased cookie sheet. Bake 8-10 minutes. Makes 100 cookies at 30 calories each.

Note: This recipe used diet margarine because it makes the batter easy to cream. The cookies are chewy and soft rather than crispy.

Doris Guimont

Raisin Oatmeal Cookies

1 cup flour
½ teaspoon baking soda
1 teaspoon salt
¼ teaspoon cinnamon
1½ cups quick cooking oats
2 egg whites, slightly beaten
1 cup brown sugar
⅓ cup canola oil
½ cup skim milk
1 teaspoon vanilla
1 cup seedless raisins

Preheat oven to 375 degrees. Sift flour, baking soda, salt and cinnamon together. Stir in oats. Combine egg whites, brown sugar, oil, milk and vanilla. Mix well. Add raisins. Combine with flour mixture. Mix well. Drop a teaspoon of batter at a time, onto an oiled cookie sheet. Bake 12 to 15 minutes, depending on texture desired. Shorter baking time results in a chewy soft cookie. Longer time results in a crisp cookie. Makes 3 dozen.

Phyllis Hickey

Where's the Fat Chocolate Sauce

¾ cup sugar
⅓ cup unsweetened cocoa powder
4 teaspoons cornstarch
⅔ cup evaporated skim milk
1 teaspoon vanilla

In small saucepan, stir together the sugar, cocoa powder and cornstarch. Add evaporated milk. Cook and stir constantly over medium heat, until sauce is thickened and bubbly. Cook and stir for 2 more minutes. Remove from heat. Stir in vanilla. Makes 1 cup. Serve the sauce warm or cool.

Serving suggestions: Drizzle over frozen yogurt or angel food cake or top fresh fruit. Makes a delicious, creamy sauce.

Note: Can be refrigerated (covered) for up to 1 week. Can be reheated in microwave until warm.

Nutrition: 47 Calories, 0g Fat, 0mg Cholesterol.

Rita Fitzgerald

Carrot Cake

3½ cups all-purpose flour
½ cup granulated sugar
1 tablespoon baking powder
2 teaspoons baking soda
2 teaspoons cinnamon
1 teaspoon ginger
¾ teaspoon salt
1 cup firmly packed brown sugar
1 cup nonfat plain yogurt
⅓ cup vegetable oil
2 large eggs
2 large egg whites
2 teaspoons vanilla
1 pound shredded carrots

Preheat oven to 350 degrees. Coat 10 cup bundt pan with vegetable cooking spray. Combine flour, sugar, baking powder, baking soda, cinnamon, ginger and salt. Whisk brown sugar, yogurt, oil, whole eggs, egg whites, and vanilla together until well blended. Stir in dry ingredients and carrots. Pour batter into pan. Bake 50-55 minutes. Cool on wire rack 10 minutes. Remove from pan. Cool completely.

Orange Glaze:
1¾ cups confectionery sugar
2 tablespoons fresh orange juice

To make glaze: stir confectionery sugar and juice in bowl until smooth. Spread glaze over cooled cake. Serves 16. Preparation time: 20 minutes.

Note: Calories per serving 305, Total Fat 5.5g, Saturated Fat 1g, Cholesterol 27mg, Sodium 394mg, Carbohydrate 58g, Protein 5g.

Suzanne Hyman

Chocolate Mint Cheesecake

½ cup crushed chocolate wafers (about 7)
1 cup low-fat cottage cheese
1 (8 ounce) package light cream cheese
1 cup sugar
⅓ cup unsweetened cocoa powder
3 tablespoons creme de menthe liqueur
1 teaspoon vanilla
½ cup (4 ounces) frozen egg product, thawed
3 tablespoons miniature semi-sweet chocolate pieces
Halved, fanned whole strawberries or other fresh fruit (optional)

Preheat oven to 300 degrees. Use 8 inch springform pan. Sprinkle wafer crumbs evenly in the bottom of the pan. Set aside. In a food processor bowl or blender container, cover and process or blend cottage cheese till smooth. Add cream cheese, sugar, cocoa powder, liqueur and vanilla. Blend or process until combined (mixture will be thick). Scrape the side of bowl often, transfer to a large mixing bowl. Stir in egg product and chocolate. Pour into prepared pan. Bake 35-40 minutes or until cheesecake appears nearly set when shaken. Cool on a wire rack for 10 minutes. Loosen sides of pan. Cool 30 minutes more. Remove sides of pan. Cool completely. Cover and chill several hours or overnight. Garnish with strawberries or other fruit, if desired. Yield 12 servings.

Note: Follow 10 minute cooling time before loosening from pan or cheesecake may crack.

Comment: Nutrition information per serving: 175 Calories (34 percent from fat), 7g Fat, 16mg Cholesterol, 6g Protein, 22g Carbohydrate, 176mg Sodium. This recipe saves about 520 calories and 32 grams of fat compared to a higher fat cheesecake and tastes every bit as good.

Rita Fitzgerald

Lemon Cheesecake

1 graham cracker, crushed
1 small package lemon flavored sugar free gelatin
⅔ cup boiling water
1 cup low fat cottage cheese
8 ounces light cream cheese
2 cups Cool Whip Lite
1 cup lite cherry pie filling

Spray 9 inch pie plate with no-stick cooking spray. Sprinkle on ½ of the graham cracker crumbs. Set aside. Dissolve gelatin completely in boiling water in a small bowl, stirring 2 minutes. Pour into blender. Add cheeses. Blend on medium speed until smooth. Put mixture in a larger bowl. Gently stir in whipped topping. Spread mixture into the pie plate. Spread remaining crumbs around the outside edge. Refrigerate 4 hours. Just before serving spread pie filling onto the center of cheesecake. Serves 8.

Note: Calories per serving 160, Fat 8g, Cholesterol 20mg, Carbohydrate 15g, Protein 7g, Sodium 280mg.

Doris Guimont

Chocolate Kahlua Brownies

1½ cups sugar
½ cup egg substitute, thawed
¼ cup melted margarine
3 tablespoons Kahlua
1¼ cups sifted cake flour
½ cup unsweetened cocoa
1 teaspoon baking powder
dash of salt
¾ cup semi-sweet chocolate morsels
vegetable cooking spray

Preheat oven to 325 degrees. Combine sugar, egg, margarine and Kahlua, stirring well. Combine flour, cocoa, baking powder and salt. Add to sugar mixture. Stir well. Stir in chocolate morsels. Coat 9 inch square pan with cooking spray. Spoon batter into pan. Bake for 30 minutes. Remove from oven and let cool on wire rack. Cut into squares. Serves 16.

Note: Calories per brownie 177, Fat 5.8g, Cholesterol 0mg, Sodium 55mg.

Doris Guimont

Bittersweet Chocolate Torte with Apricot Filling

Cake:

6 large eggs
¾ cup less 1 tablespoon sugar
1 teaspoon vanilla
½ cup plus 1 tablespoon sifted flour
½ cup sifted unsweetened cocoa powder
1 teaspoon ground allspice
1 teaspoon cinnamon
¼ teaspoon ground nutmeg

Preheat oven to 350 degrees. Spray two, 8 inch round cake pans with nonstick cooking spray. In a large bowl beat eggs, sugar and vanilla with electric mixer at high speed until thick and tripled in volume, about 7 minutes. In medium bowl sift together flour, cocoa powder, allspice, cinnamon and nutmeg. Gently fold the dry ingredients into the egg mixture. Divide the batter between the 2 prepared cake pans. Bake 15-20 minutes. Set pans on wire racks to cool.

Frosting and Filling:

1½ cups part-skim ricotta cheese
¼ cup plus 2 tablespoons unsweetened cocoa powder
2 tablespoons instant espresso powder
3 tablespoons sugar
2 teaspoons vanilla
⅛ teaspoon salt
¾ cup apricot All Fruit spread
strawberries for garnish, optional

To make the frosting, process ricotta cheese, cocoa powder, espresso powder, sugar, vanilla and salt in a food blender until smooth. Cover and chill the frosting until ready to use.

When the cake is cool take it out of the pan. Split each layer in half horizontally. Spread the bottom layers with apricot all-fruit frosting. Place the top layer over the bottom layer and spread with frosting. Stack the second filled layers on top of the cake. (Total of 4 layers.) Swirl the remaining frosting over top of the cake. Garnish, if desired. Serves 12.

Note: Calories 221, Protein 8g, Fat 6g, Carbohydrate 35g, Cholesterol 116mg, Sodium 82mg.

Doris Guimont

Lemon Torte

1 (4 serving-size) package low-calorie lemon flavored gelatin
½ cup boiling water
⅓ cup frozen lemonade concentrate, thawed
1 (12 ounce) can evaporated skim milk
2 cups cubed angel food cake
2 cups fresh raspberries
1 tablespoon sugar

Spray the bottom only, of an 8 inch springform pan with nonstick spray coating; set aside. In a large bowl dissolve lemon gelatin in boiling water. Stir in thawed lemonade concentrate and evaporated skim milk. Cover and chill in refrigerator for 1-1½ hours or until mixture mounds when spooned. After chilling, beat gelatin mixture with an electric mixer on medium to high speed for 5-6 minutes or until fluffy. Arrange angel food cake cubes in bottom of pan. Pour gelatin mixture over cake cubes. Cover and chill in refrigerator for 5 hours or until firm. Meanwhile, in a small bowl, stir together raspberries and sugar. Cover and chill at least 2 hours. To serve, cut torte into wedges and spoon raspberries on top. Yield: 12 servings.

Note: Nutrition information per serving: 80 Calories, 4g Protein, 17g Carbohydrate, 0g Fat, 0mg Cholesterol, 70mg Sodium, 190mg Potassium.

Carol Frizzell

Peach Flambe

1 (29 ounce) can sliced peaches, drained
½ cup port wine
4 sugar cubes soaked in lemon or orange extract
vanilla non fat yogurt

Place drained peaches in a glass bowl. Pour in port wine. Space soaked sugar cubes around peaches. Ignite. Spoon over yogurt.

Phyllis Hickey

New England—Tried & True

Underground Slave Railroad Network

Life was not too disrupted during the Civil War Years because the fighting did not take place in this part of the country. It is known, however, that many slaves escaping from the south traveled through Bedford on what was known as an "underground railroad," passing from one hiding place to another.

The home of Zachariah Chandler on the River Road had a hidden room upstairs, next to the chimney. The door to the room was opened by springing a loose board on the floor. Fugitives could always find refuge in this house which stood where the Manchester Country Club is now. The original house burned down in 1916. Chandler, who was born in Bedford, was a United States Senator and an outspoken abolitionist.

Gourmet Summer Barbecue

beverages

Raspberry Lime Rickey

Margaritas

hors d'oeuvres

Quesadilla with Gary's Guacamole

entrée

Spicy Marinated Salmon with Avocado Salsa

White Rice

salad

Spicy Marinated Pepper Slaw

dessert

Chilled Lime Soufflé with Strawberry Sauce

NEW ENGLAND—TRIED & TRUE

New England Clam Chowder

2 slices bacon, coarsely chopped
1 cup onions, finely chopped
2 cups potato, pared and cubed
1 teaspoon salt
dash pepper
1 cup water
2 (10½ ounce) cans minced clams
½ cup clam juice
2 cups half-and-half
2 tablespoons butter or margarine

In a large soup kettle, sauté bacon until almost crisp. Add onion and cook for 5 minutes. Add potatoes, salt, pepper and water, and cook uncovered for 15 minutes or until potatoes are fork-tender. Add clams, clam liquid, half-and-half and butter, mixing well. Cook for about 3 minutes. Do not boil. Serves 4.

Note: To thin the consistency, use 2 percent milk instead of half and half.

This recipe easily doubles or triples.

Rita Fitzgerald

Shepherd's Pie

¼ cup onion
1 pound ground beef
½ teaspoon salt
2 cups green beans
2 cups carrots
5 potatoes

Preheat oven to 350 degrees. Sauté onion, beef and salt. Boil beans, carrots and potatoes. Mash potatoes. Place onions and beef in a baking dish. Add layers of beans and carrots. Cover with mashed potatoes. Bake until potatoes are well browned, approximately 30 minutes. Serves 6.

This is an excellent way to use leftovers.

Janet Jespersen

Good Old Baked Beans

1 pound white pea beans
2 teaspoons salt
¼ teaspoon black pepper
5½ tablespoons dark molasses
¼ cup brown sugar
1 teaspoon dry mustard
1 small peeled onion, cut into chunks
2½ cups boiling water
¼ pound salt pork

Put beans in a large pot and cover with water. Soak beans overnight. Rinse with water. Drain again. Place beans in a bean pot. Mix together salt, pepper, molasses, brown sugar and mustard. Add to the beans, stirring well. Add onion and mix. Add the boiling water. Place salt pork on the top with the fat side up. Cover and cook for 6-7 hours at 325 degrees. May add more water if needed and more molasses to darken.

Christina Barley

Yankee Red Flannel Hash

1½ cups chopped, cooked corned beef
3 cups chopped, cooked potatoes
1½ cups chopped, cooked beets
⅓ cup chopped onions
⅓ cup milk
1 teaspoon salt
3 teaspoons fat for skillet

Combine the above ingredients. Cook in skillet over medium heat until underside is brown and crusty. Serves 4 to 6.

Janet Jespersen

Yankee Pot Roast

3 pounds beef (chuck or rump)
1 tablespoon flour
½ teaspoon salt
¼ teaspoon pepper
1½ tablespoons fat
1 onion
2 bay leaves
1 pint boiling water

Coat the beef with a mixture of flour, salt and pepper. Melt the fat in a heavy pan. Add meat and brown on all sides. Add boiling water, onion and bay leaves. Bring to a boil, cover and simmer for 3 hours until the meat is tender. Gravy may be made in the pan.

Janet Jespersen

Old Fashion Chicken Pie

1-2 pound chicken, boneless
10 average size potatoes
10 carrots
1 (14 ounce) can peas
2 large onions

Boil chicken. Boil vegetables. Preheat oven to 450 degrees. Cut chicken into chunks mixing with water the chicken was boiled in. Put into a 9x12x2 inch pan and add the pre-cooked potatoes, carrots, peas and onions.

Biscuits for Top:
4 cups flour
6 teaspoons baking powder
8 tablespoons shortening
½ teaspoon salt
1½ cups milk

Mix together flour, baking powder, shortening, salt and milk to make biscuit dough. Top the vegetables with the biscuit dough and bake in oven for 30 minutes. Serves 8-10.

Janet Jespersen

New England Clambake

Allow per person:

1 dozen cleaned clams
1 lobster
½ broiler chicken
2 ears of corn
1 scrubbed potato
4 small white onions, peeled

Dig a deep pit in the ground big enough to hold all the food to be cooked. Line pit with large, dry stones. Build a wood fire over the stones. When hot, add more stones and some more wood. Let this burn until the rocks are red hot. Rake off the ash embers. Place a thick layer of wet seaweed over the stones.

Place the clams, lobsters, chickens, corn cobs wrapped in husks, potatoes and onions on top of the seaweed. Cover food with more seaweed. Cover seaweed with a large tarpaulin, sealing all edges with stones or sand so steam can not escape. Food will be ready in 1½ to 2 hours.

Janet Jespersen

Crab Meat/Seafood Casserole

1 pound imitation crab meat
1 cup celery, chopped
½ cup onion, chopped
1 cup peas
2 tablespoons parsley flakes
1 cup mayonnaise
1 cup milk
2 cups stuffing

Preheat oven to 350 degrees. Mix together in casserole baking dish crab meat, celery, onion, peas and parsley. In separate bowl, mix together mayonnaise, milk and 1½ cups stuffing. Add to crab mixture. Sprinkle with ½ cup stuffing on top. Bake 30 minutes. Yield: 4 servings.

Martha Harris Gaudes
Executive Assistant to Bedford Town Manager

Boiled Lobster

1 (2 pound) lobster per person
1 tablespoon of salt for every quart of boiling water

Fill large pot with enough water to cover lobsters. Bring water to a rolling boil. Drop lobsters into water head first. Cover and wait for water to return to a boil. Simmer 15 to 18 minutes. Plunge lobsters into cold water to stop the cooking. Twist off claws, split down underside of tail, crack claws. Serve with lemon wedges, melted butter and a good supply of paper napkins.

Janet Jespersen

Lobster Rolls

2 cups diced, cooked lobster meat
⅓ cup celery
½ small onion, diced
5 tablespoons mayonnaise
salt
pepper
4 frankfurter rolls
Mayonnaise to spread

Place lobster meat, celery, and onion in bowl. Add mayonnaise and toss gently. Season with salt and pepper to taste. Spread rolls with mayonnaise and fill with lobster salad. Serve with potato chips and pickles.

Janet Jespersen

Raisin Sauce

¾ cup brown sugar
3 tablespoons cornstarch
1½ cups broth from cooked ham
¼ cup vinegar
1 lemon sliced thin
1 tablespoon butter
½ cup raisins

Mix sugar and cornstarch together, gradually adding broth. Stir to prevent lumps. Pour into a double boiler. Add the remaining ingredients. Cook until the raisins are plump and the mixture is thick. Serve hot.

Note: Good on ham.

Janet Jespersen

Hard Sauce

⅓ cup butter
1 cup powdered sugar
¼ cup wine (whiskey or rum)

Cream butter and sugar. Add liquor a little at a time and beat well.

Note: Good on fruitcake and steamed puddings.

Janet Jespersen

Heidi's Cranberry Chutney

1 (16 ounce) can Ocean Spray whole cranberry sauce
½ cup golden raisins
1 cup peeled, diced cooking apples
¼ cup sugar
¼ cup apple cider vinegar
⅛ teaspoon ground or fresh grated ginger
⅛ teaspoon cinnamon
dash of ground cloves

Combine all ingredients in a medium size saucepan. Cook over medium heat, stirring occasionally, until apples are tender and sauce has thickened slightly (about 30 minutes). Makes about 2½ cups. Chill for several hours or overnight. Bring to room temperature to serve. Serve with chicken, turkey, or pork dish.

Anne C. Hoffman

Popovers

1 cup flour
¼ teaspoon salt
1 cup milk
2 eggs, well beaten
1 teaspoon melted butter

Preheat oven to 500 degrees. Sift flour and salt together and gradually stir in milk. Add the beaten eggs and melted butter. Beat hard with a rotary beater for 2 minutes. Pour into buttered custard cups. Start baking in hot oven until popovers puff, then reduce to 350 degrees and brown. Full baking time: 30 minutes.

Janet Jespersen

Apple Crisp

5 apples
¾ cup brown sugar
1 teaspoon cinnamon
2 teaspoons lemon juice
¾ cup quick cooking oatmeal
½ cup flour
½ cup butter
¼ teaspoon salt

Preheat oven to 350 degrees. Peel and slice apples. Put into a buttered dish. Sprinkle with sugar, cinnamon and a little lemon juice. Top with the mixture of oatmeal, flour, butter and salt. Bake for 40 minutes.

Janet Jespersen

Blueberry Muffins

1½ cups flour
½ cup sugar
2 teaspoons baking powder
½ teaspoon salt
¼ cup shortening
1 egg
½ cup milk
1 cup blueberries
sugar to top the muffins

Preheat oven to 400 degrees. Sift together the flour, sugar, baking powder, and salt. Add to it the shortening, egg and milk. Stir until ingredients are blended. Mixture should not be smooth. Fold in blueberries. After batter is in the muffin tins, sprinkle each one with sugar. Bake 20 to 25 minutes.

Janet Jespersen

Best Gingerbread

½ cup butter and shortening mixed
½ cup sugar
1 egg, beaten
½ cup molasses
2½ cups sifted flour
1½ teaspoons baking soda
1 teaspoon cinnamon
½ teaspoon ginger
½ teaspoon cloves
½ teaspoon salt
1 cup hot water

Preheat oven 325 degrees. Cream shortening. Add sugar, beaten egg, molasses, and sifted dry ingredients. Lastly, add hot water. Beat until smooth. Bake 50 minutes.

Alice H. Kensall

Christmas Gingersnaps

¾ cup margarine, softened
1¼ cups sugar
1 egg
¼ cup molasses
2 cups flour
1 tablespoon ground ginger
2 teaspoons baking soda
1 teaspoon cinnamon
½ teaspoon salt

Preheat oven to 350 degrees. In large bowl beat the margarine and 1 cup sugar until it is light and fluffy. Beat in egg and molasses. Mix together flour, ginger, soda, cinnamon and salt. Stir into margarine mixture. Chill for about 10 minutes or until dough is easy to handle. Shape dough into 1 inch balls and roll in the remaining ¼ cup of sugar. Place on ungreased cookie sheet about 2 inches apart. Bake on rack in center of oven for about 11 minutes or until evenly browned. Immediately move to rack to cool. If you want crispier cookies, cook about 2 minutes longer.

Note: I call these Christmas Gingersnaps because they are a traditional favorite in our home over the Christmas Holidays. Keep stored in tightly covered container.

Christina Barley

Cream Puffs

1 cup boiling water
½ cup butter
1 cup flour
4 eggs
pinch of salt

Preheat oven 450 degrees. Boil water over low heat, add butter. Stir until butter melts. Add flour all at once and stir until mixture forms a ball. Remove from the heat and add eggs, one at a time. Beat thoroughly. Shape dough on an ungreased cookie sheet, 2 teaspoons per puff. Bake in hot oven for 20 minutes then reduce heat to 350 degrees for another 20 minutes. Remove from oven and place on a rack to cool. When cool, make a slit in each puff and fill with desired filling, usually whipped cream.

Janet Jespersen

Hermit Cookies

½ cup butter
1½ cups brown sugar
2 tablespoons sour milk
2 eggs
3 cups flour
1 teaspoon baking soda
½ cup raisins, chopped
½ cup nuts, chopped
1 cup currants, chopped
½ teaspoon ground nutmeg
½ teaspoon cinnamon

Preheat oven to 350 degrees. Cream butter and sugar together. Beat eggs and milk together. Sift half the flour and baking soda together. Mix the nuts, fruit and spices with the balance of the flour. Combine all ingredients together and beat thoroughly. Drop by teaspoonfuls on greased cookie sheet. Bake for 15 minutes.

Janet Jespersen

Whoopie Pies

½ cup butter or shortening
1 cup sugar
1 egg
1 cup milk
2 cups flour
1½ teaspoons baking powder
½ cup cocoa
1 teaspoon vanilla

Preheat oven to 400 degrees. Blend all ingredients until smooth. Drop by teaspoonfuls onto greased cookie sheet. Bake for 10 minutes. Cool on cake rack.

Filling:
½ cup butter
1 cup marshmallow fluff
½ teaspoon vanilla
1 cup confectioners sugar

Blend all filling ingredients until smooth. After cookies have cooled, spread the filling between 2 cookies. Best if kept in airtight container in the refrigerator. Can be frozen.

Janet Jespersen

1850 Suet Pudding

1 cup milk
1 cup molasses
1 cup raisins
1 cup ground suet
3 cups flour
1 teaspoon baking soda
spices, as desired

Mix all together. Pour into mold(s). Steam 3 hours.

Bedford Historic District Commission

1850 Lemon Cream

1 pint whipping cream
2 egg yolks, well beaten
½ cup sugar
juice and finely grated rind of one lemon

For best results use a double boiler pan. Mix cream, egg yolks and sugar. Cook, stirring constantly, over very low heat until just to a boil (do not boil.) Continue cooking and stirring at low temperature until thickened. Cool. Add juice and lemon rind. Cover and chill.

Marilyn Otterson, Bedford Historic District Commission

1820 Rice Pudding

⅓ cup rice, uncooked
1 quart whole milk
½ cup granulated or maple sugar
1 teaspoon salt
piece of butter
raisins
candied fruit, such as orange peel
cinnamon, vanilla, or brandy

Preheat oven to 325 degrees. In a deep baking dish place the washed rice. Add milk, sugar, salt, butter, raisins, fruit and flavoring(s). Cook slowly, stirring frequently, for about two hours.

Note: This recipe came from an old New Hampshire Cookbook.

Bedford Historic District Commission

New England Indian Pudding

5 cups milk
4¼ tablespoons cornmeal
½ cup molasses
2 eggs, beaten
½ cup sugar
1 teaspoon cinnamon
⅛ teaspoon ginger
⅛ teaspoon salt
½ cup raisins (optional)

Preheat oven to 325 degrees. Use a 2 quart flameproof casserole dish. Put 2 cups milk and the cornmeal in casserole dish or pan and cook over low heat, stirring constantly for 12 minutes. Remove from heat and stir in molasses, eggs, 2 cups milk, sugar, cinnamon, ginger and salt. Bake for 30 minutes, stirring every 10 minutes. Remove from oven and stir in remaining 1 cup of milk and raisins (if desired). Continue baking for 2 hours. Serve warm or cold with whipped cream or vanilla ice cream.

Christina Barley

1850 Bread Pudding

3 pints milk, boiled
11 ounces grated bread (crumbs)
½ pound sugar
¼ pound butter
5 eggs, well beaten
1 teaspoon vanilla, optional

Preheat oven to 325 degrees. In a 3 quart casserole dish, pour boiling milk over bread. Stir butter and sugar together well. Add to bread and milk. Cool. Add eggs. Add vanilla, if desired. Bake 45 minutes. (For richer pudding, double the butter and eggs.)

Marilyn Otterson, Bedford Historic District Commission

Yankee Trifle

Leftover white or yellow cake or jelly roll
1 small jar of raspberry jam
½-¾ cup sherry
Jell-O Americana Golden Egg Custard Mix
trace of fresh nutmeg scrapings
1 can mandarin oranges
2 bananas
1 container Creamy Cool Whip
maraschino cherries
almond, walnuts or pecans
strawberries or blueberries, in season

Spread raspberry jam on slices of cake and line bottom and sides of a punch or trifle bowl. Add sherry, soaking all cake slices. Make custard sauce, according to directions on the package, and add to mixture in bowl. Put mandarin oranges around sides of bowl, and fruits of choice on top. Top with Cool Whip, cherries, and nuts.

Alice K. Finet

Evelyn's Sweetened Condensed Milk

1 cup instant non fat dry milk solids
⅔ cup sugar
⅓ cup boiling water
3 tablespoons melted butter or margarine

Combine all ingredients in blender until smooth. Store in refrigerator until ready to use. Equals 1¼ cups - about as much as a 14 ounce can of condensed milk, but costs much less.

Margaret Rooney

Cakes

Manchester Country Club

Donald Ross, a leading authority and builder of golf courses helped choose the location of this course. Ross felt the 160-acre site of Gordon Woodbury's property would be ideal. In 1922 the property was purchased at a cost of $18,000. The cost of the golf course was $45,000, the club house $60,000 and incidentals, $7,000.

The golf course has been said to be the best of its size in northern New England. There are few if any courses that can offer such varieties of scenic beauty, more varying dips and natural billows of emerald terrain. One looks out across oaks, maples, pines and idle streams that wander aimlessly here and there. The course, hewn from the forest, was designed so that the dips and mounds would flow naturally. It is a "Donald Ross masterpiece."

Nineteenth Hole Dinner

beverage

Raspberry Lime Rickey

hors d'oeuvres

Artichoke Nibbles

Homus Dip

salad

Green Salad with

Shaker Village Salad Dressing

entrée

Beef Bourguignonne for Golfers

Irish Mashed Potato Casserole

dessert

Cran-Cherry Crisp a la mode

Frozen Lemon Mousse

CAKES

No-Bake Alaska Supreme

2 envelopes Knox unflavored gelatin
½ cup sugar
1¼ cups orange juice, heated to boiling
1 (16 ounce) can whole berry cranberry sauce
¼ cup orange or cranberry liqueur
3 cups (1½ pints) whipping or heavy cream
¼ cup coarsely chopped pecans
1 (8 inch) white cake layer
toasted flaked coconut

In medium bowl, mix unflavored gelatin with ¼ cup sugar. Add hot juice and stir until gelatin is completely dissolved. With wire whip or rotary beater, blend in cranberry sauce and liqueur. Chill, stirring occasionally, until mixture mounds slightly when dropped from spoon.

In medium bowl, whip 1 cup cream. Fold into gelatin mixture with pecans. Turn into 1½ or 2 quart bowl (about 8 inch diameter) and chill until firm. In medium bowl, whip remaining cream with sugar. To serve, unmold gelatin onto layer cake. Frost with whipped cream and sprinkle with coconut. Yield: about 10 servings.

Elisabeth P. Place

Gooey Butter Cake

1 yellow cake mix
1 stick butter or margarine, melted
1 egg
1 (8 ounce) package cream cheese, softened
3 eggs
4 cups powdered sugar

Preheat oven to 350 degrees. Grease 13x9 inch pan. Mix cake mix, butter and 1 egg and pat into pan. Combine cream cheese, 3 eggs and powdered sugar. Pour over cake mixture and bake until set, about 40 minutes. When cool sprinkle with powdered sugar. Cut into bars.

Note: Very rich. Men seem to like it.

Joan Hetland

Amazin Raisin Cake

3 cups flour
2 cups sugar
1 cup mayonnaise
1/3 cup milk
2 eggs
2 teaspoons baking soda
1 1/2 teaspoons cinnamon
1/2 teaspoon nutmeg
1/2 teaspoon salt
1/2 teaspoon ground cloves
3 cups apples, peeled and chopped
1 cup raisins
1/2 cup chopped nuts

Preheat oven to 350 degrees. Grease and flour 13x9 inch pan. In large bowl beat together flour, sugar, mayonnaise, milk, eggs, baking soda, cinnamon, nutmeg, salt, and cloves for two minutes. Batter will be thick. Stir in apples, raisins, and nuts. Bake 45 minutes. Cool in pan 10 minutes. Remove from pan. Cool. Frost with whipped cream or Cool Whip.

Jeanne Thibault

Banana Cake

1 1/2 cups sugar
1/2 cup margarine
2 eggs
1 teaspoon vanilla
1 teaspoon salt
1 cup buttermilk (or 1 cup milk with 1 tablespoon vinegar)
2 1/2 cups flour
2 teaspoons baking powder
1 teaspoon baking soda
2 cups banana
Powdered sugar

Preheat oven to 350 degrees. In food processor, cream sugar and margarine. (Can be done by hand.) Add and process for a few seconds the eggs, vanilla, salt and about 1/4 of milk. Mix together flour, baking powder and baking soda. Alternately add some flour and some milk. Process for a few seconds until all the flour and milk are used. Add bananas and process for a few more seconds until fully mixed. Put into a greased and floured bundt pan. Bake for about 45 minutes, until a toothpick comes out clean. After cake cools, remove from pan and sprinkle with powdered sugar. Yield: 12 servings.

Anne C. Hoffman

Boter Koek (Dutch Butter Cake)

½ pound butter, softened
2 cups flour
1 cup sugar
1 teaspoon vanilla
1 teaspoon water
1 egg, separated (use yolk in cake and white for topping)

Preheat oven to 250 degrees. Grease and flour 9x11 inch pan. Knead butter, flour, sugar, vanilla and egg yolk thoroughly. Press into pan. Mix egg white and water. Brush egg white mixture over cake. Bake at 250 degrees for 30 minutes and 300 degrees for 15 minutes. Let cool before cutting. Yield: 32 squares.

Note: Best when served soon but can be frozen almost indefinitely.

Jo Fearon

Chocolate Carrot Cake

2 cups flour
1½ cups sugar
1 cup salad oil
½ cup orange juice
¼ cup cocoa
4 eggs
2 teaspoons baking soda
1 teaspoon salt
1 teaspoon cinnamon
1 teaspoon vanilla extract
2 cups shredded carrots
1 (3.5-4 ounce) can flaked or shredded coconut

Preheat oven to 350 degrees. Grease and flour 10 inch bundt pan. In large bowl, with mixer at low speed, beat first 10 ingredients just until blended, constantly scraping bowl with rubber spatula. Increase speed to high and beat 2 minutes, occasionally scraping bowl. Stir in carrots and coconut. Spoon batter into pan. Bake 50 to 55 minutes, until toothpick inserted in center of cake comes out clean. Cool cake in pan on wire rack 10 minutes. Remove from pan and cool completely on rack.

Alberta Dieter

Cameo Cake

Cake Ingredients:

1½ cups butter
¾ cup water
1 (4 ounce) bar white chocolate, broken in pieces
1½ cups buttermilk
4 large eggs, lightly beaten
1½ teaspoons vanilla
3½ cups flour, divided
1 cup chopped pecans, toasted
2¼ cups sugar
1½ teaspoons baking soda

Preheat oven to 350 degrees. Use 3 greased and floured 9 inch layer pans. Combine butter and water in a medium saucepan and bring to boil over medium heat. Add white chocolate, stirring until chocolate melts. Stir in buttermilk, eggs and vanilla. Set aside. Combine pecans with ½ cup flour, stirring to coat, and set aside. Combine remaining 3 cups flour, sugar and baking soda in large mixing bowl. Gradually stir in white chocolate mixture. Fold in pecan mixture. (Batter will be thin.) Pour into pans and bake for 20-25 minutes.

White Chocolate Cream Cheese Frosting:

1 (4 ounce) bar white chocolate
1 (8 ounce) and 1 (3 ounce) package cream cheese, softened
⅓ cup butter, softened
6½ cups sifted powdered sugar
1½ teaspoons vanilla

Melt white chocolate in a heavy saucepan over low heat, stirring constantly. Remove from heat. Cool 10 minutes, stirring constantly. Beat cream cheese and butter at medium speed with an electric mixer until creamy. Gradually add white chocolate beating constantly until blended. Gradually add powdered sugar beating until smooth. Stir in vanilla.

Betty Folsom
Supervisor of Checklist

Cheese Cake

2 (8 ounce) packages cream cheese
1 pound cottage cheese
1½ cups granulated sugar
4 eggs, slightly beaten
2 tablespoons lemon juice
1 teaspoon vanilla
¼ pound butter or margarine, melted
1 pint sour cream
3 tablespoons flour
3 tablespoons cornstarch

Preheat oven to 325 degrees. Grease well a springform or tube cake pan. Have all ingredients at room temperature. Put cream cheese and cottage cheese through a sieve. Mix with slightly beaten eggs and 1 cup of the sugar. Mix well and add lemon juice and vanilla. Stir in the melted butter, mixing well. Sift together flour, cornstarch and the remaining ½ cup sugar and add to the creamed mixture. Add the sour cream and mix. Pour batter into pan and bake for one hour. When done, shut off the oven and leave cake in oven until cold. Cake will rise while baking and then deflates slightly.

Note: For variation before pouring batter into pan you may line the bottom and sides of pan with a graham cracker crust mixture.

Bonnie Venn

Hawaiian Wedding Cake

1 yellow or white cake mix
1 cup milk
1 (4 ounce) package vanilla instant pudding
1 (8 ounce) package cream cheese
1 (20 ounce) can crushed pineapple, drained
1 (12 ounce) container Cool Whip
coconut (optional)

Mix and bake cake as directed on package in a 9x13 inch pan. Cool. Mix together milk, vanilla pudding, cream cheese and pineapple. Spread on cake. Top with Cool Whip and coconut if desired.

Note: This is a very moist cake.

Pat Korcuba

Jane's Best Chocolate Cake Ever

2 cups flour
2 cups sugar
pinch of salt
2 sticks margarine
1 cup water
5 heaping tablespoons cocoa
½ cup buttermilk
2 eggs, beaten
1 teaspoon vanilla
1 teaspoon baking soda

Preheat oven to 375 degrees. Use 13x9 inch jelly roll pan. In a saucepan, bring margarine, water and cocoa to a boil. In a large bowl, mix flour and sugar together. Pour chocolate mixture over the mixture. Mix well. In a separate bowl mix together buttermilk, egg, vanilla and baking soda. Pour into first mixture and mix well. Bake for 30-35 minutes.

Frosting:
1 stick butter
3 heaping tablespoons cocoa
5-6 tablespoons milk
1 pound powdered sugar
1 teaspoon vanilla

Combine frosting ingredients and spread on cake while still hot.

Jane Charlesworth

Hot Water Sponge Cake

4 eggs, separated
1½ cups sugar
2 tablespoons cold water
½ cup boiling water
2 cups cake flour, sifted
3 teaspoons baking powder
1 teaspoon vanilla
⅓ teaspoon salt

Preheat oven to 350 degrees. Bake in a greased and floured 9x13 inch pan or 2 layer pans. Beat egg whites until peaks form. Set aside. Blend egg yolks and sugar and add cold water. Beat until creamy. Add boiling water and mix. Add cake flour, baking powder, vanilla, and salt. Fold in beaten egg whites. Bake for 30-35 minutes. When cool, split in the middle and fill center with cream filling, lemon filling, or any other desired filling. Can be topped with frosting, whipped cream or sprinkles of powdered sugar.

Nora Spitler (caterer and grandmother of Pat Nichol)

Chocolate Czech Celestial Cake

1 cup powdered sugar
6 eggs, separated
¾ cup hazelnuts, ground (reserve some for garnish)
½ teaspoon vanilla extract
zest from ½ lemon
2 tablespoons melted chocolate
2 ounces shredded hard roll

Preheat oven to 350 degrees. Butter and flour two 9-inch pans. Beat egg whites until stiff and set aside. Whip egg yolks and powdered sugar together until light. Add hazelnuts, vanilla and lemon zest. Carefully add melted chocolate and bread crumbs. Fold in egg whites a little at a time. Bake for 30 minutes. Let cool before removing from pans.

Icing:
8 ounces butter
1 cup powdered sugar
3 tablespoons melted chocolate
1 egg yolk

Cream butter with sugar. Add egg yolk and melted chocolate and mix. Frost cake and use reserved ground hazelnuts to decorate sides of cake. Yields: 12 servings.

Note: Very rich.

Hannah Perutz

Danish Aeblekage (Apple Cake)

1 (24 ounce) jar cinnamon flavored applesauce
1 teaspoon vanilla
1 cup bread crumbs or graham cracker crumbs
3 ounces melted butter

Preheat oven to 425 degrees. Use buttered casserole dish. Mix vanilla with applesauce. Place a thin layer of crumbs in casserole dish. Cover with a thin layer of applesauce mixture. Repeat, alternating layers and ending with crumb layer. Pour melted butter over all. Bake 30 minutes. Yield: 6 servings.

Note: Cake may be served hot or cold. Top with whipped cream.

Janet Jespersen

Chocolate Sheet Cake

1 stick butter
½ cup Crisco
2 tablespoons cocoa
1 cup water
2 cups sugar
2 cups flour
1 teaspoon baking soda
½ cup buttermilk
2 eggs, slightly beaten
1 teaspoon cinnamon

Preheat oven to 400 degrees. Grease and flour 11x16 inch pan. Bring butter, Crisco, cocoa and water to a boil. Add flour and sugar, mix well. Add remaining cake ingredients. Mix until well blended (batter will be thin). Bake for 15-20 minutes. Remove cake from oven and cool for 5 minutes.

Topping:
1 stick butter
2 tablespoons cocoa
1 teaspoon cinnamon
6 tablespoons milk
1 teaspoon vanilla
1 (1 pound) box powdered sugar

Five minutes after cake is done, mix topping. Combine butter, cocoa, cinnamon and milk in a pan, bring just to a boil. Remove from heat, add vanilla and powdered sugar. Beat with a whisk until blended. Spread over cake. Cool, and cut into squares. Yield: 25-30 servings.

Note: Cake can be frozen for several weeks.

Catherine Quackenbush

Fudge Cake

2 cups unsifted cake flour
1¾ cups sugar
¾ cup cocoa
1 teaspoon baking powder
1 teaspoon baking soda
½ teaspoon salt
1 cup butter or margarine, very soft
¾ cup milk
½ cup water
2 eggs
2 teaspoons vanilla

Preheat oven to 350 degrees. Grease and lightly flour two 9-inch round cake pans. Measure flour, sugar, cocoa, baking powder, baking soda, and salt into large bowl. Mix on low for one minute. Add butter, milk, water, eggs and vanilla to mixture. Mix on medium speed for one minute. Scrape bowl. Beat on high for 3 minutes Pour into pans. Bake 30-35 minutes. Cool in pans for 5 minutes. Remove from pans and cool on racks. May be frosted with Butter Cream Frosting.

Butter Cream Frosting:
½ cup cocoa
⅓ cup boiling water
3 cups powdered sugar
2 egg yolks
1 teaspoon vanilla
½ cup butter, very soft

In bowl, dissolve cocoa with boiling water. Beat sugar into cocoa mixture. Add yolks and vanilla. Beat until fluffy. Place bowl into another bowl containing ice and water. Add butter in four additions beating after each addition. Beat until frosting is lighter in color and thick enough to spread. Frost cake and refrigerate to set frosting.

Alice Asadourian

Christmas Day Dessert

Yule Log:

¼ cup unsweetened cocoa
⅛ cup sifted flour
⅛ cup sifted cornstarch
4 eggs, separated
⅛ teaspoon salt
¼ cup sugar
½ teaspoon vanilla

Set oven at 400 degrees. Grease a shallow 11x16 inch pan. Line with wax paper; grease and lightly flour paper. Sift cocoa, flour and cornstarch together. Beat egg whites with salt until they hold soft peaks. Beat in sugar, a tablespoon at a time. Continue beating until egg whites are very firm. Break up yolks with a fork. Add vanilla. Fold ¼ of egg white mixture into yolks. Pour this on top of remaining whites. Sprinkle cocoa mixture on top. Fold together gently. Do not overmix. Spread batter evenly in pan. Bake for 10 minutes or until firm to a light touch. Do not overbake. Cool cake in pan.

Mocha Butter Cream:

1 cup soft butter
12 ounces semi-sweet chocolate, melted and cooled
2 egg yolks
4 tablespoons brandy or flavoring
2 teaspoons instant coffee powder
1 teaspoon vanilla extract

Cream butter until it is fluffy. Beat in remaining ingredients and mix thoroughly.

Whipped Cream Filling:

1 teaspoon unflavored gelatin
1½ tablespoons water
1 cup heavy cream, well chilled
2 tablespoons sugar
1 teaspoon vanilla extract

Combine gelatin and water in a small metal cup and stir. Place cup over low heat for a few minutes until gelatin dissolves and looks clear. Beat cream in a chilled bowl. Add gelatin mixture and sugar as cream thickens. Beat until stiff. Add vanilla. Refrigerate

(Continued on next page)

(Christmas Day Dessert, continued)

until needed. When cake is lukewarm, loosen sides, turn cake out on rack and peel off paper. Spread thinly with ⅔ of Mocha Butter Cream, and cover with Whipped Cream Filling. Using a serrated knife, cut off a two inch strip to make cake 9x16 inch. Roll cake into a 16 inch roll. Cut remaining strip into two 8x2 inch pieces. Roll each piece, spread a little butter cream on end, and attach to cake as branches. Chill for at least one hour. Spread entire log with remaining butter cream. Use a fork to make surface bark-like. Sprinkle with nuts.

Note: Cake may be frozen for up to 1 month.

Bonnie Venn

Pistachio Inside Outside Cake

1 (18.5 ounce) package white or yellow cake mix
1 package pistachio flavor instant pudding and pie filling
3 eggs
1 cup club soda
1 cup oil
½ cup chopped nuts

Preheat oven to 350 degrees. Grease and flour 10 inch bundt pan. Blend all cake ingredients in large mixing bowl and beat 2 minutes at medium speed. Bake for 50 minutes. Cool 15 minutes. Remove from pan and cool on rack.

Frosting:
1½ cups cold milk
1 package Dream Whip topping mix, whipped
1 package pistachio flavored instant pudding and pie filling

Make frosting by blending milk, whipped topping mix and instant pudding together. Split cake into 3 layers. Spread about 1 cup of frosting between layers and spoon the rest into center of cake. Chill. Garnish with chopped nuts.

Edie Schmidtchen
Town Clerk/Tax Collector, Town of Bedford, NH

Ice Box Cake

2 sponge cakes

Filling:
¾ cup sugar
1 tablespoon potato flour
3 eggs, separated
½ cup milk
½ cup butter
juice and grated rind of 1 lemon

Put sugar, and potato flour into a double boiler. Add egg yolks and milk and beat with egg beater. Boil, stirring constantly, until thickened. Cool. Add butter and juice and rind of lemon. Beat egg whites until stiff and fold into mixture. Split each sponge cake in two and cover each layer with filling. Frost cake with whipped cream.

Edie Schmidtchen
Town Clerk/Tax Collector, Town of Bedford, NH

Italian Rum Cake

1 cup chopped pecans or walnuts
1 package yellow cake mix
1 (3¼ ounce) package instant vanilla pudding
4 eggs
½ cup cold water
1 cup granulated sugar
½ cup Bacardi dark rum (80 proof)

Preheat oven to 350 degrees. Grease and flour 9x13 inch pan. Mix together all cake ingredients. Bake 50-60 minutes until done. Let cake cool.

Glaze:
¼ pound butter
½ cup water
1 cup granulated sugar
¼ cup Bacardi dark rum (80 proof)

Heat butter, water and sugar until sugar dissolves. Add rum to glaze mixture and pour over cake. Yield: 8 to 12 servings.

Madonna Lovett Repeta

Lemon Crunch Bundt Cake

1 package yellow cake mix
1 package lemon instant pudding and pie filling
½ cup oil
1 cup water
1 tablespoon grated lemon rind
4 eggs, beaten
½ cup flaked coconut
½ cup ground walnuts

Preheat oven to 350 degrees. Use heavily buttered 10 inch bundt pan. Put cake and pudding mix into a large bowl. Add oil, water and lemon rind and mix well. Stir in eggs and blend well. Sprinkle bottom and sides of bundt pan with coconut and nuts (most will settle to bottom). Pour batter into pan. Bake for 55 minutes, or until toothpick comes out clean. Cool completely.

Glaze:
½ cup lemon juice
2½ cups sifted powdered sugar

Combine glaze ingredients and mix well. Drizzle over cake. Yield: 12-16 servings.

Beth Squeglia

Milkless, Eggless and Butterless Cake

1 cup brown sugar
1⅓ cups water
⅓ cup oil
1 cup seedless raisins
½ teaspoon nutmeg
1 teaspoon cinnamon
2 cups flour
1 teaspoon baking soda
½ teaspoon salt
cherries and nuts, optional

Preheat oven to 350 degrees. Bake in a layer pan. Sift flour, baking soda, and salt together and set aside. In a saucepan mix brown sugar, water, oil, raisins, nutmeg and cinnamon, and boil for 3 minutes. When thoroughly cool, add flour mixture. May add cherries and nuts, if desired. Bake for 35 minutes.

Note: This recipe came from Canada where it was served with cream when the men were through cutting Christmas trees.

Claire Labonville

Lemon Poppy Seed Cake

½ pound butter, softened
2 cups granulated sugar
3 eggs
3 cups all purpose flour, sifted
½ teaspoon baking soda
½ teaspoon salt
1 cup buttermilk
2 tightly packed tablespoons grated lemon zest
2 tablespoons fresh lemon juice
3 tablespoons poppy seeds

Preheat oven to 325 degrees. Grease and lightly flour a 10 inch tube pan. Cream butter and sugar until light and fluffy. Beat in eggs, one at a time, blending well after each addition. Sift together flour, baking soda and salt. Stir dry ingredients into egg mixture alternately with buttermilk, beginning and ending with dry ingredients. Add lemon zest and juice. Pour batter into pan. Set pan on the middle rack of the oven and bake for 1 hour or until done. Cool cake in the pan on a rack for 10 minutes. Remove cake from pan and spread on icing at once, while cake is still hot.

Lemon Icing:
½ pound powdered sugar
½ stick butter, softened
1½ tightly packed tablespoons grated lemon zest
¼ cup fresh lemon juice

Cream sugar and butter thoroughly. Add lemon zest and juice. Spread on warm cake. Yield: 8-10 servings.

Martha Glasheen

Peanut Butter Chocolate Chip Cheesecake

1¼ cups graham cracker crumbs
⅓ cup sugar
¼ cup cocoa
⅓ cup butter or margarine, melted
3 (8 ounce) packages cream cheese, softened
1 (14 ounce) can sweetened condensed milk (not evaporated)
1 (10 ounce) package peanut butter chips, melted
4 eggs
2 teaspoons vanilla extract
1 cup mini semi-sweet chocolate chips

Preheat oven to 300 degrees. Use 9 inch springform pan. Stir together crumbs, sugar, cocoa and butter. Press onto bottom of pan. In large mixing bowl, beat cheese until fluffy. Gradually beat in sweetened condensed milk then melted peanut butter chips until smooth. Add eggs and vanilla. Beat well. Stir in mini chocolate chips. Pour over crust. Bake 55 to 65 minutes or until center is set. Cool. Refrigerate. Garnish as desired. Cover. Refrigerate leftover cheesecake. Yield: 12 servings.

Doris Guimont

Sour Cream Pound Cake

3 cups flour
¼ teaspoon salt
¼ teaspoon baking soda
3 cups sugar
1 cup butter (no substitute)
6 eggs
2 teaspoons vanilla extract
¼ teaspoon almond flavoring
Juice of half lemon
1 jigger Bourbon whiskey
1 cup sour cream

Preheat oven to 325 degrees. Grease and flour a tube pan (may also be divided into loaf pans.) Sift flour, salt, and baking soda together and set aside. Cream butter and sugar together. Add eggs, one at a time, beating vigorously after each addition. Add flavorings. Add flour and sour cream alternately. Mix and pour into pan. Bake for one hour and 10 minutes. Yield: 15-20 servings.

Note: Freezes nicely.

Catherine Quackenbush

Pumpkin Cheesecake

Crust:

¾ cup graham cracker crumbs
½ cup pecans, ground
2 tablespoons sugar
2 tablespoons brown sugar
¼ cup butter or margarine, melted

Preheat oven to 350 degrees. Use 9 inch springform pan. Combine crust ingredients, mixing well. Firmly press mixture into pan.

Filling:

¾ cup sugar
¾ cup canned pumpkin
3 egg yolks
1½ teaspoons ground cinnamon
½ teaspoon ground mace
½ teaspoon ground ginger
¼ teaspoon salt
3 (8 ounce) packages cream cheese, softened
¼ cup plus 2 tablespoons sugar
1 egg
1 egg yolk
2 tablespoons whipping cream
1 tablespoon cornstarch
½ teaspoon vanilla extract
½ teaspoon lemon extract
Whipped cream (optional)
Pecan halves (optional)

Combine ¾ cup sugar, pumpkin, 3 egg yolks, spices, and salt in a medium bowl. Mix well and set aside. Beat cream cheese with an electric mixer until light and fluffy, gradually adding sugar and mixing well. Add egg, egg yolk, and whipping cream, beating well. Add cornstarch and flavorings. Beat until smooth. Add pumpkin mixture, mixing well. Pour into crust and bake for 50-55 minutes. Center may be soft but will firm when chilled. Let cool on a wire rack. Chill thoroughly. Garnish with whipped cream and pecans, if desired.

Rose Marie Borelli

Pumpkin Roll Cake

¾ cup flour
1 teaspoon baking powder
2 teaspoons cinnamon
1 teaspoon ginger
½ teaspoon nutmeg
½ teaspoon salt
3 eggs
1 cup granulated sugar
⅔ cup pumpkin
1 teaspoon lemon juice
1 cup finely chopped walnuts

Preheat oven to 375 degrees. Grease well and flour a 15x10x1 inch pan. Mix together dry ingredients and set aside. Beat the eggs on high speed for 5 minutes, gradually beating in sugar. Stir in pumpkin and lemon juice. Fold dry ingredients into the pumpkin mixture. Spread in pan and top with walnuts. Bake for 15 minutes. Turn out onto a towel sprinkled with powdered sugar. Starting at the narrow end, roll towel and cake together and cool.

Filling:
1 cup powdered sugar
2 (3 ounce) packages cream cheese
4 tablespoons butter or margarine
½ teaspoon vanilla

Meanwhile, beat the powdered sugar, cream cheese, butter and vanilla until smooth. Unroll cake and towel and spread filling over the cake. Re-roll cake and chill. Yield: 8 or more servings.

Jeanne Thibault

Queen Elizabeth 25th Jubilee Cake

1 cup boiling water
1 cup dates
½ cup butter or margarine
1 cup sugar
1 egg, well beaten
½ cup chopped walnuts or pecans
1½ cups flour
1 teaspoon soda
1 teaspoon baking powder
1 teaspoon vanilla

Preheat oven to 350 degrees. Pour boiling water over chopped dates. Simmer 3 minutes. Cream together butter and sugar; add egg and vanilla. Combine with date mixture. Add nuts. Sift flour, soda, and baking powder. Add to date mixture, blending thoroughly. Bake 40-50 minutes.

Topping:
5 tablespoons brown sugar
2 tablespoons cream
3 tablespoons butter
¾ cup coconut

Mix together brown sugar, cream, butter and coconut. Boil 3 minutes. Cover cake and return to oven to brown. Caution: Make topping just before returning to the oven. It browns quickly.

Alice Asadourian

Cherry Sauce for 50

6 (1 pound) cans water packed red sour pitted cherries
3 cups water
½ cup cornstarch
2 cups sugar
1 teaspoon salt
2 teaspoons grated lemon rind
1 teaspoon almond flavoring
1 teaspoon red food coloring

Drain cherries, add water to cherry liquid. Combine cornstarch, sugar and salt in deep saucepan and mix well. Stir in liquid. Bring to a boil, stirring constantly. Boil 5 minutes. Remove from the heat. Add lemon rind, food coloring and drained cherries. Serve over cake or custard, hot or cold.

Cookies

The Currier Gallery of Art

The Currier Gallery of Art, considered one of the finest small museums in America today, is located in neighboring Manchester. This museum, open since 1929, is recognized internationally for the quality of its permanent collection of fine and decorative arts. On view are celebrated paintings and sculpture pieces by European and American masters, with works spanning the 13th - 20th centuries. Collections also include The Zimmerman House, a 1950 Usonian home designed by Frank Lloyd Wright, as well as glass, silver, pewter, and American furniture. The Currier also offers changing exhibitions, films, lectures and concerts. Many of our club members volunteer at this museum.

High Tea

beverages

Assorted teas

Sherry

tea sandwiches

Ham & Spinach Wheels

Chicken Salad Sandwiches

sweets

English Rich Scones

Cherry Cheese Tarts

Healthy Carrot Cake

English Trifle

Lace Cookies

COOKIES

Apple Squares

1¼ sticks butter
2 cups sugar
1 teaspoon vanilla
2 eggs
2 cups flour
1 teaspoon baking soda
1 teaspoon baking powder
½ teaspoon cinnamon
dash nutmeg
1 cup raisins, optional
1 cup chopped nuts
2 cups firm apples, peeled and cubed

Preheat oven to 350 degrees. Grease and flour 13x9 inch pan. Cream butter and sugar. Add vanilla. Add eggs, one at a time. Sift flour, baking soda, baking powder, cinnamon and nutmeg together. Add gradually to butter mixture. Add apples, raisins and nuts. Mix by hand. Spoon mixture into pan, spreading evenly. Bake 25-35 minutes. Cool slightly before cutting into squares.

Bess Morrison

Apricot Squares

3 sticks of sweet butter, melted
1 egg
1 cup powdered sugar
3½ cups flour
1 (18 ounce) jar Smucker's apricot preserves

Preheat oven to 350 degrees. Bake in 8½x12½ inch Pyrex dish. Mix together butter, egg, sugar, and flour until dough sticks together. Spread ¾ of dough in dish, bringing up four sides ½ inch. Spread apricot preserves on top of dough. Drop remaining dough as slivered pieces on top of jam. Cook over 30 minutes. Broil a few minutes on top for color. Cool and cut into squares.

Sharlene Genest

Chocolate Squares

graham crackers
2 sticks butter
1 cup brown sugar
1 cup chopped nuts
1 cup chocolate bits

Preheat oven to 350 degrees. Grease and flour 17½x11½ inch shallow pan. Line pan with graham crackers. Bring to boil 2 sticks of butter and add 1 cup brown sugar. Remove from heat and add 1 cup chopped nuts. Pour over crackers and sprinkle on chocolate bits. Bake for 10-15 minutes. Cool 1 hour.

Sheila Roberge
New Hampshire State Senator, District 9

Cranberry Nut Squares

½ cup oil
1 cup granulated sugar
2 eggs
½ teaspoon vanilla
1 cup flour
½ teaspoon baking powder
½ teaspoon salt
½ cup chopped nuts
½ cut-up cranberries

Preheat oven to 375 degrees. Grease and flour 8 inch square pan. Stir together oil, sugar, eggs and vanilla. Sift together flour, baking powder and salt and add to mixture. Fold in nuts and cranberries. Pour into prepared pan and bake for 25 minutes. Yield: 9 servings.

Janet Jespersen

Brownies

½ cup flour
1 stick Fleishman's margarine (no other kind will do)
2 (1 ounce) squares bitter-sweet chocolate, melted
½ teaspoon vanilla
2 eggs
1 cup sugar
½ teaspoon salt
nuts, amount to your liking
chocolate chips, amount to your liking

Preheat oven to 350 degrees. Stir first seven ingredients into a pan. Sprinkle nuts and chocolate chips on top. Bake for 20-30 minutes.

Alice Asadourian

Creme de Menthe Bars

1 cup sugar
1½ sticks butter plus 6 tablespoons
4 eggs
1 cup flour
½ teaspoon salt
1 (16 ounce) can Hershey's chocolate syrup
1 teaspoon vanilla
2 cups powdered sugar
4 tablespoons green creme de menthe
1 cup chocolate chips

Preheat oven to 350 degrees. Grease and flour 13x9 inch pan. Cream sugar with ½ cup butter. Add eggs, flour, salt. Then add chocolate syrup and vanilla. Bake for 35 minutes or until done. Cool cake completely. Cream powdered sugar with 1 stick of butter and creme de menthe. Spread over cooled cake and refrigerate. Melt 6 tablespoons butter and 1 cup chocolate chips and spread over cooled cake. Chill before serving.

Madonna Lovett Repeta

Old Fashioned Raisin Bars

1 cup seedless raisins
1 cup water
½ cup shortening or salad oil
1 cup sugar
1 slightly beaten egg
1¾ cups sifted flour
½ teaspoon salt
1 teaspoon soda
1 teaspoon cinnamon
1 teaspoon nutmeg
1 teaspoon allspice
½ teaspoon cloves
½ cup chopped nuts

Preheat oven to 375 degrees. Grease 13x9x2 inch pan. Combine raisins and water in a pan and bring to a boil. Remove from heat and stir in shortening or salad oil. Cool to lukewarm. Stir in sugar and egg. Sift together the dry ingredients and beat into the raisin mixture. Stir in the nuts. Pour into pan and bake for 20 minutes or until done. Cool. Cut into bars and dust with powdered sugar. Yield: 24 bars.

Elisabeth P. Place

Pecan Pie Squares

Crust:
3 cups flour
¼ cup plus 2 tablespoons sugar
¾ cup softened margarine
¾ teaspoon salt

Preheat oven to 350 degrees. Grease 10x15 inch jelly roll pan. Beat crust ingredients until crumbly. Mixture will be dry. Pat into pan and bake until light golden brown, approximately 20 minutes.

Filling:
4 eggs, slightly beaten
1½ cups sugar
1½ cups Karo syrup, light or dark
3 tablespoons melted margarine
1½ teaspoons vanilla extract
2½ cups chopped pecans or walnuts

To slightly beaten eggs add sugar, Karo syrup, melted margarine and vanilla extract. When well blended, mix in nuts. Pour filling over baked layer and bake 25 minutes or until set. Cool before cutting into 1½ inch squares. Yield: 70 squares.

Doris Guimont

Toffee Bars

½ pound sweet butter
1 cup light brown sugar
1 egg yolk
2 cups all-purpose flour
1 teaspoon vanilla extract
12 ounces semi-sweet chocolate chips
1 cup walnuts or pecans, coarsely chopped

Preheat oven to 350 degrees. Grease a 9x12 inch baking pan. Cream butter and sugar. Add egg yolk, beating well. Sift in flour, mixing well, then stir in vanilla. Spread batter in prepared pan. Bake for 25 minutes. Cover with chocolate chips and return to oven for 3-4 minutes. Remove from oven and spread melted chocolate evenly. Sprinkle with nuts. Cool completely before cutting. Yield: about 30 bars.

Beth Squeglia

Toll House Marble Squares

½ cup soft butter
6 tablespoons granulated sugar
6 tablespoons brown sugar
½ teaspoon vanilla
¼ teaspoon water
1 egg
1 cup plus 2 tablespoons sifted flour
½ teaspoon baking soda
½ teaspoon salt
½ cup chopped nuts
1 cup chocolate morsels

Preheat oven to 375 degrees. Grease and flour 13x9x2 inch pan. Beat butter, sugars, vanilla extract and water until creamy. Beat in egg. Sift together and mix in the flour, baking soda, and salt. Stir in the nuts. Spread in pan. Sprinkle with the chocolate morsels. Bake for about one minute. Remove pan from oven and run knife through dough to marbleize. Bake 12-14 minutes more. Yield: 24 squares.

Elisabeth P. Place

Applesauce Cookies

2 cups flour
¼ teaspoon salt
¼ teaspoon cloves
1 teaspoon cinnamon
1 teaspoon soda
½ cup shortening
¾ cup sugar
1 egg
1 cup applesauce
½ cup raisins
½ cup walnuts or pecans, if desired

Preheat oven to 350 degrees. Use lightly greased cookie sheet. Sift dry ingredients together and set aside. Cream together shortening and sugar. Beat in the egg. Stir in the applesauce. Add dry ingredients and mix well. Add raisins and walnuts or pecans if desired. Drop by teaspoonfuls onto cookie sheets. Bake 12-15 minutes.

Note: This easy recipe makes a soft moist cookie which keeps well and freezes well.

Donna Powell

Walnut Raspberry Brownies

3 (1 ounce) squares unsweetened chocolate
½ cup shortening
3 eggs
1½ cups sugar
1½ teaspoons vanilla extract
¼ teaspoon salt
1 cup flour
1½ cups chopped walnuts
⅓ cup raspberry jam

Preheat oven to 325 degrees. Grease and flour 8 or 9 inch pan. Melt chocolate with shortening over warm water. Blend together eggs, sugar, vanilla and salt. Stir in chocolate mixture along with the flour. Fold in walnuts. Bake for 40 minutes. Spoon jam over the hot brownies. Cool.

Glaze:
1 (1 ounce) square unsweetened chocolate
2 tablespoons butter
2 tablespoons light corn syrup
1 cup powdered sugar
1 tablespoon milk
1 teaspoon vanilla extract

Melt the unsweetened chocolate and blend in the butter and corn syrup. Stir in powdered sugar, milk and vanilla. Spread over brownies and cut in squares. Yield: 12.

Doris Guimont

Anise Slices

8 eggs
2 cups sugar
1½ cups cooking oil
1 teaspoon anise oil or 2 teaspoons anise extract
2 tablespoons baking powder
4 cups flour

Bake at 350 degrees. Use 3-4 greased loaf pans and cookie sheets. Mix ingredients in the above order. Pour 1 inch layers in loaf pans. Bake for 20 minutes. Cool. Cut in slices about 1 inch thick. Place on greased cookie sheets and bake about 10 minutes. Remove from oven. Turn cookies and bake an additional 10 minutes.

Note: These cookies keep up to 3 weeks in a closed container.

Dorothy Czopek

Brown Sugar Cookies

2 cups light brown sugar (packed)
1 cup margarine
2 eggs
3 cups sifted all-purpose flour
1 teaspoon salt
1 teaspoon baking soda
1 cup chopped walnuts

Bake at 350 degrees on ungreased cookie sheet. Cream shortening and sugar together. Add eggs and mix. Sift dry ingredients together and add to creamed mixture; add nuts. Form dough into rolls. Cover with wax paper and chill overnight or put in freezer until firm. Slice dough ¼ inch thick and place on ungreased cookie sheet (cookies will spread when baking). Bake 10-12 minutes until medium brown. Yield: 6 dozen or more.

Note: Dough will keep a long time in freezer if well wrapped. Shorter rolls are handy if freezing, as a small number can be baked as needed. Bake still frozen.

Margaret G. Comiskey

Eleanor's Casserole Cookies

2 eggs
1 cup sugar
1 cup dates, chopped
1 cup coconut
1 cup walnuts, chopped
1 teaspoon vanilla
¼ teaspoon almond extract
15 cherries for decoration

Preheat oven to 350 degrees. Beat eggs in a 2 quart buttered casserole dish. Add sugar and mix well. Add dates, coconut, walnuts, vanilla and almond extract, mixing well. Bake mixture 25-30 minutes, stirring occasionally. Let cool. Form into walnut size balls and roll in sugar. Flatten, add ½ cherry for decoration. Yield: about 30 cookies.

Joan Hetland

Cheese Cake Cookies

1 cup butter or margarine
1 cup brown sugar
3 cups flour
1½ cups chopped walnuts

Preheat oven to 350 degrees. Use jelly roll pan. Mix first four ingredients for pie dough. Separate dough into 2 parts, reserving 3 cups for topping. Pat the rest on the bottom of the pan. Bake for 10 minutes.

Filling:
1 cup sugar
3 eggs
6 tablespoons milk
1 teaspoon vanilla
¼ cup flour
3 (8 ounce) packages cream cheese, softened
6 tablespoons lemon juice
½ cup sour cream

For filling, cream the sugar and cream cheese. Add eggs, milk, juice and vanilla. Beat well. Fold in sour cream and flour. Pour over baked crust. Sprinkle saved flour mixture over the top. Bake for 25-30 minutes. Cool. Cut into squares. Refrigerate.

Note: Freezes well.

Marge McNamee

Chocolate Pinwheel Cookies

½ cup shortening
½ cup brown sugar
½ cup granulated sugar
½ cup peanut butter
1 egg
1¼ cups flour
½ teaspoon baking powder
½ teaspoon salt
1 (12 ounce) package chocolate chips, melted on low heat

Preheat oven to 375 degrees. Use greased cookie sheets. Mix flour, baking powder, salt and set aside. Cream shortening and sugar. Add peanut butter and egg. Mix well. Add flour mixture and mix well. Divide dough into 2 parts. Roll out into oblong sheets. Spread melted chocolate onto cookie dough and roll up as for a jelly roll. Makes two rolls. Chill in refrigerator 15-20 minutes. Slice into ¼ inch pieces and bake for 10-12 minutes.

Kay Warner

Gram's Cookies

2 cups sugar
1 cup shortening
6 eggs
1 tablespoon flavoring (lemon, vanilla, almond)
6 cups flour
6 teaspoons baking powder

Bake at 350 degrees. Cream sugar and shortening, add eggs then flavoring. Sift flour and baking powder and add to egg mixture to make soft dough. Remove dough to pastry board and fold in small amounts of flour until dough can be rolled and handled easily (too much flour will make hard cookies). Roll dough into ½ inch strips to make letters or ¼ inch thick to use cookies cutters. Make any shaped cookies, top with colored sugars if desired and use your imagination!

Using the same ingredients you can make Cinnamon Cookies. On a piece of floured waxed paper, take piece of dough and roll out to ¼ inch thick rectangular shape. Cover dough with sugar and sprinkle cinnamon all over it. If you want to add walnuts, sprinkle lightly on dough (crush nuts first). Take up edge of waxed paper to help start roll. Cut in ¼x½ inch slices and bake in oven for 10 minutes until lightly browned.

Dorothy Czopek

Lace Cookies

1 cup uncooked quick cooking oatmeal
1 cup sugar
1 stick margarine
2 heaping tablespoons flour
¼ teaspoon salt
¼ teaspoon baking powder
1 egg, beaten
1 teaspoon almond extract

Preheat oven to 325 degrees. Bake on greased heavy duty aluminum foil. Melt margarine in pan. Remove from heat and add remaining ingredients. Drop by ½ teaspoonfuls on foil 4 inches apart (they spread a lot). Bake 6 minutes. Cool 1 minute before removing from foil.

Janis Galeucia

My Mother's Favorite Italian Cookies (Biscotti)

6 eggs
1 cup sugar
5 cups flour
9 teaspoons baking powder
½ cup oil
2 teaspoons anise oil

Preheat oven to 375 degrees. Use a greased cookie sheet. Mix eggs with sugar, one at a time. Add to this mixture the rest of the ingredients and mix. If dough is sticky, add more flour. Pick up small amounts of dough and roll thin as a pencil. Can make in rounds, like a wreath, or twists. Bake 10-12 minutes. Cool.

Frosting:
powdered sugar
water
colored sprinkles

Frost and decorate.

Natalie Granchelli

Kisses From The Oven

2 egg whites
pinch of salt
½ teaspoon vinegar
½ teaspoon vanilla
½ cup light brown sugar
1 (6 ounce) package semi-sweet chocolate bits, melted and slightly cooled
walnuts, finely chopped

Preheat oven to 350 degrees. Line a cookie sheet with parchment paper. Beat egg whites with salt, vinegar and vanilla until soft peaks form. Gradually add sugar and beat until mixture forms stiff peaks. Fold in chocolate bits. Pipe in little balls onto cookie sheet. Sprinkle generously with walnuts and small amount of brown sugar. Bake for 10 minutes. Cool and store in a tight fitting container.

Claire Labonville

Koulourakia (Greek Butter Cookies)

5 cups flour
2 teaspoons baking powder
½ teaspoon baking soda
½ pound butter
1½ cups sugar
3 eggs
½ cup orange juice
1 tablespoon vanilla
1 egg (additional for basting)
1 tablespoon milk

Bake at 400 degrees on buttered cookie sheets. Sift flour with baking powder and baking soda three times and set aside. Cream butter, adding sugar gradually. Add 3 eggs, one egg at a time, alternately with orange juice. Add flour mixture gradually. Add vanilla. Shape into 3½ inch finger shaped forms. Dough should be soft. Place on cookie sheet. Brush with mixture of one egg beaten with one tablespoon milk. Sprinkle with sesame seeds. Bake 15-20 minutes.

Doris Guimont

Crisp Peanut Butter Balls

1 (18 ounce) jar peanut butter
3 cups Rice Krispies cereal
2¼ cups powdered sugar, sifted
½ cup margarine, softened
1 (12 ounce) package chocolate chips
½ cake paraffin wax

Mix peanut butter, cereal, sugar, and margarine together with hands and form into 1 inch balls. Melt chocolate chips and paraffin wax in top of double boiler over boiling water. Dip formed balls into melted chocolate. Place on wax paper on cookie sheet. Cool. Pack in tin box. No refrigeration needed.

Note: Won't last long!

Margaret K. Rooney

Macaroon Kiss Cookies

⅓ cup butter or margarine, softened
1 (3 ounce) package cream cheese, softened
¾ cup sugar
1 egg yolk
2 teaspoons almond extract
2 teaspoons orange juice
1¼ cups unsifted all-purpose flour
2 teaspoons baking powder
¼ teaspoon salt
5 cups (14-ounce package) flaked coconut
54 Hershey's Kisses chocolates (9-ounce package), unwrapped

Preheat oven to 350 degrees. Use an ungreased cookie sheets. Cream butter, cream cheese and sugar in large mixer bowl until light and fluffy. Add egg yolk, almond extract and orange juice; beat well. Combine flour, baking powder and salt; gradually add to creamed mixture. Stir in 3 cups of the coconut. Cover tightly; chill 1 hour or until firm enough to handle. Shape dough into 1 inch balls. Roll in remaining coconut. Place on cookie sheets and bake for 10-12 minutes or until lightly browned. Remove from oven; immediately press unwrapped Kiss on top of each cookie. Cool 1 minute. Carefully remove from cookie sheets. Cool completely on wire rack. Yield: about 4½ dozen cookies.

Elisabeth Place

Kate Hepburn Brownies

2 squares unsweetened chocolate
¼ pound butter
1 cup granulated sugar
2 eggs
½ teaspoon vanilla
1 cup chopped walnuts
¼ cup all-purpose flour
¼ teaspoon salt

Preheat oven to 325 degrees. Grease well and flour 8 inch square pan. Melt unsweetened chocolate and butter over very low heat. Remove from heat and stir in granulated sugar. Beat in the eggs and vanilla. Quickly stir in chopped walnuts, flour and salt. Spread batter in pan and bake for 40-45 minutes. Cool on a rack and cut into squares. Yield: 12 squares.

Bonnie Venn

Desserts

Sheraton Tara Wayfarer Inn

The Sheraton Tara Wayfarer Inn in Bedford, NH is located on the historic site of John Goffe's Grist Mill. The Wayfarer is the largest motel, not only in Bedford, but in the surrounding area. Many of the 194 guest rooms and 10 meeting and conference rooms overlook the picturesque water fall, mill pond and covered bridge. When building began in 1961, John Goffe's mill was left intact and opened as a gift shop. A covered bridge was built across the brook to connect the motel and the parking lot. The old falls of Bowman's Brook are accentuated by floodlights at night. It was built by the Dunfey family, which consisted of eight boys and four girls. The Wayfarer won the Lumber Association of New England's award for unusual use of wood in construction and design.

Lighter Fare

soup

Basil Bean Soup

salad

Green Salad with Poppyseed Dressing

entrée

Chicken Tarragon with Asparagus

Angel Hair Pasta

dessert

Rum Mousse

DESSERTS

Apple Crunch

½ cup sugar
1 teaspoon cinnamon
8-9 large apples, sliced
1 cup flour
¾ cup sugar
1 teaspoon baking powder
¾ teaspoon salt
1 egg
⅓ cup butter melted
chopped walnuts (optional)

Preheat oven to 350 degrees. Grease and flour 8x8 or 11x7 inch pan. Mix together ½ cup sugar and cinnamon. Sprinkle over sliced apples. In another bowl mix together flour, cup sugar, baking powder and salt. Beat egg. Pour into flour mixture and mix until crumbly. Place apples in baking pan and spread flour mixture evenly over the apples. Pour melted butter evenly over all and sprinkle with more cinnamon. Chopped walnuts can be spread on top if desired. Bake for about 35 minutes.

Jackie Lavoie

Baked Devils Float

1 cup flour
½ teaspoon salt
1 teaspoon baking powder
3 tablespoons cocoa
1 cup sugar
1½ cups water
12 marshmallows, quartered (or mini marshmallows)
2 tablespoons shortening
1 teaspoon vanilla
½ cup milk
½ cup chopped walnuts

Preheat oven to 350 degrees. Use a 9 inch square baking pan. Sift flour with salt, baking powder and cocoa and set aside. Cook ½ cup sugar with water for 5 minutes and pour into baking pan. Top with marshmallows (if using mini marshmallows, cover water with them). In mixing bowl, cream shortening with remaining ½ cup sugar and add vanilla. Add dry ingredients, alternately with milk. Add nuts. Drop batter from spoon over marshmallow and sugar mixture. Bake for 45 minutes. Serve with whipped cream or vanilla ice cream.

Mary Dambach

Apple Flan

Applesauce:

8 tart apples
water (enough to keep apples from burning)
½ cup sugar
¼ teaspoon nutmeg
¼ teaspoon cinnamon

Peel apples and slice thin. Place in saucepan and add water. Bring to boil, lower heat and simmer covered for 20 minutes, or until soft. Add sugar and spices, and mix.

Flan:

1 uncooked pie crust
3 cups homemade applesauce
4 -5 cooking apples, Macintosh or Cortlands, peeled and sliced thin
⅔ cup apricot jam
⅓ cup warm water

Preheat oven to 425 degrees. Use a 12 inch flan pan. Spread the pie crust in pan and cover with applesauce. Lay sliced apples in overlapping concentric circles over entire surface. Mix apricot jam with warm water and pour over the top of apples. Bake 30 minutes. Serve with vanilla ice cream.

Evelyn Letendre
New Hampshire State Representative

Pineapple Marshmallow Cream

1 (8½ ounce) can crushed pineapple
1 tablespoon lemon juice
2 cups miniature marshmallows
½ cup whipping cream, whipped

Combine crushed pineapple, lemon juice, and marshmallows in saucepan. Place over low heat, stirring until marshmallows are dissolved. Remove from heat and cool. When partially set, fold in whipped cream. Spoon into sherbet dishes and chill 2 hours or overnight. Yield: 4 servings.

Mrs. Richard J. McDonald
(wife of founder of McDonald's)

Apple Pizza

2 cups flour
7 to 8 tablespoons water
⅔ cup shortening
1 teaspoon salt
7 Macintosh apples, peeled, sliced and cut in small pieces
½ cup sugar
1 teaspoon cinnamon
¼ teaspoon nutmeg

Preheat oven to 375 degrees. Use a pizza pan. Mix flour, water, shortening and salt to make dough. Spread on pan, making a ridge around edge. Cover with apples. Mix sugar, cinnamon and nutmeg and sprinkle over apples.

Topping:
¾ cup flour
½ cup margarine
½ cup sugar

Combine topping ingredients and top with this mixture. Bake 35-40 minutes.

Frosting:
½ cup powdered sugar
butter
milk

Combine powdered sugar with enough butter and milk to make a light frosting and drizzle on pizza.

Marsha Lee, friend of Bonnie Venn

Anne's Viennese Apple Cobbler

1 sheet of Pepperidge Farm frozen puff pastry
7 medium-sized cooking apples (Cortland, Pippin or Granny Smith)
1-2 ounces dark rum (Meyers rum)
¾ cup sugar
1 tablespoon ground cinnamon
zest and juice of 1 large lemon
1 cup plain white bread crumbs
1 cup golden raisins
½ cup pecans
egg wash: 1 egg beaten with 1 teaspoon water

Thaw pastry 20 minutes. Preheat oven to 350 degrees. Peel, core and thinly slice the apples. Mix them with rum, sugar, cinnamon, lemon zest and juice. Set aside. Butter a 9x13 inch Pyrex baking dish. On a flour surface roll pastry sheet to rectangular shape to fit baking dish and set aside. Pour a layer of apple mixture in baking dish. Sprinkle white bread crumbs, raisins and pecans. Repeat the layer. Normally mixture makes two layers. Cover the apple mixture with pastry sheet. If desired, decorate top with pastry scraps. Brush with egg wash. Bake until crust is a medium-dark golden brown, about 40-45 minutes. Serve warm. This dessert can be topped with non-fat vanilla frozen yogurt or vanilla ice cream. Yield: 12-15 servings.

Anne C. Hoffman

Baklava (Greek Pastry)

2 packages frozen patty shells, thawed in refrigerator
3 cups walnuts, finely chopped
1 cup honey, warmed

Preheat oven to 425 degrees. Line 8 inch square pan with foil; grease lightly. Stack 3 thawed patty shells, one atop the other, on lightly floured surface. Roll out into 9 inch square. With a sharp knife, trim down to 8½ inch square. Place in bottom of prepared pan. Sprinkle with 1 cup chopped nuts and dribble with ¼ cup honey. Repeat process three times making the top layer plain pastry. Mark pastry into diamond pattern with tip of sharp knife. Bake 20-25 minutes. Cool slightly in pan. Brush surface with last of warm honey. Remove from pan and peel away foil.

Doris Guimont

Blueberry Buckle

Crumb Topping:
1 cup sugar
⅔ cup flour
1 teaspoon cinnamon
½ cup butter, softened

Preheat oven to 375 degrees. Grease and flour a 13x9x2 inch pan. Prepare crumb topping by blending dry ingredients together. Mix in butter with a fork until a crumbly mixture forms. Set aside.

Cake:
4 cups flour
4 teaspoons baking powder
1 teaspoon salt
1½ cups sugar
½ cup shortening
2 eggs
1¼ cups milk
1 quart fresh blueberries, washed and drained

Sift together flour, baking powder and salt. Set aside. Using medium speed on electric mixer, mix together sugar, shortening and eggs. Stir in milk. Using low speed on electric mixer, add flour mixture. Gently stir in blueberries being careful not to smash the berries. Spread topping over cake. Bake for 45-50 minutes.

Pat Lauer

Cherry Berries in the Snow

Meringue layer:
6 egg whites
½ teaspoon cream of tartar
¼ teaspoon salt
1½ cups sugar

Day 1: Preheat oven to 275 degrees. Lightly grease 13x9 inch pan. Beat egg whites, cream of tartar and salt. Gradually add 1½ cups sugar. Beat 15 minutes or until stiff. Spread in the pan. Bake 1 hour. Turn off oven and leave there overnight.

Filling:
6 ounces cream cheese
½ cup sugar
1 teaspoon vanilla
2 cups whipped cream cheese
2 cups miniature marshmallows

Day 2: Mix together cream cheese, sugar and vanilla. Fold in whipped cream cheese. Add marshmallows. Spread on top of the meringue and refrigerate 12 hours.

Topping:
1 (1 pound 5 ounce) can cherry pie filling
1 tablespoon lemon juice
1 (16 ounce) box frozen strawberries

Cut into squares and top with cherry pie filling, lemon juice and frozen strawberries. Yield: 18 or more servings.

Note: Prepare 2 days ahead.

Margaret K. Rooney

Cherry Dessert

¼ pound margarine
30 single saltines
nuts, optional
4 egg whites
dash of salt
½ teaspoon vanilla
1 cup sugar
1 can cherry pie filling
1 (12 ounce) container Cool Whip

Preheat oven to 350 degrees. Use a 9x13 inch pan. Melt margarine in baking pan. Crush saltines into crumbs. Add nuts, if desired, to crumbs and spread crumbs in pan. Beat egg whites until stiff. Add salt and vanilla and blend in sugar. Spread mixture over cracker crumbs. Bake for 10 minutes or until light brown. Cool. Spread with cherry pie filling. Cover with Cool Whip. Yield: 12 servings.

Fran Wiggin

Chocolate Truffle with Raspberry Sauce

Truffle:
2 cups heavy cream, divided
3 egg yolks, slightly beaten
2 (8 ounce) packages semi-sweet chocolate
½ cup Karo syrup
½ cup butter
¼ cup confectioners sugar
1 teaspoon vanilla

Line a loaf pan with plastic wrap. Mix ½ cup cream and egg yolks together. In a saucepan combine chocolate, Karo syrup and butter until melted. Add egg mixture. Stir constantly over medium heat about 3 minutes. Cool to room temperature. Beat remaining cream, sugar and vanilla until soft peaks form. Fold into chocolate mixture until no streaks remain. Pour into loaf pan and refrigerate overnight. Cut in thin slices and serve with raspberry sauce.

Raspberry Sauce:
10 ounces thawed raspberries
½ cup Karo syrup

In a blender, puree raspberries. Stir in Karo syrup. Strain if desired. Yield: 12-14 servings.

Note: A very rich treat.

Cathy Sullivan

Mother's Chocolate Bread Pudding

1 quart milk, scalded
2 (1 ounce) squares unsweetened chocolate
¾ standard size loaf white bread, cut into large cubes
¼ cup sugar
½ teaspoon salt
2 eggs, beaten
1 teaspoon vanilla
¼ teaspoon nutmeg
3 tablespoons butter, melted

Preheat oven to 350 degrees. Use a large greased baking dish. Heat milk to scalding in a large pan and melt the chocolate in the milk. Beat until well blended. Add the bread to the milk mixture. Mix sugar and salt with eggs. Gradually stir this egg mixture into bread mixture. Add vanilla, nutmeg and butter, stirring well. Pour into baking dish. Set the dish in a pan filled to about ¼ inch with warm water. Bake for 75 minutes. Yield: 12 servings.

Sauce:
powdered sugar
1 egg, well beaten
1 teaspoon vanilla
½ pint heavy cream, whipped medium thick

To well beaten egg, add as much powdered sugar as needed to make it thick and smooth. Add vanilla and whipped cream, stirring until well blended. Double recipe for more than four servings.

Christina Barley
Pat Baldwin

Chocolate Mousse

6 eggs, separated
6 ounces semi-sweet chocolate
1 teaspoon vanilla
heavy cream
walnuts or pecans

Use 8 glasses. Separate eggs and beat whites until stiff. Set aside. Melt chocolate. Add vanilla to egg yolks and beat well. Combine yolks and chocolate. Combine beaten egg whites carefully with chocolate mixture. Whip cream and fold in. Put a few nuts in the bottom of glasses, spoon on the mousse.

Bonnie Venn

Chocolate Mousse

1½ pints (3 cups) whipping cream
8 ounces semi-sweet chocolate (or 12 ounces white chocolate)
¾ cup egg yolks
1 cup sugar
water (enough to dissolve sugar)
2 ounces rum (or Grand Marnier)

Whip cream and set aside. Melt chocolate and set aside. With mixer on high, whip egg yolks with a little sugar until fluffy. Meanwhile, boil sugar and water to 249 degrees (medium ball stage). Slowly pour sugar mixture into whipped yolks in a steady stream while whipping at medium speed. When mixture has cooled to body temperature, mix in by hand, the liquor, then the chocolate, and lastly the cream. Pour into glasses and refrigerate.

Sheila Roberge
New Hampshire State Senator, District 9

Four Layer Dessert

1 stick margarine
1 cup flour
1 cup pecans, chopped
1 (8 ounce) package cream cheese, softened
1 cup powdered sugar
1 (12 ounce) container Cool Whip
2 packages pistachio instant pudding
3 cups cold milk
coconut

Bake at 350 degrees in 9x13 inch Pyrex dish. Mix together margarine, flour, and pecans. Put in dish and bake for 30-25 minutes. Cool. Mix cream cheese, powdered sugar, and ½ of Cool Whip and spread on cooled crust. (May use food coloring with this layer, such as green for Christmas, yellow for Easter). Mix pudding with milk and spread over the other layers. Spread remaining ½ container of Cool Whip (also tinted) over all. Refrigerate. Top with coconut.

Sharlene Genest

Chocolate Pears

1 cup sugar
4 cups water
juice of 1 lemon
2 cinnamon sticks
4 whole cloves
6 firm, ripe pears with stems
6 ounces semi-sweet chocolate squares
4 tablespoons sweet butter
2 teaspoons creme de menthe or Grand Marnier
fresh mint leaves
whipped cream with liqueur

Dissolve sugar in water. Add lemon juice and spices. Bring to a boil. Peel pears leaving stems intact and cut a slice off the bottom so they will stand upright. Poach pears in gently boiling syrup for 20-40 minutes, or until tender. Cool pears in syrup and chill overnight. In a double boiler, melt the chocolate. Add butter and liqueur and stir over low flame until mixture is smooth. Remove the pears from syrup and dry carefully with paper towels. Dip pears in the chocolate until evenly coated. Lift pears to drain off excess chocolate. Arrange on serving dish or individual dishes and decorate with mint leaves and a dab of whipped cream.

Note: May be made 24 hours in advance. Very showy dessert.

Bonnie Venn

Heath Bar Chocolate Trifle

1 package chocolate cake mix
⅔ cup Kahlua
2 (4 ounce) packages instant chocolate pudding
2 containers Cool Whip, or 1 pint sweetened whipped cream
6 Heath bars, crushed

Bake as directed on cake package. Use 13x9 inch pan. Mix cake as directed on package and bake. Cool. Crumble cake into 1 inch chunks. Put half of chunks into a clear glass serving bowl. Sprinkle with half the Kahlua. Make pudding as directed on package. Cover cake in bowl with ½ of the pudding. Add half the Cool Whip (or whipped cream). Sprinkle with half the Heath bars. Repeat all layers. Yield: serves 10.

Priscilla Van Wagner

Cran-Cherry Crisp

Fruit Mixture:
1 (16 ounce) can whole berry cranberry sauce
1 (16 ounce) can pitted tart red cherries, drained
½ teaspoon almond extract
⅓ cup sugar
1 tablespoon cornstarch

Preheat oven to 350 degrees. In ungreased 8 inch square baking dish, combine cranberry sauce, cherries and extract. Mix well. In small bowl, combine sugar and cornstarch, mixing well. Stir into fruit.

Topping:
½ cup all purpose flour
½ cup quick-cooking rolled oats
⅓ cup firmly packed brown sugar
¼ teaspoon nutmeg
¼ cup margarine or butter
½ cup chopped almonds

Lightly spoon flour into measuring cup. In medium bowl, combine flour, oats, brown sugar and nutmeg. Using pastry blender or fork, cut in margarine until mixture is crumbly. Stir in almonds. Sprinkle topping evenly over fruit. Bake 30-35 minutes or until topping is golden brown. Serve warm with whipped cream or ice cream, if desired. Yield: 9 servings.

Catherine Liotta

English Trifle

Lady Fingers
sherry or fruit juice
jam or jelly
jello
fruit
cream
almonds
1 package Bird's English Custard mix
glacé cherries

Use a large glass bowl. Split Lady Fingers, spread with jam or jelly and put in bottom of bowl. Pour sherry or fruit juice over Lady Fingers, soaking them. Place fruit on top. Make jello and pour over fruit. Let set. Make custard as directed on package. Cool and pour over jello. Put a few chopped almonds on top of custard. Cool in refrigerator. When cool and ready to serve, whip cream and decorate top with glacé cherries.

Caroline Williams

English Trifle

1 package strawberry jello
1 package raspberry jello
1 package instant vanilla pudding
1 large angel cake
1 cup orange juice
1 package frozen strawberries, thawed
1 package frozen raspberries, thawed
1 cup walnuts, chopped
2 bananas, sliced
1 regular container Cool Whip

Prepare both packages of jello as directed on packages in large bowl. Refrigerate for about 20 minutes to cool. Prepare instant pudding as directed on the package. Refrigerate. Pull half of the angel cake apart and place in the bottom of a bowl in chunks. Pour ½ cup of orange juice over cake. To cooled jello add thawed fruit, walnuts and sliced bananas. Stir. Ladle ½ of this mixture on top of cake. Fold pudding and Cool Whip together. Spoon ½ over jello and fruit mix. Repeat all layers and garnish if desired. Chill at least four hours before serving.

Note: Easy, no-bake dessert.

Pat Baldwin

Flan

Caramel:
6 tablespoons sugar
2-3 tablespoons water

Preheat oven to 275 degrees. Bake in ring mold pan. Place sugar in pan with just enough water to moisten it. Put pan over heat (if electric range, you can leave the pan on burner; if gas, hold pan and rotate) until sugar becomes a caramel color, consistent, but not too dark. Set aside.

Custard:
2 cups milk
large piece of lemon rind
4 eggs
4 tablespoons sugar
1 teaspoon vanilla

In a saucepan, bring milk and lemon rind just to boiling point. Meanwhile, beat eggs with sugar using a whisk. When milk is scalding, pour it slowly into egg mixture, beating constantly. (If poured too fast the eggs will curdle with the heat.) After thoroughly mixed, add vanilla, continuing to beat the mixture. Pour into ring mold over the caramel. Put mold into pan of water (about 1½-2 inch deep) and bake for 1-1½ hours. (If cooked too fast, it will have air holes, if cooked too long, it will be tough.) Done when knife comes out clean. Remove from oven and pan of water and let cool. Serve cold. Loosen around the edges of pan with a knife. Place serving plate on top of the mold and invert. The flan and caramel sauce should come out easily. Garnish with fruit. Yield: 6-8 servings.

Anne C. Hoffman

Holiday Hot Curried Fruit

¼ cup butter or margarine
¾ cup light brown sugar, packed
2 teaspoons curry powder
1 (16 ounce) can pear halves, drained
1 (16 ounce) can peach halves, drained
1 (20 ounce) can pineapple chunks, drain and reserve juice
1 can mandarin oranges, drained
1 small bottle maraschino cherries, drained

Bake at 350 degrees in a flat casserole dish. In a small saucepan, combine butter, brown sugar, curry powder, and one tablespoon of reserved pineapple juice. Heat until sugar is dissolved. Place fruits in dish. Pour syrup over all, and bake for 45 minutes. Serve hot. Yield: 12 servings.

Jeanene Procopis

Lemon Delight

1 cup flour
1 cup nuts, chopped and divided into 2 parts
1 stick margarine
1 (8 ounce) package cream cheese, at room temperature
1 cup powdered sugar
1 (8 ounce) container Cool Whip
2 packages lemon instant pudding
3 cups whole milk

Bake at 375 degrees using 9x13 inch baking dish. For first layer blend flour, ½ cup nuts, and margarine. Dip hand in flour and spread mixture over bottom of baking dish. Bake for 15 minutes, then cool. Make second layer by beating together the cream cheese, powdered sugar and 1 cup of Cool Whip until smooth. Pour over the first layer. Next, blend the lemon pudding and whole milk and pour over the second layer. Spread remaining Cool Whip on top. Sprinkle ½ cup chopped nuts over top. Refrigerate 1 day before serving. Cut into squares. Yield: 12 servings.

Note: Freezes well.

Catherine T. Liotta

Chilled Lime Soufflé with Strawberry Sauce

Soufflé:

1½ teaspoons unflavored gelatin
¾ cup lime juice
1 cup sugar
6 eggs, separated
2 tablespoons unsalted butter
½ teaspoon vanilla
Zest of 1 lime
Strawberry Sauce to serve (recipe below)
Fresh berries for garnish

Combine gelatin and ¼ cup lime juice. Allow to soften. Set aside. Whisk ½ cup sugar, egg yolks, remaining ½ cup lime juice in a large saucepan. Whisk over low heat until mixture thickens slightly. Remove from heat and continue stirring. Add butter, softened gelatin, vanilla, and lime zest. Whisk until thoroughly blended. Chill for 30 minutes. Beat egg whites. Add remaining sugar gradually when whites start to form stiff peaks. Beat until sugar is dissolved and peaks are thick and shiny. Add a little of the egg white to the lime mixture to lighten it. Fold in remaining egg whites gently. Turn mixture into a soufflé dish and gently cover with plastic wrap. Refrigerate for at least 4 hours or overnight. Serve with Strawberry Sauce and garnish with fresh berries.

Strawberry Sauce:

3 cups fresh strawberries, hulled
¼ cup sugar
Dash lemon juice
2 tablespoons Chambord (raspberry liqueur)

Place strawberries in a food processor or blender and puree. Add sugar, lemon juice, and liqueur. Blend until sugar is dissolved, about 1½ to 2 minutes. Preparation time: 1 hour and 10 minutes. Yield: 8 servings.

Note: Make Strawberry Sauce only a few hours before serving and always keep refrigerated. It does not keep. Strawberry Sauce also makes an excellent base for strawberry ice cream.

Anne C. Hoffman

Scrumptious Mocha Ice Cream Dessert

24 Oreo or Hydrox chocolate cream sandwich cookies, crushed
⅓ cup butter, melted
½ gallon coffee ice cream, softened
3 ounces unsweetened chocolate
2 tablespoons butter or margarine
1 cup sugar
dash of salt
2 (5½ to 6 ounce) cans evaporated milk
½ teaspoon vanilla extract
1½ cups heavy cream, whipped
1½ ounces Kahlua liqueur
powdered sugar to taste
½-¾ cup nuts, chopped

Use 9x13 inch buttered pan. Combine cookie crumbs and butter. Press into the bottom of pan. Refrigerate. When chilled, spoon on softened ice cream and freeze. Melt chocolate and butter. Add sugar, salt, and milk. Bring to a boil, stirring until thickened. Remove from heat and add vanilla. Chill. Spread on top of ice cream. Freeze. Whip cream. Add Kahlua and powdered sugar to taste. Spread over chocolate layer and sprinkle top with chopped nuts. Freeze. Yield: 25 servings.

Note: A dessert to keep in the freezer for unexpected guests. Excellent with peppermint stick ice cream, garnished with cookie crumbs or shavings of semi-sweet chocolate.

Bonnie Venn

Raspberry Cream

1 (3 ounce) package raspberry flavored gelatin
1 cup boiling water
1 (10 ounce) package frozen raspberries, unthawed
½ pint vanilla ice cream, softened

Dissolve gelatin in water. Stir in raspberries and ice cream. Refrigerate until set, about 20 minutes. Spoon into serving dishes. Yield: 4 servings.

Mrs. Richard J. McDonald
(wife of McDonald's founder)

Rum Mousse

1½ pints whipping cream
4 dozen large marshmallows
½ cup milk
7 tablespoons rum
32 Lady Fingers
pecans, chopped

Use springform pan. Whip cream and set aside. In the top of a double boiler pan, melt marshmallows in milk. Add rum and fold into whipped cream. Line bottom and sides of pan with split Lady Fingers. Pour mixture into pan. Cover with pecans and crumbled Lady Fingers. Refrigerate at least 8 hours. Yield: 12 servings.

Note: Lasts several days.

Mary Brambilla

Scandinavian Baked Pears

4 fresh Anjou, Bosc or Comice pears
2 tablespoons lemon juice
⅔ cup sugar
1 (16 ounce) can red tart cherries
1 tablespoon cornstarch
¼ teaspoon cinnamon
toasted slivered almonds
whipped cream
nutmeg, optional

Preheat oven to 375 degrees. Bake in a shallow baking dish. Wash, halve, core and peel pears. Combine lemon juice, sugar and cherries in dish. Arrange pears cut side down over fruit mixture. Bake for 25-30 minutes or until pears are tender. Remove pears from dish. Add cornstarch and cinnamon to fruit mixture and cook over medium heat until thickened. Pour over pears. Serve warm or chilled with a spoonful of whipped cream. Sprinkle with almonds and dash of nutmeg, if desired. Yield: 8 servings.

Note: The pears can be prepared up to 10 hours ahead.

Anne C. Hoffman

Strawberry-Yogurt Dessert

3 cups Kix cereal, crushed (about 1½ cups)
¼ cup plus 2 tablespoons margarine or butter, melted
2 tablespoons sugar
1 envelope unflavored gelatin
1 (10 ounce) package frozen sweetened strawberries, thawed and drained (reserve liquid)
⅔ cup boiling water
2 cups vanilla flavored yogurt
1 teaspoon vanilla

Heat oven to 350 degrees. Use ungreased 8 inch square pan. Mix cereal, margarine and sugar. Press firmly in bottom of pan. Bake 10 minutes. Cool completely. Sprinkle gelatin over reserved strawberry liquid; let stand 1 minute. Pour boiling water over gelatin. Stir until gelatin is dissolved. Cool completely. Place strawberries in blender container or in food processor workbowl fitted with steel blade. Cover and blend on high speed until smooth. Mix gelatin mixture, yogurt and vanilla until smooth. Stir in strawberries until well blended. Pour over crust. Refrigerate uncovered until set, at least 4 hours. Refrigerate any remaining dessert. Yield: 9 servings.

Doris Guimont

Tortoni

1 (12 ounce) container Cool Whip
10 or 12 macaroon cookies, crushed
12 maraschino cherries, chopped
⅓ cup rum, or to desired taste
chopped almonds

Mix Cool Whip with crushed macaroon cookies and chopped cherries. Add rum and mix. Fill paper or foil muffin cups. Sprinkle with chopped almonds and place cherry (or half) in center. Freeze overnight. Remove from freezer about ½ hour before serving. Yield: 10 servings.

Note: Great light dessert after an Italian dinner. Always a hit!

Rose Marie Borelli

Sunshine's Grapenut Custard

4 eggs
4 cups milk
1 teaspoon vanilla
1 pinch salt
2 teaspoons cinnamon
½ cup sugar
¾ cup grapenuts

Bake at 350 degrees. Use 8x11 inch baking dish. Beat eggs and milk until foamy. Add vanilla, salt, and cinnamon. Slowly beat in sugar. Pour mixture into baking dish and sprinkle grapenuts evenly over the top. Place dish in pan of hot water and bake for 1¼ hours or until silver knife inserted 1 inch from edge comes out clean. Serve hot or cold with whipped cream or Cool Whip.

Melanie Finet Dadura

Summer Pudding

1 loaf of sliced white bread
2 packages of frozen fruit (strawberries, raspberries, blackberries)
6 plastic cups or molds
cream

Remove crusts of sliced bread. Completely cover the inside of mold. Fill with defrosted fruit and plenty of juice. Top with slice of white bread, cut to size of mold. Cover with something heavy and leave in refrigerator overnight. Juices should have soaked through the bread, if not, add more juice. Tap each mold onto a plate and drizzle with leftover blended juices and fruit. Drizzle with cream and serve immediately. Can also be made as one large pudding. Yield: 6 servings.

Finola Murphy
wife of D. Patrick Murphy,
Senior Vice President, Bank of Ireland/First NH Banks

Trifle

1 box (6-serving size) vanilla pudding, not instant
1 pound cake
strawberry jam
Amaretto or brandy
whipping cream
1 tablespoon sugar

Use a large glass bowl. Prepare pudding according to directions on package. Set aside to cool slightly (cover with wax paper to prevent film from forming). Slice pound cake into 16 pieces and spread with jam, making jam sandwiches. Slice each sandwich into 4 pieces. Line bowl with the sandwiches. Sprinkle with Amaretto or brandy. Pour warm pudding over sandwiches. Cool completely. Whip cream, adding sugar and small amount of Amaretto or brandy. Spread whipped cream over pudding. Garnish and chill.

Dennis Pope
Superintendent of Schools, Bedford School District

Frozen Lemon Mousse

lemon or vanilla wafers
4 eggs, separated
½ cup lemon juice
1 cup sugar, divided
1½ tablespoons grated lemon zest
1½ cups heavy cream

Line bottom and sides of 8 or 9 inch springform pan with lemon or vanilla wafers. Combine egg yolks, lemon juice, ¼ cup sugar and lemon zest in a large bowl and blend well. Let stand at room temperature. Beat egg whites until soft peaks form. Gradually add ¾ cup sugar, beating until stiff and glossy. Whip heavy cream and gently fold egg whites and heavy cream into egg yolk mixture. Spoon into pan. Cover with foil and freeze overnight. Let soften in refrigerator one hour before serving.

Note: A very refreshing dessert for the summer months.

Caroline Williams

Pies

McDonald's

Dick and Mac McDonald, of Bedford, opened their first restaurant in 1948. The first billionth hamburger was sold on the Art Linkletter Show in 1963. By 1970, McDonald's grew at the rate of 500 restaurants per year. 1972 marked the beginning of the Quarter Pounder. In 1974 the first Ronald McDonald House was established as a residence for families of hospitalized children. Chicken McNuggets arrived in 1983.

McDonald's is the world's largest food serving organization serving people in 65 countries. Today there is also McSpaghetti, a noodle dish for the Philippines and McLak, a salmon sandwich in Norway. Recently, a McDonald's opened in Casablanca.

Children's Birthday Party

beverage

Non-alcoholic Punch

hors d'oeuvres

Fresh Vegetables with

Puree of White Bean Dip

entrée

No Fuss Lasagna

desserts

Chocolate Sheet Cake with Ice Cream

Chewy Popcorn Balls

PIES

Basic Pastry

2½ cups flour (do not use King Arthur)
4 teaspoons sugar
1 teaspoon salt
9 tablespoons cold butter
5 tablespoons cold shortening (if limiting cholesterol, may substitute 14 tablespoons margarine in place of butter and shortening)
5-6 tablespoons ice water

Combine flour, sugar, salt, butter and shortening. Blend well with pastry blender or 2 knives until crumbly. Add ice water and mix with fork to form a ball. Chill at least 1 hour.

Note: This flaky, tasty, crust rolls out and handles beautifully.

Dianne Russell

Salad Oil Pie Crust

2 cups sifted flour
1½ teaspoons salt
½ cup salad oil
¼ cup whole milk

Mix flour and salt. Combine oil and milk in measuring cup and add to flour. Mix and form pastry ball. Divide pastry and roll out crust between two layers of wax paper. Makes 2 crusts.

Note: Crust is difficult to roll out unless you use wax paper. Cooking time depends on the filling that is used.

Eunice Brine

Dutch Apple Pie

Filling:

4 cups of pared, cored, thinly sliced cooking apples (Cortland, Pippin, Granny Smith)
juice of ½ lemon
¼ cup sugar
¾ teaspoon cinnamon
⅛ teaspoon salt

Preheat oven to 400 degrees. Put prepared apples in large mixing bowl. Pour lemon juice over apples. Mix sugar, cinnamon and salt. Add to apples and mix well. Arrange apples in pie shell.

Topping:

¾ cup brown sugar
¾ cup flour
⅓ cup butter

Blend the sugar and flour for the topping in a small bowl. Cut in butter with knife until crumbly. Spread topping over apples. Bake for 30 to 35 minutes. Serve warm with vanilla ice cream or vanilla frozen yogurt. Yield: 8 servings.

Note: For a deep dish pie use 6 cups of apples. Freezes well.

Anne C. Hoffman

Spicy Apple Crunch Pie

1 (9 inch) unbaked pie shell
3 eggs, separated
1½ cups sugar
1 tablespoon flour
⅛ teaspoon ground cloves
1 teaspoon cinnamon
1 tablespoon butter, melted
1 tablespoon vinegar
1 cup grated peeled apple (2-3 medium)
½ cup chopped pecans (or walnuts)

Preheat oven to 350 degrees. Beat yolks until thick and lemon colored. Combine sugar, flour and spices. Add egg yolks alternately with butter and vinegar. Mix well. Stir in apple and nuts. Beat egg whites until stiff peaks form. Fold into apple mixture, blending well. Pour into pie shell. Bake 50 minutes or until a knife inserted in center comes clear.

Tish Smith

Norwegian Apple Pie

¾ cup sugar
½ cup flour
1 egg
½ teaspoon vanilla
¼ teaspoon salt
1 teaspoon baking powder
½ cup walnuts, chopped
1 cup diced apples

Preheat oven to 350 degrees. Bake in buttered pie pan. Combine flour, sugar, salt, and baking powder and stir well. Beat in egg and vanilla, stir in nuts and apples. Mixture will be thick. Spoon into pie pan and spread evenly. Bake 30 minutes. Serve warm or cold, plain or with ice cream or whipped cream. Yield: 6 servings.

Doris Spurway

Banana Cream Pie

Crust:
1½ cups graham cracker crumbs (20 squares)
⅓ cup margarine
3 tablespoons sugar

Preheat oven to 350 degrees. Combine crust ingredients and press into pie pan. Bake for 10 minutes.

Filling:
¼ cup cornstarch
⅔ cup sugar
½ cup flour
½ teaspoon salt
3 cups milk
4 egg yolks
2 tablespoons butter, softened
1 tablespoon vanilla
2 large bananas

Combine cornstarch, sugar, flour, salt, milk, egg yolks, butter and vanilla in the top of a double boiler and cook, stirring until thick. Slice two bananas into pie shell and pour filling over fruit.

Topping:
2 cups whipped cream
1 large banana

Top pie with whipped cream, and refrigerate at least two hours. Garnish with one sliced banana just before serving. Yield: 8-10 servings.

Christina Barley

Chewy Caramel Brownie Pie

Brownie Layer:
½ cup butter or margarine
2 squares unsweetened chocolate
1 cup sugar
¾ cup all-purpose flour
2 eggs, slightly beaten
½ teaspoon salt
½ teaspoon baking powder
1 teaspoon vanilla

Preheat oven to 350 degrees. Bake in a greased 9 inch pie pan or springform pan. In a 2 quart saucepan, combine butter and unsweetened chocolate. Cook over medium heat, stirring occasionally, until melted (4-6 minutes). Stir in remaining brownie ingredients. Spread batter into pan and bake for 20-25 minutes or until brownie is firm to the touch.

Caramel Layer:
8 ounces (30) caramels, unwrapped
3 tablespoons whipping cream
½ cup chopped pecans
¼ cup semi-sweet chocolate chips
Ice cream, optional but a real plus

Meanwhile, in 1 quart saucepan cook caramels and whipping cream over medium low heat, stirring occasionally, until caramels are melted (5-6 minutes). Remove brownie from oven. Spread melted caramel mixture over top of brownie. Sprinkle with pecans and chocolate chips. Return to over and bake 3-5 minutes or until caramel mixture is bubbly. Let stand 30-45 minutes. Cut into wedges. Serve warm with ice cream. Yield: 8-10 servings.

Note: This brownie pie is exceedingly rich, chewy and gooey!

Pat Nichol

Mud Pie

½ package Nabisco chocolate wafers
½ stick butter, melted
1 quart coffee ice cream, softened
1½ cups fudge sauce

Use 9 inch pie plate. Crush wafers and add butter, mix well. Press into pie plate. Cover with ice cream. Put into freezer until ice cream is firm. Top with cold fudge sauce (it helps to place in freezer for a time to make spreading easier). Store in freezer approximately 10 hours. Presentation: Slice mud pie into eight portions and serve on a chilled dessert plate with a chilled fork. Top with whipped cream and slivered almonds.

Alice Asadourian

Don's Chocolate Birthday Pie

1 (9 inch) graham cracker crust
⅔ cup butter
1 cup sugar
3 eggs, well beaten
2 (1 ounce) squares unsweetened chocolate
½ cup semi-sweet chocolate bits
½ pint heavy cream
crushed candy cane or peppermint candies

Cream butter and sugar, mixing in eggs until blended. Melt unsweetened and semi-sweet chocolate together in double boiler. Add to creamed mixture. Mix well and pour into pie shell. Chill until firm (at least four hours.) When ready to serve, whip cream and sweeten slightly. Spread cream over pie and sprinkle top with peppermint.

Note: This is a very sweet dessert for real chocolate lovers.

Christina Barley

Chocolate Peanut Butter Pie

Crust:

1⅓ cups graham cracker crumbs
⅓ cup sugar
1 stick unsalted butter, melted

Preheat oven to 350 degrees. Use a deep 9 inch pie plate. Prepare the crust by combining the graham cracker crumbs, sugar and melted butter in a mixing bowl. Stir together thoroughly. Press the mixture onto the bottom and sides of the pie plate. Bake the crust for 8 minutes. Set aside to cool completely.

Filling:

12 ounces cream cheese, at room temperature
1½ cups peanut butter
1½ cups sugar
1 cup heavy cream or whipping cream

Make the filling by mixing the cream cheese, peanut butter and sugar together in a large bowl until well blended. Whip the cream with an electric mixer until stiff and fold it into the cream cheese mixture. Spoon the filling into the cooled crust.

Topping:

½ cup sugar
½ cup heavy cream or whipping cream
2 ounces good quality unsweetened chocolate
4 tablespoons unsalted butter
½ teaspoon vanilla extract

In a saucepan combine the sugar and cream for topping and bring to a boil. Reduce the heat and simmer, without stirring for 6 minutes. Remove from heat. Add the chocolate and butter and stir until melted. Stir in vanilla. Carefully pour the topping over the pie and refrigerate, uncovered, for at least 4 hours. Yield: 8-10 servings.

Mary Hamrock
Virginia Larson

Chocolate Funny Cake Pie

1 (9 inch) unbaked pie shell
1½ cups sugar
¼ cup butter
½ cup milk
1 egg, beaten
1 cup flour
1 teaspoon baking soda
1 teaspoon vanilla
4 tablespoons unsweetened cocoa
6 tablespoons water

Preheat oven to 350 degrees. Cream 1 cup sugar and butter until fluffy. Mix the milk and egg. Add to sugar mixture. Combine, along with flour and baking powder, stirring as you add. Add ½ teaspoon vanilla, mix and pour into pie shell. Then mix cocoa with ½ cup sugar. Gradually add water and ½ teaspoon vanilla, mixing well. Pour this mixture over batter in pie shell. Bake for 35 minutes or until firm. Yield: 8-10 servings.

Note: May garnish with dollop of whipped cream or spoonful of warm fudge sauce or both.

Christina Barley

Cranberry Pie Cake

2 cups whole cranberries
½ cup raisins
½ cup sugar
2 eggs, beaten
1 scant cup sugar
1½ sticks butter or margarine (¾ cup), melted
1 cup flour

Preheat oven to 325 degrees. Use a 10 inch pie plate. Spread cranberries, raisins and ½ cup of sugar in pie plate. Beat eggs, gradually add one cup of sugar. Add melted butter and flour. Mix and pour over the fruit. Bake 40-50 minutes. Serve warm or cold.

Note: Good with vanilla ice cream or whipped cream.

Priscilla Van Wagner

Cranberry Raisin Pie

1 uncooked pie crust
1 cup cranberries, raw
1 cup raisins
1 cup sugar
1 cup water
1 rounded tablespoon flour or tapioca
2 tablespoons butter or margarine, softened
1 teaspoon vanilla

Preheat oven to 400 degrees. Use an 8 inch pie pan. Chop cranberries and raisins finely in cuisinart or blender and add water. Put in a saucepan and add sugar, flour and butter. Cook for 20 minutes, stirring often. Cool and add vanilla. Line pie pan with pie crust. Add filling. Top with a lattice crust. Bake for 10 minutes at 400 degrees then reduce heat to 350 degrees and continue baking for 20 minutes.

Wesley Maloney
Eunice Brine

Daiquiri Pie

1½ cups water
1 (3½ ounce) package vanilla pudding and pie filling (not instant)
1 (3 ounce) package lime or strawberry flavor gelatin
⅓ cup light rum
1 tablespoon lime juice
1 envelope whipped topping mix
1 baked and cooled 9 inch graham cracker crumb crust

Combine pudding mix, gelatin, and 1½ cups water in a saucepan. Cook over medium heat, stirring constantly, until mixture comes to full boil and is thickened and clear. Remove from heat. Stir in rum and lime juice. Chill until slightly thickened. Prepare whipped topping mix according to package directions, reducing water by 2 tablespoons. Blend into chilled pudding mixture. Spoon into pie crust. Chill about three hours or until firm. Garnish with additional prepared whipped topping and lime slices or strawberries.

Alberta Dieter

Fudgey Mocha Nut Pie

6 tablespoons butter or margarine
⅓ cup Hershey's cocoa
1 (14 ounce) can sweetened condensed milk
⅓ cup water
2 eggs, beaten
2 to 3 tablespoons powdered instant coffee
1 cup semi-sweet chocolate chips
1 cup coarsely chopped pecans
1 teaspoon vanilla extract
1 unbaked 9 inch pie crust

Preheat oven to 350 degrees. In medium saucepan over low heat, melt butter. Add cocoa, stirring until smooth. Stir in sweetened condensed milk, water, eggs, instant coffee and chocolate chips. Whisk until well blended. Remove from heat. Stir in pecans and vanilla. Pour into unbaked pie crust. Bake 50 minutes or until center is set. Cool completely. Garnish as desired. Refrigerate leftover pie. Yield: 8 servings.

Doris Guimont

Grasshopper Pie

24 large marshmallows
½ cup milk
½ pint whipped cream or Cool Whip
1½ ounces green creme de menthe
1 ounce white creme de cocoa
1 crumb pie crust (chocolate crumb is best)

Melt marshmallows in milk in double boiler. Remove from heat and cool. Add liquors. Cool until partially set. Add whipped cream and pour into pie shell. Refrigerate.

Martha Harris Gaudes
Executive Assistant to Bedford Town Manager

Kahlua Whipped Cream Pie

2 packages Pepperidge Farm Bordeaux cookies
1 pint heavy cream
¼ cup Kahlua
chopped pecans

Use 10 inch springform pan. Do not make more than 5 hours ahead. Whip cream with Kahlua. Spread cookies in a single layer in the bottom of pan. Break cookies into pieces to fill in. Cover with a layer of whipped cream, then another layer of cookies and whipped cream. On third layer of cookies, top with another layer of whipped cream. (There will be a few cookies left over.) Spread nuts on top and refrigerate until serving time.

Priscilla Van Wagner

Mocha Almond Fudge Pie

1 (9 ounce) package chocolate wafer cookies
7 tablespoons melted butter
¾ cup butterscotch or caramel sauce
½ gallon mocha almond fudge ice cream, softened
1 (16 ounce) jar hot fudge topping, slightly warmed
1 cup chopped Heath bars (about 5 ounces English toffee bars)

Preheat oven to 325 degrees. Use 9 inch deep pie plate. Finely grind chocolate cookies in food processor, add butter and process until crumbs are moist and stick together. Firmly press crumbs onto bottom and up sides of pie plate. Bake crust 10 minutes. Freeze until cold, about 15 minutes. Spread butterscotch (or caramel) sauce over bottom crust and freeze 15 minutes more. Spoon ice cream into crust, pressing to compact, and mound slightly in center. Freeze 15 minutes. Spread fudge topping over ice cream. Freeze 5 minutes. Press chopped Heath bars (or toffee) over top. Cover and freeze 6 hours. Let stand at room temperature 15 minutes before serving. Yield: 10-12 servings.

Molly Rooney O'Connor
Mary Hamrock

Pecan Pie

3 eggs, well beaten
½ cup sugar
3 tablespoons butter or margarine, melted
1 cup white Karo syrup (may use dark or half white and half dark)
1 teaspoon vanilla
pinch salt
1 cup pecans
1 unbaked pie shell

Preheat oven to 350 degrees. Mix together eggs, sugar, butter, Karo syrup, vanilla and salt. Put pecans into pie shell and cover with mixture. Bake 45 minutes.

Mary Dambach

Pumpkin Chiffon Pie

Crust:
42 vanilla wafers, finely rolled
2 tablespoons sugar
⅓ cup margarine, melted

Preheat oven to 375 degrees. Combine wafer crumbs and sugar. Stir in margarine. Press onto bottom and sides of pie pan. Bake for 8-10 minutes. Cool before filling.

Filling:
1 cup pumpkin
32 marshmallows
1 tablespoon nutmeg
1 tablespoon cinnamon
1 teaspoon allspice
½ teaspoon salt
1 small can evaporated milk, chilled

Cook pumpkin and marshmallows in microwave until smooth. Add spices. Cool. Whip milk. Fold in pumpkin mixture. Pour into shell and chill in refrigerator until cool. Serve with whipped cream topping, if desired.

Betty Ann Barnes

Pumpkin Ice Cream Pie

1 quart vanilla ice cream, softened
¾ cup canned pumpkin
¼ cup honey
½ teaspoon cinnamon
¼ teaspoon ground ginger
¼ teaspoon salt
¼ teaspoon nutmeg
⅛ teaspoon ground cloves
1 (9 inch) pie shell, baked and cooled
⅓ cup chopped pecans
whipped cream and pecans for decoration

Combine ice cream, pumpkin, honey, cinnamon, ginger, salt, nutmeg and cloves in mixing bowl and blend. Pour into pie shell. Sprinkle with chopped nuts. Freeze until serving time. Garnish with whipped cream and nuts. Yield: 6-8 servings.

Wesley Maloney

Pumpkin Pie

2 cups of cooked or canned pumpkin
½ teaspoon salt
2 cups milk (can be skim milk)
2 eggs, slightly beaten
⅔ cup brown sugar
2 tablespoons white sugar
1¼ teaspoons cinnamon
½ teaspoon ginger
¼ teaspoon cloves
½ teaspoon nutmeg
pastry for 1 pie crust
whipped cream
honey

Preheat oven to 450 degrees. Mix the first 10 ingredients together in order given. Stir and strain through a sieve. Pour into deep 10″ pie dish lined with plain pastry. Bake for 10 minutes at 450 degrees. Reduce oven temperature to 325 degrees and cook 45-55 minutes. Pie is done when a knife cut 1 inch from edge, comes out clean. Serve cold with a bit of whipped cream and a small spoonful of honey on each serving. Yield: 8-10 servings.

Anne C. Hoffman

Sour Cream Apple Pie

1 unbaked pie shell
2½ cups diced apples
¾ cup sugar
2 tablespoons flour
¼ teaspoon salt
1 egg plus 1 egg yolk, slightly beaten
1 cup sour cream
1 teaspoon vanilla

Preheat oven to 400 degrees. Place apples in unbaked pie shell. Mix sugar, flour, salt and eggs. Add sour cream and vanilla to the flour mixture and mix well. Pour batter over apples and bake for 25 minutes.

Topping:
½ cup brown sugar
¼ cup butter or margarine
2 teaspoons cinnamon, optional

Mix topping ingredients and spread over apples. Bake 20 minutes longer.

Nora Spitler (caterer and grandmother of Pat Nichol)

Ritz Cracker Pie

3 eggs whites
½ teaspoon baking powder
1 cup sugar
16 Ritz crackers, crumbled coarsely
½ teaspoon vanilla
⅔ cup walnuts, chopped (optional)

Bake at 325 degrees in a buttered 8 inch pie plate. Beat egg whites with baking powder until stiff peaks form. Add sugar and beat until mixed. Stir in vanilla and crackers. Nuts may be added if desired. Turn mixture into pie plate and bake for 35 minutes. Serve topped with strawberries and whipped cream. (Pie will settle and crack as it cools.)

Note: This recipe was handed down from my aunt who lived in New Hampshire all her life. She made it for me when I was a little girl. I was so fascinated that Ritz crackers could be turned into a pie! It was a special treat!

Christina Barley

Squash Pie

1 cup cooked squash (or 1 can One Pie squash)
1 cup cream
¼ cup white sugar
½ cup brown sugar
3 eggs
½ teaspoon ginger
½ teaspoon nutmeg
½ teaspoon salt
¼ teaspoon mace
½ teaspoon cinnamon
3 tablespoons vanilla

Bake at 425 degrees for 20 minutes and 375 degrees for 45 minutes. Use greased 9 inch pie pan. To the squash add cream and sugar and slightly beaten eggs and mix. Add ginger, nutmeg, salt, mace and cinnamon and mix. Add vanilla and mix. Bake for 20 minutes. Reduce heat and bake for 45 minutes or until knife inserted in center comes out clean.

Cathy Sullivan

Cherry Cheese Tarts

Crust:
1½ cups graham cracker crumbs
⅓ cup melted butter
3 tablespoons sugar

Preheat oven to 350 degrees. Use tiny muffin papers. Make a mixture for a graham cracker crust. Set the muffin papers on an ungreased cookie sheet. Put one teaspoon of mix in each cup and press down. Set aside.

Filling:
½ pound cream cheese
¼ cup sugar
1 egg
½ teaspoon vanilla extract
1 can cherry pie filling

Mix ingredients for the filling with a hand mixer until well blended. Put some of the mixture in each cup. Bake about 10 minutes. When cool, top each tart with a teaspoon of cherry pie filling.

Note: Any kind of pie filling can be used or served plain.

Carol Molitoris

Individual Cheese Tarts

24 vanilla wafers
½ cup sugar
1 pound cream cheese
2 eggs
2 teaspoons vanilla
1 can cherry (or other fruit) pie filling

Preheat oven to 375 degrees. Line cupcake tin with papers liners. Crumble 1 wafer into each cupcake liner. Beat ingredients together for five minutes. Fill each liner ½ full with filling. Bake for 15-18 minutes. Cool. Top with pie filling. Store in refrigerator. Yield: 24.

Sally Balog

Linzertorte

1 cup butter or margarine
1 cup sifted flour
1½ cups unpeeled almonds, ground with metal blade in cuisinart
½ cup sugar
⅛ teaspoon cloves
⅛ teaspoon cinnamon
2 egg yolks
½ cup raspberry jam
½ egg white, slightly beaten
1½ tablespoons powdered sugar

Preheat oven to 325 degrees. Use 9 inch ungreased cake pan with removable bottom. Chop butter into flour. (May use cuisinart steel blade). Add almonds. Mix sugar with the cloves, cinnamon and egg yolks. Add to flour mixture and blend thoroughly. Turn ⅔ of the dough into pan, pressing over the bottom and halfway up the sides. Spread with jam. Roll egg-sized balls of the remaining dough between the palms to make long rolls about ⅓-½ inch in diameter and about 8 inches long. Place the rolls on a baking sheet and chill until firm. Using a spatula, lift the rolls and arrange lattice style over the jam. Fasten to the dough around the rim of the pan by pressing lightly. Brush with egg white and bake on the lower shelf of oven about one hour. Set the pan on wire rack and partly cool the cake before removing the rim of the pan. Sprinkle with powdered sugar.

Barbara Weigold

Granny Smith Apple Tarts

2 Granny Smith apples, peeled, quartered and cored
1 teaspoon lemon juice
1 tablespoon melted butter
4 (2½ inch) frozen round puff pastry shells, thawed in the refrigerator
½ teaspoon cinnamon
2 tablespoons sugar
powdered sugar

Preheat oven to 400 degrees. Slice apples into ¼ inch thick slices; toss with lemon juice and butter. Roll out puff pastry shells into 5 inch circles. Cut a circle ½ inch from the outer edge of dough, cutting almost all the way through the dough. Prick the inside circle with a fork. Divide apples between pieces of dough and arrange in center of dough, staying inside cut circle. Refrigerate 20 minutes, or until dough is chilled. Toss together cinnamon and sugar and sprinkle evenly over apples. Bake for 12 minutes, or until pastry is golden brown. Dust with powdered sugar before serving. You may also top with Cool Whip, whipped cream or ice cream. Yield: 4 servings.

Note: This easy dessert can be made ahead. Other fruits in season may be substituted for apples such as peaches, plums, etc.

Louise Langley

Fruit Torte

½ cup butter
1 cup sugar
1 cup flour, sifted
1 teaspoon baking powder
salt
2 eggs
fruit: 1 pint blueberries, sliced apples, peaches or combination of these

Bake at 350 degrees. Use a 9 inch springform pan. Cream butter and sugar. Add flour, baking powder, salt and eggs. Place in pan and cover entire surface with fruit. Sprinkle top with sugar, cinnamon, lemon juice and flour (if fruit is very juicy). Bake one hour.

Bonnie Venn

Pecan Tarts

1 (3 ounce) package cream cheese, softened
½ cup butter or margarine, softened
1 cup all-purpose flour
¼ teaspoon salt

Preheat oven to 325 degrees. In a mixing bowl, beat cream cheese and butter, blending in flour and salt. Chill for 1 hour. Shape into 1 inch balls. Press into the bottom and up the sides of greased mini muffin cups.

Filling:
1 egg
¾ cup packed dark brown sugar
1 tablespoon butter or margarine, melted
1 teaspoon vanilla extract
⅔ cup chopped pecans
maraschino cherry halves, optional

For filling, beat the egg in a small mixing bowl. Add and mix well the brown sugar, butter and vanilla. Stir in pecans. Spoon into shells. Bake 25-30 minutes. Cool in pan on a wire rack. Decorate with maraschino cherries, if desired. Yield: about 20.

Sharlene Genest

Key Lime Pie

1 (14 ounce) can condensed milk
½ cup sugar
½ cup lime juice
½ pint whipping cream
green food coloring
1 baked pie shell

Beat cream until stiff. Mix condensed milk, sugar, lime juice and food coloring with half of the whipped cream. Pour into pie shell and top with the balance of the whipped cream. Chill.

Fran Wiggin

Swiss Nut Torte

Crust:

1 cup flour
⅛ teaspoon salt
¾ teaspoon sugar
½ cup butter

Preheat oven to 375 degrees. Use buttered springform pan. Combine crust ingredients. Press onto bottom and just a little up sides of the pan.

Filling:

½ cup shredded coconut
3 tablespoons flour
1 teaspoon salt
1¼ cups brown sugar
1 cup walnuts, chopped
1 teaspoon vanilla extract
2 eggs, beaten

Combine all filling ingredients and pour on top of crust. Bake 35-40 minutes.

Frosting:

1¼ cups powdered sugar
½ cup butter
2 tablespoons heavy cream
½ teaspoon almond extract

Mix together powdered sugar, butter cream and almond extract. When cool frost and refrigerate. Yield: 8 servings.

Beth Squeglia

Diet Pineapple Cream Pie

2 graham cracker pie shells
1 (8 ounce) package cream cheese
1 (3½ ounce) package instant vanilla pudding
½ cup milk
1 (20 ounce) can unsweetened crushed pineapple
1 (12 ounce) container Cool Whip

Soften cream cheese and add vanilla pudding, milk and crushed pineapple. Beat 3 minutes. Fold Cool Whip into this mixture until fluffy. Pour into pie shells. Refrigerate overnight. Makes 2 pies.

Jacqueline Aiken

Restaurant Specialties

Bedford Village Inn

The Bedford Village Inn was built on land cleared in 1774 by John Gordon, who raised his fourteen children here. His eldest son Josiah joined the Continental Army at the start of the Revolutionary War, wearing a linen shirt made by his mother from flax grown and woven on the farm. Upon his return, he became a gentleman farmer and businessman — and built the present farmhouse in 1810.

The decline in farming and the advent of residential and commercial growth met. The "farm" was purchased in 1981 with the intention of renovating the house as a restaurant and the old livestock barn as an inn. Over the next three years, delicate preservation work and substantial new construction began before the opening in 1985. Original and reproduction antiques make this a fine approximation of Federal Era splendor — with all the modern conveniences.

Moonlight and Roses

soup

Vichyssoise

bread

Homemade Dinner Rolls

salad

Waldorf Salad

entrée

Boursin Chicken

Lemon Glazed Carrots

White Rice

dessert

Cheesecake with Strawberries

RESTAURANT SPECIALTIES

Pan Braised Chicken Breast

12 ounces skin on boneless chicken breast
½ cup small diced red bliss potato
¼ cup chopped fresh tomato
1 cup fresh spinach leaves
1 teaspoon chopped rosemary
1 teaspoon chopped garlic
1 tablespoon chopped shallot
¼ cup white wine
¼ cup chicken or veal stock
2 ounces goat cheese

Preheat oven to 350 degrees. Season chicken breast with salt and pepper. Preheat sauté pan until smoking, then add chicken breast skin side down. Sauté both sides until golden brown. Add to sauté pan diced potatoes. Sauté until golden brown. Add to sauté pan tomato, garlic, shallot, rosemary, and salt and pepper to taste. Deglaze with white wine, then reduce heat. Deglaze again with stock, then reduce heat. Add spinach and goat cheese to sauté pan and place in 350 degree oven. Bake for 20 to 30 minutes depending on thickness of breasts. Serves 2.

Atherton Café & Grille
Clayton Nash, Chef/Owner
Salzburg Square
Amherst, NH

Steak with Onion Bourbon Sauce and Mushroom Cheese Grits

Sauce:

2 tablespoons (¼ stick) butter
2 onions, cut in half, thinly sliced
¼ cup balsamic vinegar
1 cup canned beef broth
1 cup canned low-salt chicken broth

Melt butter in heavy large skillet over medium-low heat. Add onions and sauté until golden and tender, about 12 minutes. Add vinegar and boil until reduced by half, about 1 minute. Add both broths and boil until slightly thickened, about 10 minutes. (Can be made 1 day ahead. Cover; chill.)

Grits:

2 tablespoons (¼ stick) butter
3 ounces crimini or button mushrooms, thinly sliced
3 ounces shiitake mushrooms, thinly sliced
¼ cup chopped onion
3 cups water
¾ cup quick-cooking grits
½ cup grated cheddar cheese (about 2 ounces)
¼ cup Romano cheese (about ¾ ounce)

Melt butter in heavy large saucepan over medium-high heat. Add all mushrooms and onion and sauté until mushrooms are tender, about 3 minutes. Add 3 cups water and bring to boil. Gradually stir in grits. Reduce heat to medium-low, cover and cook until grits are tender and liquid is absorbed, about 7 minutes. Remove from heat and stir in both cheeses. Season grits to taste with salt and pepper. Cover to keep warm.

Steak:

2 tablespoons olive oil
4 (12-ounce) New York sirloin steaks (about 1 inch thick)
2 tablespoons bourbon
2 tablespoons (¼ stick) butter

(Continued on next page)

(Steak with Onion Bourbon Sauce and Mushroom Cheese Grits, continued)

Heat oil in heavy large skillet over medium-high heat. Season steaks with salt and pepper. Add to skillet and cook to desired doneness, about 3½ minutes per side for rare. Transfer to plates. Tent with foil to keep warm. Reduce heat to medium-low. Add bourbon to skillet (mixture may ignite) and boil until almost all liquid evaporates, about 30 seconds. Add sauce to skillet and bring to boil. Remove from heat. Add butter and whisk just until melted. Season with salt and pepper. Divide grits equally among plates. Spoon sauce over steaks and serve. Yield: 4 servings.

Bedford Village Inn
Bedford, NH

Cranberry Crisp

1 bag fresh cranberries
zest and juice of two oranges
1 cup sugar
1½ tablespoons instant tapioca
½ cup chopped walnuts
1 teaspoon vanilla extract

Preheat oven to 350. Combine all filling ingredients in mixing bowl. Pour into shallow baking dish, quiche dish or pie pan.

Topping:
1 cup flour
½ cup brown sugar
1 stick of butter - cold and cut into small pieces
½ cup chopped walnuts
½ cup old fashioned oatmeal

Combine flour and brown sugar in a mixing bowl or bowl of a food processor. Cut butter in until it is the size of peas. Pulse your food processor. If using a processor dump into mixing bowl. Add nuts and oatmeal. Pour topping over filling. Bake crisp for 45-50 minutes, until filling bubbles around the edges. Yield: 6-8 servings.

The Black Forest Cafe
Amherst, NH

Curried Butternut Squash with Apple Soup

½ stick (4 tablespoons) unsalted butter
1 medium onion, coarsely chopped (can be frozen onion)
2 teaspoons curry powder
2 butternut squashes—peeled, seeded, coarsely chopped (4-6 cups)
4 apples, peeled and coarsely chopped (recommend cooking apples)
6 cups chicken stock (or unsalted canned chicken stock)
1 teaspoon salt (omit if using salted chicken stock)
½ teaspoon pepper
2 cups heavy cream (do not use milk, it will curdle)

Melt butter in soup pot. Over low heat add onions; cover. Stir occasionally until onions are transparent. Add curry powder. Stir over heat 1 minute. Add squash, apples, chicken stock, and 1 teaspoon salt and ½ teaspoon pepper. Bring to a boil and boil gently for 20 minutes. Strain solids, reserving liquid. Puree solids in a food processor or blender with enough of the reserved stock to moisten. Recombine the solids with the remaining liquid. Heat to a boil. At this point the soup can be cooled and frozen for future use and reheated. Remove from heat. Add cream. Check seasoning. Add more stock if too thick. Garnish with croutons or toasted squash seeds. Yield: 12 one cup servings.

The Black Forest Cafe
Amherst, NH

A chef is a person with a large enough vocabulary to give the soup a different name every day.

Grilled Salmon with a Raspberry Coulis

For the fish:
4 salmon fillets or steaks
1 lemon
2 tablespoons olive oil
dash Kosher salt
dash coarse ground pepper

Squeeze lemon onto fish, brush with olive oil and season. Grill to desired doneness using a lower heat for steaks.

For the Sauce:
1 shallot
1 teaspoon vegetable oil
3 ounces cassis or red wine
2 pints fresh raspberries or 1½ pints frozen
½ pint cranberries
2 teaspoons sugar
4 ounces orange juice

Sauté minced shallot in oil until translucent. Deglaze with cassis. Add raspberries, cranberries, sugar and orange juice. Cook over medium heat until cranberries pop. Let cool and puree in blender or food processor; strain if desired and may be refrigerated for up to three days.

For the Garnish:
2 tablespoons citrus yogurt
4 mint sprigs
12 raspberries
1 tablespoon orange zest

For the presentation, ladle sauce onto plate (either hot or cool) and dot with citrus yogurt. Lay salmon on the sauce and garnish with mint, raspberries and orange zest. Yield: 4 servings.

C.R. Sparks
Bedford, NH

Chocolate Sheet Cake

2 cups sugar
2 cups flour
pinch of salt
1 stick butter
½ cup shortening
4 tablespoons cocoa
1 cup water
2 eggs, beaten
1 teaspoon baking soda
1 teaspoon vanilla
½ cup milk

Preheat oven to 400 degrees. Mix sugar, flour and salt in bowl and set aside. Bring 1 stick butter, ½ cup shortening, 4 tablespoons cocoa and 1 cup water to boil and pour over flour and sugar mixture. Mix eggs, baking soda, 1 teaspoon vanilla, and ½ cup milk and combine with other ingredients. Pour into greased cookie sheet. Bake for 15-20 minutes.

Frosting:
6 tablespoons milk
1 stick butter
3 tablespoons cocoa
3½ cups powdered sugar
1 teaspoon vanilla
1 cup chopped nuts

Boil milk for a few minutes. Add butter, cocoa, powdered sugar, vanilla and nuts. Mix and spread on cake as soon as it comes out of oven.

The Flower Cart
Bedford, NH

New England Clam Chowder

3 cups chopped clams; drain liquid and reserve
6 potatoes, diced, steamed (do not overcook)
1 large onion, diced
4 sticks celery, diced
4 strips bacon, chopped
¼ pound butter or margarine
3 tablespoons vegetable oil
8 ounces all-purpose flour
½ cup light cream
8 ounces clam juice
1 bay leaf
salt to taste
pepper to taste
1 teaspoon rosemary
½ teaspoon leaf thyme
½ teaspoon granulated garlic
dash Tabasco sauce
dash Worcestershire

Open and drain clams; save liquid. Cook potatoes, steaming is best, about ¾ done. Do not overcook. In a stock pot or large saucepan sauté bacon, add butter, oil, onions and celery. Cook until transparent. Add flour and mix, should look like mashed potatoes. Lower heat to medium; add liquid from clams and stir until smooth. Add clam juice and stir until smooth. Add spices and allow mixture to thicken. Add clams and potatoes; lower heat to low. Add cream a little at a time; adjust thickness by adding more or less cream.

Manchester Country Club - Chef John Hutchison
Bedford, NH

Pecan Chicken

Maple Butter:
¼ pound butter
2 ounces maple syrup
2 tablespoons finely chopped pecans

Soften butter and place in bowl of an electric mixer, at about medium speed. Begin to mix the butter while slowly adding the maple syrup. When butter becomes smooth add the pecans and mix well. Chill the butter mixture about half an hour, then scoop out with a melon baller.

Coating:
½ cup all purpose flour
½ cup Panco style bread crumbs
2 tablespoons brown sugar
½ cup chopped pecans

For the coating: mix flour, bread crumbs, brown sugar and pecans in a bowl and set aside.

4 (6-ounce) boneless chicken breasts
½ stick butter
2 ounces vegetable oil

Cut chicken breasts in half, remove any fat and pound each breast flat, to about ¼ inch thick. Melt butter in frying pan and add the vegetable oil over medium high heat. Take the chicken breast and press them into the coating mix, being sure that chicken is fully coated. Add the coated chicken to the frying pan and sauté until golden brown on both sides. Remove chicken and drain on a paper towel. To finish chicken, place on a baking sheet in a 350 degree oven for about 10-15 minutes (depends upon oven). Chicken should have 155 degrees internal temperature. Chicken needs to be served right out of the oven. Plate chicken and top with maple butter and enjoy!

Manchester Country Club - Chef John Hutchison
Bedford, NH

Chicken Marsala

4 (6-ounce) boneless chicken breasts
1 cup all-purpose flour
2 tablespoons butter
3 ounces Marsala wine
4 large mushrooms
4 ounces beef stock, canned is ok

Coat each chicken breast in flour. In a sauté pan heat the butter; sauté chicken 3 or 4 minutes on each side or until golden brown. Remove chicken from the pan and place on paper towels. Remove pan from stove and carefully add the wine. The wine may flame so be careful. Replace pan on stove; mushrooms may be added at this time. Allow mushrooms to sauté and then add the beef stock stirring until mixture is smooth. Return chicken to the pan and simmer for about 4 to 5 minutes. Serve with rice.

Manchester Country Club - Chef John Hutchison
Bedford, NH

Homemade Dinner Rolls

8 cups flour
¾ cup sugar
½ cup Crisco shortening
1 teaspoon salt
1 tablespoon dry yeast
¼ cup warm water (105-115 degrees)
2½ cups water
1 tablespoon melted butter

In large bowl thoroughly mix flour, sugar, Crisco and salt to remove all lumps. Dissolve yeast in warm water; add to batter and mix. Add water 1 cup at a time, mixing with hands until malleable. Add more water if necessary. Do not knead. Cover bowl with plastic wrap and refrigerate overnight.

When ready to bake, form into balls 2 inches in diameter and arrange around the outside of greased pie plates. Cover loosely with plastic wrap and let rise in warm place until doubled in size, about 2 hours. Preheat oven to 400 degrees. Remove plastic wrap; brush rolls with melted butter and bake until lightly browned, 15-20 minutes. Turn out onto racks to cool.

Maplehurst Inn - Chef Garret Sullivan
Antrim, NH

New England Crab Cakes

3 pounds snow crab meat, drained
5 ounces mayonnaise
1 heaping tablespoon Dijon mustard
1 tablespoon Worcestershire sauce
1 teaspoon Tabasco
1 teaspoon old bay seasoning
1 teaspoon garlic powder
½ teaspoon white pepper
½ teaspoon black pepper
2 ounces flour
4-6 ounces bread crumbs (plain)

Mix all wet ingredients. Add spices, flour and bread crumbs until it is moist and bound together. Shape into ½ inch thick silver dollar size portions. Sauté with butter over medium heat until browned. Serve over mixed greens with balsamic vinegar.

Maplehurst Inn - Chef Garret Sullivan
Antrim, NH

Grilled Swordfish "Steak Out"

¼ cup olive oil
1 tablespoon lemon juice
1 tablespoon chopped garlic
1 tablespoon chopped onion
½ cup butter or margarine
¼ teaspoon parsley
salt and pepper to taste
4 (8-ounce) center cut swordfish fillets (or substitute halibut or salmon steaks)

In a large bowl, whip the olive oil and lemon juice with a whisk until it thickens. Combine the other ingredients and brush on, or pour over, the fillets. Let marinate for one to four hours in the refrigerator. After marinating, prepare the grill. To keep the fillets from sticking, brush the rack with vegetable oil. For a smoky, outdoor flavor, add wood chips of apple, oak, hickory or mesquite to the coals. For an electric grill, sprinkle a few chips over the lava rocks. Use medium heat to cook the fillets, and set the rack about four inches above the coals. Allow ten minutes cooking time per one inch of fillet. Turn fillets once to ensure even cooking. Do not overcook.

The Weathervane
Bedford, NH

Maplehurst Sugar Cake

1 egg yolk
1 cup light brown sugar with 2 teaspoons maple flavoring
1 cup sour cream
1 teaspoon baking soda
1 teaspoon salt
½ teaspoon warm water
1½ - 2 cups flour
1 egg white
1 cup chopped walnuts (or butternuts if available)
¼ cup pure maple syrup

Preheat oven to 350 degrees. In large mixing bowl beat well egg yolk, sugar and sour cream. Dissolve baking soda and salt in water to make a paste, blend into mixture. Add half of the flour until well combined, then add remaining flour—it will be thick. Fold in one stiffly beaten, but not dry, egg white, along with nuts if desired. Bake in greased 9-inch cake pan until toothpick inserted in center comes out clean, approximately 40 minutes.

Maple Glaze:
1 cup sugar
1 cup maple syrup
¼ cup heavy cream
¼ stick butter

Boil together and then completely cool. Top cake with maple glaze.

Maplehurst Inn - Chef Garret Sullivan
Antrim, NH

Lobster and Crab Chowder

1 stick of butter
1 medium onion
3 ribs of celery, diced small
2 each bay leaves
3 sprigs fresh thyme, remove leaves and chop
½ cup flour
1 quart lobster stock
2 each medium potatoes, diced
1 cup heavy cream
½ pound crabmeat
cayenne, black pepper and celery salt — to taste

Melt butter in large saucepan over medium heat. Add onion and celery and sauté until translucent. Add bay leaves, thyme and flour to make roux. Cook for 5 minutes. Add lobster stock and cook until thick. Add potatoes and cook until tender. Add heavy cream. Do not boil. Add crabmeat and seasoning to taste.

The Woodstock Inn & Resort
Woodstock, VT

Boursin Chicken

2 boneless skinless chicken breasts
2 eggs
½ cup milk
2 tablespoons chopped fresh parsley
1 cup fresh grated Parmesan cheese
salt & pepper to taste
½ cup flour
2 tablespoons butter
1 package boursin garlic & herb cheese (not Au Poivre with pepper)
light cream

Cut each breast in half and pound to ⅛-¼ inch thickness between layers of plastic wrap. In a bowl mix eggs, milk, parsley and Parmesan; set aside. Place ½ cup flour in a separate bowl with a little salt and pepper. Heat 2 tablespoons butter in large frying pan on low heat. Heat half package boursin cheese with about ½ cup light cream in separate saucepan (should be consistency of medium white sauce) until warm - hold.

Dredge each breast fillet in flour and then dip into egg mixture and pan fry in butter until lightly brown. Place each fillet on warm serving plates and top with boursin mixture. Goes especially well with asparagus. Enjoy!

Parker's Maple Barn - Chef John Sullivan
Mason, NH

Tomato Juice - Used in sauces to serve with bland foods, such as potato croquettes or with foods having distinctive flavor, such as fish, also in beverages.

Basil Bean Soup

½ pound dried white kidney beans
6 cups water
3 medium zucchini, diced
3 large potatoes, peeled and diced
6 medium carrots, peeled and thinly sliced
2 celery stalks, thinly sliced
2 onions, coarsely chopped
4 whole cloves
1 bay leaf
1 (17-ounce) can whole tomatoes, undrained
5 tablespoons fresh basil, snipped
4 drops Tabasco sauce

Soak the beans overnight in cold water to cover. Drain and rinse in cold water. Place in a large pan and add the 6 cups of water. Bring to a boil and add all the vegetables. Place the cloves and bay leaf in muslin bag and add to the pot. Add the tomatoes, 3 tablespoons of the basil, and the Tabasco sauce. Reduce heat and simmer until the beans are tender, about 2½ hours. When serving, sprinkle with the remaining 2 tablespoons basil.

Pickity Place
Mason, NH

Shrimp Scampi

9 large shrimp, peeled and deveined
1 tablespoon butter or margarine
2 tablespoons olive oil
½ medium tomato, dried
1 pinch oregano
1 pinch basil
1 tablespoon chopped garlic (1 teaspoon if dried, minced garlic)
4 ounces dry sherry
1 scallion, chopped fine
cooked pasta of your choice

Sauté items 1 through 8. When shrimp are done, add scallions. Then toss with pasta of your choice.

Note: For interesting alternatives try chicken, scallops, or clams instead of shrimp. Don't forget a nice bottle of white wine with dinner. Enjoy!

Anni Etelli's Owner-Chef David Canavan
Merrimack, NH

East/West Stir Fry

¼ cup vegetable oil
1 pound chicken breast, diced
1 garlic clove, peeled and minced
1 onion, peeled and sliced thin
2 jalapeño peppers, seeds removed and minced
½ pound snow peas, strings removed
1 cup fresh mushrooms, sliced
1 cup broccoli florets
1 cup carrots, sliced and peeled
2 cups sweet n' sour sauce
1 tablespoon fresh cilantro, chopped
4 cups crisp flour tortilla strips
4 teaspoons sesame seeds

This dish is cooked quickly just before serving, so organization is essential. Have all your vegetables cut and in separate bowls. For a Southwestern touch, serve over crisp tortilla strips (see recipe below), and accompany with rice.

A few vegetables require some steaming while others are fine only stir fried. In a steamer, steam broccoli until just crisp, tender and fragrant. Broccoli should be bright green, which should only take 5 minutes. The carrots should steam for about 8 minutes. When they are done, remove them from heat and set aside. Heat oil over medium-high heat in a large frying pan or wok and stir-fry chicken until it is no longer pink, 3 to 4 minutes. Add in the garlic and onion and continue cooking until the onion becomes translucent. Add in the jalapeños, snowpeas and mushrooms, cook 2-3 minutes. Now add in the steamed vegetables, toss together. Stir together for a minute until the vegetables are heated through. Add the sweet n' sour sauce to the pan, stir until the sauce thickens and the vegetables are glazed. Stir in the cilantro. Serve over the crisp tortilla strips and sprinkle sesame seeds on top.

Crisp Tortilla Strips: Using 6 or 8-inch flour tortillas, stack a dozen tortillas and cut in half. Cut each new stack in half. You should now have four stacks. Cut each stack into strips no more than ¼ inch wide. Separate strips to prevent clumping together while frying. Heat 1 inch of oil in a skillet until hot. Place a few strips at a time into the oil and fry until crisp and golden brown. Remove from pan and drain on paper towels. Yield: 4-6 servings.

Shorty's Mexican Roadhouse
Bedford, NH

Gifts from the Kitchen

Little Leaguers, 1993

It started as the season always does — games of catch with friends, pitching with Dad, and pickup games. But this year was going to be different!!!!

In July, the Bedford Little League competed in the district championship games. Winning, they were in the running for state championship. Winning, they were in the Eastern Regional Tournament. Winning, they were on their way to a three game World Series.

Over 6,000 fans watched as our 11, 12, and 13 year olds won over Richmond, VA. The second game in the World Series was a 1-0 win over Hamilton, Ohio. California was the only team in the United States to beat our Little Leaguers. Bedford Police escorted our champs from the Massachusetts border to the Bedford Mall on their triumphal return where the entire town celebrated our Number Two Spot in the Nation.

Little Leaguers Barbecue

entrées

Teriyaki Marinade with

Boneless Chicken Breasts

Mexican Sauce with

Hamburgers and Hot Dogs

vegetables

Baked Beans

Corn on Cob

desserts

Crispy Peanut Butter Balls

Toll House Marble Squares

Whoopie Pies

Orange-Cashew-Cranberry Sauce

1 (11 ounce) can mandarin orange segments
1 (12 ounce) package fresh cranberries
¾ cup sugar
1 teaspoon ground ginger
1 (6-8 ounce) package cashew nuts

Drain oranges. Reserve ¼ cup syrup. Cook cranberries, sugar, ginger and reserved syrup, covered, on high for 7-11 minutes until cranberries pop. Stir twice during cooking, making sure sugar does not stick on bottom of pan and burn. Stir in oranges and nuts. Chill overnight to let flavors mingle. Yield: 3 cups.

Note: Serve with fowl.

Barbara Fox Friedman

Carrot Marmalade

4 cups carrots
2 lemons
2 oranges
6½ cups sugar

Peel and grate raw carrots. Cut up seeded lemons and oranges, rind included. Be sure to save all juice. Put in saucepan. Add sugar and cook slowly until thick. Pour immediately into hot sterilized jars and seal at once. Yield: about 3 pints.

Note: This marmalade has a rich color and excellent flavor.

Janet Jespersen

Caraway Seeds - have a spicy smell and aromatic taste. Used in baked fruit, in cakes, breads, soups, cheese and sauerkraut.

Raspberry Jam

3 cups sugar
5 cups raspberries
½ cup lemon juice

Place sugar and berries into a large saucepan and boil hard for 5 minutes. Add lemon juice and mix. Pour into hot, sterilized jars immediately. Remove any foam from the top and any drips inside of the top. Immediately cover with melted wax. After the wax has hardened but while the jars are still warm add covers and tighten. Preparation time is 20 minutes.

Note: This jam will not harden like the commercial jams. A half package of Surejell will solidify it somewhat if you prefer, but the jam will lose the free flowing texture. This is a delightful raspberry indulgence.

Eunice Brine

Rhubarb Jam

5 cups rhubarb, cut in 1 inch pieces
1 cup drained, crushed pineapple
4 cups sugar
1 (3 ounce) package strawberry gelatin

Mix rhubarb, pineapple and sugar and allow to stand 30 minutes. Cook slowly, bringing to a boil. Let cook for 12 minutes, stirring constantly. Remove from heat and stir in 1 package of dry strawberry gelatin. Pour into sterilized glasses and cover with melted paraffin. Yield: 8 glasses.

Marion Jenkins

Chives - Leaves are used in many ways. May be used in salad, in cream cheese, in sandwiches, omelets, soups, and in fish dishes. Mild flavor of onion.

Fruit and Nut Chocolates

6 ounces chocolate bits
1½ cups toasted almonds
½ cup dried cranberries
1 tablespoon butter

Melt the chocolate bits, stir in nuts, cranberries and butter. Using spoons, drop small clusters onto a waxed paper covered surface. Let cluster sit until the chocolate has hardened. Yield: Approximately 2 cups.

Barbara Fox Friedman

Easy Fudge

2 cups granulated sugar
2 squares bitter chocolate
1 small can (5½ ounces) evaporated milk
1 piece butter, size of a walnut
1 cup semi-sweet chocolate bits
½ cup walnuts

Bring sugar, chocolate, milk and butter to a boil. Boil 5 minutes. Remove from heat. Stir in chocolate bits and walnuts. Pour into an 8x8 inch square buttered pan. Score and cool. Never fails.

Marion Jenkins

Happy Pistachios

2 cups shelled pistachio nuts
2 tablespoons butter, melted
1 teaspoon salt
1 teaspoon sugar

Preheat oven to 275 degrees. Mix all ingredients together, spread on non-stick cookie sheet and roast for 20 minutes. Allow to cool and store in air tight container. Yield: 2 cups.

Note: May use colored sugar for a holiday mood.

Barbara Fox Friedman

Spicy Bourbon Pecans

1 pound pecan halves
¼ cup bourbon
½ cup sugar
½ teaspoon Angostura bitters
1 tablespoon Worcestershire sauce
1 tablespoon corn oil
½ teaspoon cayenne pepper
½ teaspoon salt
¼ teaspoon freshly ground black pepper
1 teaspoon cumin

Preheat oven to 325 degrees. Drop the pecans into a pan of boiling water and cook for 1 minute. Drain and set aside.

Pour the bourbon into a small saucepan and bring to a boil. Reduce to 3 tablespoons. In a bowl, combine the bourbon and sugar and stir. Add the bitters, Worcestershire sauce and corn oil. Stir in the pecans and mix thoroughly. Let the nuts sit for 10 minutes. Spread the nuts and liquid on a rimmed baking sheet. Bake for 35 minutes, tossing nuts every 10 minutes until all liquid is absorbed.

Combine the cayenne pepper, salt, black pepper and cumin. In a bowl, toss the hot pecans with the seasonings, adding a small amount of the seasoning mix at a time as it is very spicy. Season to taste and mix well to coat all of the nuts. Return the pecans to the baking sheet until cool and dry. Store in an air tight container. Yield: 6 servings.

Pat Lauer

Muddy Buddies

9 cups Chex cereal
1 cup chocolate bits
½ cup peanut butter
¼ cup margarine
1½ cups confectioners sugar
1 teaspoon vanilla

Put cereal in bowl. Melt chocolate bits, peanut butter and margarine until smooth, stirring often. Remove from heat and stir in vanilla. Pour over cereal to coat. Place in plastic bag with confectioners sugar and shake. Spread on wax paper to cool. Store in airtight container.

Martha Harris Gaudes
Executive Assistant to the Bedford Town Manager

Nibbler's Delight

1 cup sugar
¼ teaspoon salt
½ teaspoon cinnamon
6 tablespoons milk
½ teaspoon vanilla
2 cups pecan or walnut halves

Mix first four ingredients together and cook slowly until sugar is dissolved. Increase heat slightly and cook to soft ball stage, stirring occasionally. Remove from heat. Add vanilla and nuts. Beat until mixture thickens. Turn onto waxed paper and quickly separate nuts into individual pieces using two forks. When cool, pack into a decorative jar or box. Preparation time 15 minutes.

Note: These are outstanding. Makes a lot! A nice gift.

Bonnie Venn

Candy Toffee: A Candy/Cookie

¾ cup brown sugar
2 sticks butter
Unsalted saltines
1 (12 ounce) bag of chocolate bits
Topping choices: chopped pecans, walnuts, almonds or coconut

Preheat oven to 400 degrees. Layer a cookie sheet with saltines. Melt brown sugar and butter. Bring to a boil for 3 minutes. Stir continuously while boiling to prevent burning. Pour and spread the sugar and butter mixture over the saltines. Bake for 5 minutes. Spread the chocolate bits over all and let melt. Immediately top with the topping of your choice. Let cool. Crack to original cracker size. Store in a tin.

Note: A Nice Treat!

Cathy Rooney Ashley

Artie's Garlic Dills

pint sized wide mouth canning jars
pickling cucumbers
elephant garlic cloves, cut in quarters
alum
fresh dill

In each jar place one piece of garlic, and alum equal to the size of a large pea. Pack with clean cucumbers. Top with one dill flower, and 2-3 sprigs of the side leaves or weed.

Boiling hot brine:
¼ cup canning salt
1 cup white vinegar
4 cups water

Fill jar to one quarter inch from the top with boiling hot brine. Seal with lids and bands immediately. Let sit for about two weeks before eating. Garlic will turn blue, this is natural.

Note: Use fresh cucumbers, 2-3 inches long. Make them one jar at a time or as many jars as you want.

Artie Robersen
Bedford Town Manager

Chewy Popcorn Balls

½ cup sugar
½ cup light corn syrup
4 tablespoons butter
½ teaspoon salt
8 cups popped popcorn

In a saucepan combine sugar, corn syrup, butter and salt and cook on medium high heat until mixture starts to boil. Remove from heat. Add popcorn and mix to coat. Cool 5 minutes. Dip hands into cold water and form popcorn into balls. May add food coloring to sugar mixture before adding to the popcorn. Yield: 8-10 tennis ball size popcorn balls.

Brian Ross
Recreation Director, Town of Bedford

Green Tomato Mince Meat for Pies

2 quarts sliced apples
2 quarts green tomatoes
½ cup vinegar
¼ cup molasses
1 orange with juice and fine cut rind
2 tablespoons minced peel
5 cups sugar
1 teaspoon salt
2 teaspoons cinnamon
½ teaspoon ground cloves
1 teaspoon nutmeg
2 pounds seeded raisins, chopped fine or halved

Combine first five ingredients and bring to a boil. Add the remaining ingredients and boil until thick and apples are cooked. Freeze in plastic bags, enough for a pie or pudding in each bag.

Note: This makes a lot of meatless mincemeat and is very tasty. It takes a lot of time chopping by hand so it is a great project to share with others. I did it in the fall at a cottage on Prince Edward Island with my sister and it is a great memory of working together with her.

Eunice Brine

Italian Basil Oil

⅓ cup lightly packed fresh basil leaves
5-6 garlic cloves, peeled and left whole
3 cups (approximately) extra virgin olive oil

Wash the basil leaves and remove the stems. Pat dry. Place the basil leaves with garlic cloves and olive oil in an air-tight glass container. Leave at room temperature for 2-3 days and then refrigerate. It will keep in the refrigerator for several months. Bring to room temperature before serving.

Note: Serve with Italian bread for dipping or use on salads or pasta. When most of the oil is gone, the leaves and garlic may be chopped and sautéed for use in tomato sauce or added to salad and pasta dishes directly.

Roseann Paolini

Roasted Peppers in Olive Oil

6-8 red peppers
8-10 cloves of garlic, coarsely chopped
4 cups (approximately) extra virgin olive oil

Wash peppers (leaving them whole and uncored) and pat dry. Rub a little olive oil on each and place on a baking sheet. Broil the peppers until soft, turning them constantly until the skins become dark and bubbled all over, about 30 minutes. Carefully place the peppers in a sturdy paper bag for 15-20 minutes. This will allow them to steam and sweat so the skin can be easily removed. Take each pepper and carefully (and patiently) remove all of the skin. Pull out the core and drain well. Cut the peppers in half and remove all the seeds, etc. Cut the peppers into 1-2 inch strips.

Place the pepper strips in an air-tight glass container. Add the garlic and olive oil. They will last for several months in the refrigerator and get better with age as the oil absorbs the garlic and peppers. Just bring to room temperature before serving. Use in salads, on pasta, in sandwiches or straight out of the jar with a good loaf of Italian bread to dip in the oil.

Note: It is excellent. Makes a lot.

Roseann Paolini

Rum Balls

1½ cups vanilla wafer crumbs (about 50 cookies)
¼ cup Bacardi dark rum
¼ cup honey
2 cups walnuts, ground
powdered sugar

Combine all ingredients, except sugar. Blend thoroughly. Shape into small balls about 1 inch in diameter. Roll in sugar. Store in tightly covered container. Yield: about 2½ dozen.

Janet Jespersen

Index

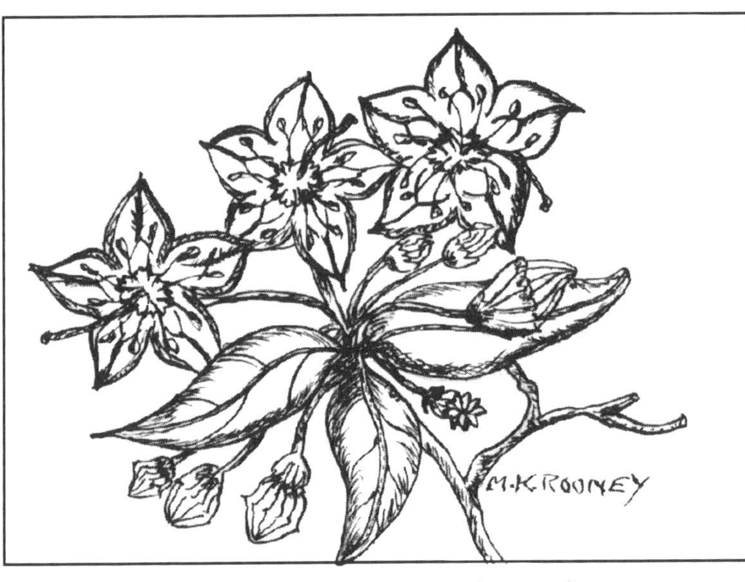

Our Mountain Laurel Stands

One of the unusual features with which nature has endowed Bedford, especially in the northwest section of town, is an abundance of Mountain Laurel (Kalmia latifolia). The leaf is evergreen, wide and leathery. In June and July, the shrub is covered with delicate light pink or white blossoms that brighten the woods and the roadsides. For many years, Bedford was on the route of laurel tours for motorists. The developers and contractors have been kind to the laurel bushes, not cutting more than necessary when building new roads and homes. So renown is this shrub that we have "Laurel Drive," "Laurel Hill," "Laurel Acres," and "Kalmia Way" within our town.

Spring Fling

soup

Prize Winning Split Pea Soup

bread

Irish Soda Bread

salad

Broccoli Salad

Entrée

Valentine Lamb Shank

Rice Pilaf

dessert

Grasshopper Pie

Scrumptious Mocha Ice Cream Dessert

INDEX

D

E

F

G

Q

R

T

V

W

Y

Z

ZUCCHINI

Egg Doggie Treats

1/2 cup oatmeal
1 TBSP Peanut Butter
1/2 TBSP Water
1 large egg
1/8 tsp Cinnamon
1/2 tsp Honey
Cook 20 min @ 350°F
Spoon onto cookie sheet
(± 9 large treats)